The *Not So* Wild, Wild West

TERRY L. ANDERSON *and* PETER J. HILL

The *Not So* Wild, Wild West

Property Rights on the Frontier

Stanford Economics and Finance

AN IMPRINT OF STANFORD UNIVERSITY PRESS

STANFORD, CALIFORNIA

2004

Stanford University Press
Stanford, California
www.sup.org

Library of Congress Cataloging-in-Publication Data

Anderson, Terry Lee, 1946–
    The not so wild, wild west : property rights on the frontier / Terry L. Anderson and Peter J. Hill.
        p.   cm.
    Includes bibliographical references and index.
    ISBN 0-8047-4854-3 (alk. paper)
    1. West (U.S.)—Economic conditions.   2. Right of property—West   (U.S.)—History.   3. Property—West   (U.S.)—History.   4. Public   lands—West   (U.S.)—History.   5. Common   good—History.   6. West (U.S.)—Economic policy.   I. Title: Property rights on the frontier.   II. Hill, Peter Jensen.   III. Title.
HC107.A17A85 2004
333.3'0978'09034—dc22   2004001038

Printed in the United States of America on acid-free, archival-quality paper.

Original Printing 2004

Last figure below indicates year of this printing:
13   12   11   10   09   08   07   06   05   04

Designed and typeset at Stanford University Press in 10/14 Janson.

To our children—Sarah, Peter, Jennifer, Josh, and Lisa. May they always be blessed with the freedom and spirit of the West.

Contents

Illustrations and Tables

TABLES

Acknowledgments

This book has been a long time in the making. We first began thinking about the evolution of property rights on the frontier in the early 1970s. The subject became a major part of the economic history course we co-taught at Montana State University for two decades. Consequently, we must thank our many students who listened to our half-baked ideas and helped us refine them.

During the long gestation of this project, the list of seminars where we have presented papers and of discussions we have had with colleagues has grown too large to detail here. The short list of friends and colleagues to whom we owe thanks for their comments includes Dan Benjamin, Bruce Benson, James Buchanan, David Friedman, David Haddock, Ron Johnson, Gary Libecap, Fred McChesney, Andrew Morriss, Seth Norton, Richard Stroup, and Bruce Yandle. We also thank Anna Nordberg for her research assistance and her editing of the manuscript. Of course, flaws that remain in our analysis or evidence remain our responsibility.

We are fortunate to have had foundations and individuals support our research through PERC (Property and Environment Research Center), the Hoover Institution, and Wheaton College. We are particularly grateful for support from the Earhart Foundation, which allowed us to start pulling together our many disparate ideas and papers on this subject and to collect the artwork that is included in the book. Andy Morriss organized a Liberty Fund Colloquium centered around several book chapters. We thank him, the participants, and the Liberty Fund for their contribution to making this a better book. Idea entrepreneur Bill Dunn has provided generous general support for PERC that has helped in the production of this book. At the Hoover Institution, John Raisian gave Terry the flexibility to work on this project, and Marty and Illie Anderson have supported Terry's position as a senior fellow. At Wheaton College, the Bennett family has supported Peter's endowed chair.

Thinking about the evolution of property rights on the frontier and researching the fascinating history of the West were the easy parts of this project. Putting all our results together in a manuscript for publication was the hard part. This would not have been possible without Michelle Johnson's hard work and attention to detail. We can't thank her enough for keeping us organized, correcting our errors, and smiling the whole time. In addition we wish to thank Monica Lane Guenther for juggling staff time at PERC to allow production of this manuscript, and Michelle McReynolds for helping secure the necessary artwork.

Finally, we thank our families for their patience, interest, and support. They were always "lovingly critical" when we seized easy opportunities to try new ideas out on them. No doubt our children, Sarah and Peter and Jennifer, Josh, and Lisa, would not want to tally the many dinner-table lectures they have had to digest. We especially thank our wives, Janet and Lois, for their love and moral support during the ups and downs of writing this book.

The *Not So* Wild, Wild West

ONE

Heroes, Villains, and Real Cowboys

On a cold April morning in 1892, Peter Jensen walked to a Denver livery stable, saddled the horse he had just bought, tied on all his earthly belongings, and set off to seek his fortune in Montana. Five years earlier, the 22-year-old Danish immigrant had left the family homestead in Nebraska to work in Cheyenne, Wyoming; Cripple Creek, Colorado; and Denver. He had enjoyed his adventures, but now he felt he must acquire land if he was going to make much of a living. Eastern Montana, only a decade into its cattle-ranching era, seemed to offer bountiful opportunities.

Jensen's northward journey would prove arduous, though apparently he didn't expect it to be dangerous. On the very first day, finding his newly purchased six-gun awkward, he threw it into a stream, never again to carry a sidearm. As the journey continued, Jensen and his two traveling companions encountered a spring snowstorm that left them walking and leading their horses for two days and hungry for three. On the second night after the storm, they took refuge in a vacant cabin they had come across, and were able to cut cottonwood limbs for the horses to eat, but still could find no food for themselves. At last, on the third night, a trapper and his family offered the travelers food and rest in their remote cabin.

When Jensen arrived in Montana, he worked on the Biddle and Ferdon Ranch in the southeastern part of the state. Later that year he moved to their Powder River ranch, where he would stay for two years. In 1894 he purchased from that ranch a pasture called the "bull camp," where bulls were kept when they were not mixed with the cows. That property, located on Crow Creek, became the headquarters for Jensen's operation, the P J Ranch, which would stay in the family for 98 years. Although Jensen owned a cabin, a set of corrals, and several hundred acres of creek bottom, he ran his cattle on the open range with other ranchers in the area.

At about the same time, halfway around the world from Jensen, a young Serbian named Novak Kapor boarded a ship bound for New York City. He arrived there with his brother in 1896, planning to cross the vast continent to work in the Montana mines. Having cleared immigration on Ellis Island, the two brothers, while awaiting their transcontinental train, flipped a coin to see who would go to Red Lodge, Montana, to work in the coal mines and who would go to Butte to work in the copper mines. Novak became the coal miner.

When he arrived in Red Lodge, it was a thriving ethnic town supplying coal to the Northern Pacific Railroad. Many other ethnic enclaves, such as Finn Town, Little Italy, and Slav Town, dotted this remote western wilderness. Few frictions existed among these communities, even though the immigrants tried to maintain their cultural identities while learning English and working side-by-side in the mines. For Novak, the Serbian lodge and Yugoslavian picnics remained an important part of his life well into the twentieth century.

Working in the mines, Novak made a fortune compared to what his family earned back in Serbia. When he returned home for a visit before World War I, he became a local folk hero by purchasing a farm for his family. During prohibition, he added to his wealth by distilling whiskey in the basement of a fellow Serbian's house in Red Lodge and selling it throughout the region. With his mining and bootlegging proceeds, he moved 27 miles to Bridger, Montana, where he built a hotel, bar, and café that became an important business anchor on the short main street.

The two individuals discussed above are our grandfathers—Peter Jensen is P. J. Hill's, and Novak Kapor is Terry Anderson's. Thus we come to this book both as professional economists interested in questions of institutional design and as grandsons of newcomers to the western frontier.

The experiences of our grandfathers raise several questions that we attempt to answer in this book. Was Pete Jensen foolish to throw away his six-gun as he entered the supposedly violent society of cattle towns and open-range cattle ranching? How did he expect to defend himself and his property? And when he started his own ranch with the bull camp, did he really have any property rights to the open range that was necessary for his survival? How could he be assured that his capital improvements, such as the water reservoir for stock that he built with a two-horse scraper, would not become worthless as more and more cattle were put on the range? Did Novak Kapor encounter ethnic discrimination in the mining communities where he worked, and thus lose opportunities? How could this non-English-speaking emigrant who started out as a common laborer become an entrepreneur (albeit an illegal one in the case of bootlegging) and a property owner? Why didn't violence reign? How were mining claims established? What kept a rough-and-tumble community of diverse immigrant groups from degenerating into a chaos of warring gangs?

To this personal curiosity we add our professional interest in the economic history of the American West.

In 1893, Frederick Jackson Turner started historians thinking about the significance of the frontier in American history. Before the American Historical Association, Turner argued that the closing of the frontier in 1890 was also "the closing of a great historic moment,"[1] a moment that he believed had displayed the best of American character. Through rugged individualism and heroic action, the settlers had tamed a lawless frontier and a hostile natural environment. Generations of historians adopted and expanded Turner's thesis, making it the dominant paradigm for interpreting western-American history. They portrayed the West as a place that "promoted individualism, self-reliance, practicality, optimism, and a democratic spirit that rejected external constraints."[2] In this setting, the heroic individual became the focal point of an analysis that showed him subduing the natural environment, indigenous peoples, and outlaws to transform the West from a place of anarchy to one of law and order. Violence was simply part of the transition to civilization.[3]

In contrast to heroic individualism, revisionist historians have more recently developed the domination thesis.[4] This new perspective focuses on conquest, environmental disruption, and antagonism between classes and ethnic groups. Terms such as "invasion," "colonization," and "exploitation" have replaced "manifest destiny," "progress," and "civilization."[5] Patricia Nelson Limerick, arguably the most noted of the new western historians, states that "the history of the West is a study of a place undergoing conquest and never fully escaping its consequences."[6] Here the heroic portrayal of hardy settlers improving human welfare has given way to a depiction of a ruthless, power-hungry elite grasping for control of natural resources and human populations. As in previous interpretations, violence plays an important role in this interpretation of western history, but it becomes the tool of the powerful to oppress and exploit.

Though both of these interpretations offer useful insights into the development of the American West, neither explains how individuals—heroes or villains—shaped their institutional environment and how the institutional environment, in turn, shaped the way people interacted. We fill this gap.

Our approach is that of the "new institutional economics," which explains how institutions evolve and how they affect economic activity.[7] By "institutions" we mean the rules that govern how people interact with one another. More specifically, they are the property rights that determine who may use resources (including natural resources, capital, and labor), how they may use those resources, and whether they may trade them. For example, we will explain how property rights evolved to govern grazing on the vast Great Plains, how miners racing to gold fields hammered out rules for claiming mining sites along streams or mineral veins, and how irrigators divvied up water in the arid West.

In our institutional explanation, violence (a negative-sum game) generally is supplanted by trade and cooperation (positive-sum games). We consider how the rules determined the benefits and costs that individuals faced and how individuals attempted to change those rules or institutions. If rules governing water use did not allow irrigators to reap the rewards from building dams and canals, there would have been little investment in irrigation infrastructure. Conversely, if grazing rules allowed cattlemen to reap the benefits of good grazing practices, resource stewardship was more likely. The lack of rules to encourage investments in water infrastructure or to encourage stewardship of the range provided an incentive for entrepreneurs to change the rules and capture the benefits of those changes.

To the extent that institutions encouraged cooperation and gains from trade, the "wild, wild West" was really the "*not* so wild, wild West." For this reason, institutional entrepreneurs become the heroes who promoted law and order, efficient use of the natural and human resources, and good resource stewardship. These institutional entrepreneurs saw opportunities in the abundant grass, scarce water, rich ore veins, and the geysers in Yellowstone, all of which offered rewards to those who could hammer out new rules.

The importance of institutional entrepreneurs is best understood in the context of their ability to prevent the "tragedy of the commons."[8] The tragedy of the commons occurs when there are no limits on access to a resource, with the result that the resource is overused. Overgrazing of the village commons is often cited as the typical example. If customs and traditions do not limit access to the commons, individuals will overgraze it because any grass left will simply be eaten by someone else's livestock. The entrepreneur who can develop rules to restrict grazing will capture part of the increased value of the pasture rather than seeing that value dissipated through the tragedy of the commons. In such cases the entrepreneur is a hero because he not only prevents the destruction of resources but also creates opportunities for gains from trade, thus making the overall pie larger.

This is not to deny the violence of the West. Violence certainly occurred, and when it did, it usually took one of two forms. First, violence, or more precisely coercive power, was used by private persons and institutions to defend property rights against intruders. For example, cattlemen's associations flexed their muscle to exclude newcomers from the open range, and vigilante groups acted to enforce laws. Second, violence manifested itself through the exercise of governmental power to take assets from others. The Indian wars of the late nineteenth century were a quintessential example.

If the West was not the wild and woolly place depicted by some historians and in western novels and movies, the question becomes, What conditions promoted cooperation rather than conflict on the frontier? We argue that cooperation dominated conflict because the benefits and costs of institutional change redounded to small, well-defined groups or communities. As long as new institutions evolved locally and voluntarily, the costs of conflict and the benefits of cooperation were internalized by the decision makers. Hence, local institutions adapted efficiently to new environmental and economic conditions. However, as the state and national governments began to take over the role of rule makers, the calculus changed since individuals bore fewer costs from conflict and reaped fewer benefits from cooperation. If you could get a standing army paid from the national treasury to take land from Indians, or if you could get the federal government to subsidize uneconomic irrigation projects, you would do so regardless of the net benefits to society. This transformation occurred because a centralized government located farther from the impacts of institutional change was able to spread the costs over the general population while concentrating the benefits in the hands of special interest groups.

The American West offers abundant examples of how institutional entrepreneurs created and adapted harmonizing rules to fit natural and technological constraints on the frontier:

- Prior to the arrival of Europeans, American Indians hammered out cooperative institutions that went beyond mere survival by recognizing and capturing gains from trade and specialization. Though not thought of as capitalistic societies, the institutions of American Indians harnessed incentives that promoted the same "wealth of nations" described by Adam Smith. This recognition of the economic benefits from trade extended to relationships with whites after their arrival on the scene. With the rise of standing armies, however, whites shifted to taking Indian lands rather than trading for them.

- In pursuit of "soft gold," fur traders exchanged manufactured goods with Indians for beaver pelts and organized complex firms to bring the pelts to market even though transportation and marketing costs were quite high. Although entrepreneurs were able to solve most of the problems of harvesting and selling beaver pelts, dealing with bison was more difficult. Costs were high for defining property rights to live bison, which would have encouraged their preservation. Instead, individuals on the frontier eliminated bison and replaced them with cattle.

- Miners in the gold camps of California and Nevada developed property rights in an orderly fashion that discouraged conflict and promoted efficient extraction of gold and silver.

- Similarly, miners and early farmers responded to arid conditions where water had to be stored and delivered off the stream by developing prior-appropriation water rights to replace the riparian rights that had evolved in regions where water was abundant.
- Migrants on the wagon trains understood the importance of cooperation to their ability to survive the harsh conditions on the trail and hence entered into constitutional agreements that promoted efficiency and justice.
- Cattlemen's associations quickly formed to define and enforce property rights to the cattle and the grass. The common roundup and branding sufficed to close access to valuable grazing lands until the arrival of sheep and sheep herders disrupted the enforcement system and prompted range wars.

The lessons from the American West transcend the era by providing insights into the causes of efficient and inefficient institutional evolution. By the time the Berlin Wall fell and communism collapsed, it was obvious to most observers that institutions were crucial determinants of economic performance. Several recent studies have quantified the influence of property rights and rule of law[9] and have allowed estimates of the nexus between economic growth and property rights. Seth Norton summarizes these studies, concluding that "recent evidence is unambiguous. Property rights and its related construct, the rule of law, and the more general category, freedom from property rights attenuation, are all positively related to economic growth. Their absence leads to economic stagnation and decline."[10]

Though formal property rights, rules, and laws can be important determinants of economic prosperity, their effectiveness in promoting harmony depends a great deal on how the formal rules interact with informal institutions. Customs and culture can be important determinants in the growth process. If people respect property rights because it is the right thing to do, or if a handshake is as good as a legal contract, the costs of transacting will be lower and the potential for gains from trade higher.

The process through which institutions evolve also affects their potential to promote capital formation and gains from trade. This is the basic theme of Hernando de Soto's book, *The Mystery of Capital: Why Capitalism Triumphs*

in the West and Fails Everywhere Else. De Soto emphasizes that we now understand the importance of property rights to the growth process, but that we
have not fully appreciated the importance of having property rights evolve
from the bottom up. Regarding the American frontier, de Soto observes:
"Information about property and the rules that governed it were dispersed,
atomized, and unconnected. It was available in rudimentary ledgers, personal notes, informal constitutions, district regulations, or oral testimony in
every farm, mine, or urban settlement."[11]

Property rights that evolve from the bottom up—as opposed to the top
down—are much more likely to conserve resources and promote investment. The opposite is also true; when property rights are dictated from central authorities with less stake in the outcome, time and effort are often
wasted in the process of creating the property rights, and productive investment suffers. Just as technological change is usually incremental rather than
discontinuous, effective institutional change evolves slowly, taking into account specific conditions of time and place. Developing countries generally
and the former communist countries in particular are finding out just how
hard it is to nurture this evolutionary process. We believe that important lessons can be learned from the American West, where institutional evolution
trumped institutional revolution.

TWO

The Institutions That Tamed the West

Studying the history of the U.S. frontier through its institutions shifts the focus from the autonomous strivings of traditional heroes to the cooperative efforts of communities and interest groups. Using such an institutional approach, we examine how people came together to establish rules, formal or informal, that assigned benefits and costs to their actions. If valuable resources such as land and water are left up for grabs in a world where the mightiest take what they want, life will surely be "nasty, brutish, and short," as Hobbes predicted. In that world, the frontier would have resembled Hollywood cowboy movies. But if rules can be established to define and enforce property rights and encourage peaceful trade, order can replace fighting, and prosperity can replace hardship.

Traveling to the United States in the 1830s, Alexis de Tocqueville was the first to recognize that the frontier was a crucible for institutional evolution emphasizing cooperation.[1] Moving beyond the pale of formal government, facing new climatic and environmental constraints, and developing new production techniques, pioneers had to create and implement rules and organizations that fit their needs.

Consider, for example, water use (which we treat fully in Chapter 10). In the eastern United States, where water was abundant, the English common law that gave landowners along a stream a right to an undiminished quantity and quality of water worked well. Because this rule did not allow diversions, however, it was not appropriate for the arid West, where water had to be moved out of the stream for mining and farming. Not surprisingly, miners and farmers abandoned the riparian rule and devised a new system called the prior-appropriation doctrine, which divided up the scarce stream flows and accommodated the need to divert water.

The problem of developing appropriate rules was not unique to water. Trappers, members of wagon trains, ranchers, cattle drovers, and even the Plains Indians faced conditions that called for new rules. In each case individuals and groups had to devise institutions to govern their interactions among themselves and with others.

In examining these rules and organizations we ask: What motivated people to change the rules? Why did they choose one set of rules over another? Who got the new property rights that were being formed? How did the new rules affect whether people engaged in peaceful, productive trade or in violent takings?

Defining the Frontier

Before providing a framework for thinking about these questions, we must define what we mean by the frontier. For an individual or group, the frontier is the margin between the time or place where resources have no value and the time or place where they have positive value.[2] Consider, for example, the status in 1821 of a hypothetical piece of land located in what is now known as Montana. In 1821, that land might have had value to American Indians living there because it had unique characteristics that made it a sacred place or an excellent buffalo jump.[3] For those people, that land was within rather than beyond their frontier.

But what counts as the frontier for one individual or group might not do so for another because it depends on values rather than on geographic fea-

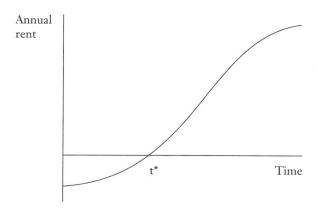

FIGURE 2.1 The Path of Land Rents over Time.
"Rent" is the value of a unique, nonreproducible asset.

tures. The piece of land that has value for Indians might have no value for non-Indians. Indeed the land could have negative value to non-Indians if they actually had to occupy it far from their society and economy. Such land would be beyond the frontier for non-Indians.

Figure 2.1 depicts a conceivable path of the value of this hypothetical piece of land to non-Indians over time. In 1821 the land would have had negative value, but as the non-Indian population grew and pushed west, bringing its civilization and economy closer to the land, the land's value would have risen, and eventually would have become positive. That turning point would occur at t^*, the time when the land becomes the frontier to non-Indians.

Think about the frontier in the context of outer space. Mars is a planet we are exploring with unmanned probes, but it is not yet a place we are likely to inhabit in the near future. Any value that might be had from habitation would be offset by travel costs, risks, and distance from family and friends. Just as railroads increased the value of western land to non-Indians and shifted the frontier, we can imagine that improvements in space travel will increase the value of property on Mars. Eventually the value of that property may become positive. When it does, that property will lie within rather than beyond the frontier.

Frontier Resources and Economic Rents

The land value we are talking about is called "rent" by economists. Rent is simply the value of a unique asset that cannot be reproduced. Let us return to the value of our hypothetical piece of land, considered this time as a buffalo jump.[4] Cliffs over which Indians drove bison had to have special characteristics. First, they had to be in the vicinity of bison migration paths because the bison had to be lured near the cliffs. Second, the cliff had to offer no easy escape route for the bison. A cliff with an hourglass shape was particularly valuable because, once bison were lured through the narrow gap, escape became very difficult. Such special characteristics meant that certain cliffs were more valuable than others; they earned more rents. Similarly, box canyons into which bison could be driven, confined from behind, and slaughtered would earn rents.

While box canyons might not be valuable to non-Indians for procuring bison, they could be valuable for keeping cattle from wandering and for protecting them from rustlers. However, if a canyon was so far from the market that moving fattened cattle from it to the market was impossible, that unique piece of land would not command a positive rent and would lie beyond the frontier. As markets moved closer to the land or as transportation costs fell, say because of the approach of railroads, the rent associated with the land would rise.

Obviously rents accrue to all kinds of unique resources. Land at the confluence of rivers earns rents because of its proximity to transportation and trade. That is why it was so important for the Mandan Indians in what is now North Dakota to control land at the confluence of trade routes between the Great Plains and the Midwest. The unique geysers and canyons of Yellowstone were originally dubbed "Colter's Hell" (suggesting a negative value) because of the horrific description given by John Colter, the first white man to see them. But when the transcontinental railroads lowered the transportation cost of visiting Yellowstone, the rents turned positive (i.e., Yellowstone was no longer beyond the frontier). Gold-rich streams obviously commanded more rents than streams without gold. In a modern context, wavelengths in the electromagnetic spectrum, talented athletes, and unique internet names all earn rents.

Rents should not be confused with profits. The difference is that rents cannot be competed away because they arise as a result of uniqueness; profits can be competed away. For example, when Ray Kroc "invented" McDonald's, some of the earnings from his idea were rents and some were profits. His production techniques and his fast, consistent service were new and unique and therefore earned rents. To the extent that he could keep those techniques secret and establish the "golden arches" and Ronald McDonald as trademarks, he could earn rents from his ideas. However, to the extent that his ideas could be closely replicated, his earnings were profits that could be competed away. Competition would lower profits for McDonald's, but it would not eliminate the rents associated with the ideas and the unique locations for which McDonald's was famous. Similarly, athletes tried to replicate Michael Jordan's skills and compete away some of his profits, but to the extent that his athletic ability was unique, it could not be replicated and hence command rents.

It is important to note that though rents cannot be competed away, they can be dissipated.[5] Rents cannot be competed away because they result from unique asset characteristics to which property rights can be established. They can be dissipated or destroyed, however, if the property rights are poorly defined and enforced and thus allow unique assets to be overused or fought over. Particularly valuable grazing land will command a rent because it can fatten cattle, but, if available to all comers, it will be overgrazed in a tragedy of the commons. The tragedy is that the rents are dissipated by overgrazing. Similarly, unfettered access will dissipate rents of valuable fisheries through overfishing, of valuable oil pools or groundwater basins through overpumping, and of freeways through congestion.

If the rents of unique resources are not dissipated through overuse, they can be dissipated through races to control or possess the resources.[6] The race to homestead land, for instance, induced people to move beyond the frontier and settle before the land commanded a positive rent. To wait meant to risk losing out to others who got there first. But the suffering endured by the early homesteaders was a cost that dissipated part if not all of the valuable land rents. Racing to beat others to catch fish, to pump oil or groundwater, and to occupy satellite orbits are other examples of how rents can be dissipated.

Rents can also be dissipated through war.[7] When Indian lands lay beyond the non-Indian frontier and hence were of negative value to non-Indians, there was no competition for the land between Indians and non-Indians (though there was competition and fighting among different Indian tribes). But when the land came within the non-Indian frontier (say because transportation costs fell) and commanded positive rents for non-Indians, fighting sometimes erupted. Eventually the spoils were divided, but the effort expended in fighting dissipated some, if not all, of the rents, to say nothing of the injustice inflicted upon Indians.

The story of the western frontier is a story of rents and how they were captured or dissipated. The "wild, wild West" image suggests that rents were dissipated through racing and fighting. In contrast, the "not so wild, wild West" image suggests that rents were captured and nurtured as individuals and groups peacefully defined and enforced property rights and engaged in market transactions in which those rights were exchanged. The establishment of mining claims, water rights, and grazing rights to the open range are all examples upon which we will elaborate in chapters that follow. Understanding the conditions under which the West would be wild or not requires understanding how property rights were defined and enforced.

The Costs of Transacting

Whether people fight over valuable resources or engage in cooperation and trade depends on how well property rights are defined and enforced. Property rights determine who has access to valuable goods and services, who reaps the benefits from them, and who must pay the costs of utilizing them. In other words, they are the rules that govern who gets what and who pays for what.

Transaction costs are the most important factor in determining whether people can define and enforce property rights without dissipating the rents they are trying to capture through those rights.[8] Transaction costs are the costs of specifying, monitoring, enforcing, and trading property rights. Higher transaction costs make it more costly for people to cooperate, less likely that they will gain from trade, and more likely that conflict will ensue.

Suppose Tex agrees with Hoss to trade some of his cows for some of Hoss's land. This transaction requires that the two specify which cows and which land are being traded, how many cows will exchange for how much land, how performance of the contract will be monitored to ensure that each is abiding by the terms of the agreement, and how disagreements about performance will be resolved. If Tex and Hoss know one another well, know the goods to be exchanged, and expect to have repeat dealings, the transaction costs are likely to be low. But if they do not have this specific knowledge of one another and of the cows and land, they will have to put more effort into specifying, monitoring, and enforcing the contract. That is, they will have higher transaction costs.

Transaction costs in markets can be likened to friction in a machine. Just as friction reduces the efficiency of an engine and diverts valuable energy into unwanted by-products, transaction costs reduce the net gains from trade. If Tex and Hoss have to hire a lawyer to draw up the contract, a veterinarian to examine each cow, and a surveyor to survey the land, these costs must be subtracted from their expected gains from the trade. Further, if either side violates the terms of the agreement, say by substituting inferior cows or by misrepresenting the quality of the land to be traded, efforts to force the offending party to deliver as agreed will incur additional costs, such as legal fees. Enough costly friction will cause Tex and Hoss's trade agreement to break down like a gritty, unlubricated engine.

Whether business partners can be trusted, whether people lie, and whether they cheat or steal depends on more than just the legal consequences of violating contracts. Moral and cultural constraints that encourage people to honor contracts and property rights also provide important lubricant for economic transactions. Religious commandments and doctrines, fraternal ceremonies that bond individuals together, moral precepts inculcated through education, and a teamwork ethic instilled through coaching all discourage opportunistic behavior. "Thou shalt not steal," "working for the good of the order," "do unto others," "team spirit," and similar tenets urge individuals to set aside narrow self-interest for a common good. In economic transactions, moral constraints reduce transaction costs by inducing people to abide by their contractual obligations and to refrain from taking other people's property. To the extent that such moral precepts make it less necessary to monitor contract performance or defend property rights, transaction costs will be lower and potential gains from trade higher.

Because cultural and moral values reduce transaction costs, people often deal within homogeneous communities, wear certain types of clothing, or participate in rituals that inculcate moral precepts.[9] Fraternal organizations such as the Masons,[10] religious sects such as the Mormons, and voluntary groups such as cattlemen's associations all played a role in lowering transaction costs on the western frontier.

When moral constraints are not sufficient to make people abide by contracts or respect property rights, force must be used to punish violators. Whether force comes from social sanctions, vigilante groups, or governmental police, it becomes a part of transaction costs.

Suppose Tex and Hoss know and trust one another, so their transaction costs are low, but Jesse, who cannot be trusted, tries to rustle Tex's cattle or graze his own herd on Hoss's customary range. Tex and Hoss will capture fewer gains from their trade and will have to incur some cost to enforce their rights against Jesse's taking.

Transaction costs also exist between groups as well as individuals. Legal, cultural, and linguistic barriers can make it difficult for groups to interact. Land disputes between Indians and whites offer an example in the West. Because Plains Indians generally did not have property rights to small parcels of land that white farmers needed for farming and cattle ranching, it was virtually impossible for one group to trade with another. The bloody Indian wars were, in part, dramatic examples of what can happen if transaction costs are so high that trade cannot occur.

The costs of enforcing property rights and contracts can be reduced through collective action for two reasons.[11] First, collectives can often take advantage of economies of scale. Instead of each homeowner hiring his or her own guard to enforce his or her property rights, a group of homeowners can hire one guard to protect several homes at a lower cost. Second, collectives can reduce the potential free-rider problem associated with enforcement of property rights against theft. If the guard hired by the homeowners sees a burglar but does not know which house is the target, the guard would be derelict in his duties if he did not stop the burglar. But suppose the targeted house belonged to a person who was not part of the homeowner collective; that homeowner would be a free rider because he would have his property rights protected without paying for the guard services. The cost of enforcing his property rights would fall on the paying homeowners. By obliging all homeowners in an area to be paying members, the collective can eliminate the free-rider problem and thus reduce each participant's enforcement costs. Without such an obligation, all the homeowners would have an incentive to try free riding, in which case there might be no guard service.

More generally, collective action offers a potential solution to free-rider problems associated with public goods, which, once provided for one individual, are available to all. Fire protection in urban areas has a public-good element because it is impossible to protect one building without providing at least some protection to other buildings. Likewise, it is difficult to reduce flood damage by building dams and levees for one person without providing protection for his neighbors.

Wagon trains illustrate how collective action reduced transaction costs on the trip across the Great Plains (see Chapter 7). By banding together in a train, migrants could hire a leader to guide them, to coordinate defense, to facilitate river crossings, and to adjudicate disputes. Once people voluntarily joined the train, they were required to contribute to the production of public goods so that all were better off for having joined.

Thus far we have been talking about transaction costs that cannot be avoided entirely. Returning to the friction analogy, just as no machine is frictionless, no exchange is without transaction costs. Buyers must be found, sellers must be monitored, and contracts must be enforced. Each of these requires resource expenditures and hence reduces the net value of exchange. Friction can never be totally eliminated, but lubrication can reduce its effects. Similarly, some transaction costs can never be totally eliminated, but they can be lowered through repeat dealings, customs and morals, careful specification of contracts, and collective action. Just as lubrication can convert more energy into useful outputs, lower transaction costs convert more human ingenuity into valuable production. Institutions that clarify existing property rights or create property rights where they are lacking lower the transaction costs associated with measurement and monitoring. For example, rules for branding livestock made the cattle market more efficient, and surveys and land records made transferring land less costly.

Like some friction, however, some transaction costs are unnecessary or artificial. Running a car without sufficient air in the tires or without oil to lubricate the engine increases friction and reduces useful output. Similarly, rules that restrict exchange can discourage profitable trades and encourage conflict, and laws that prevent private ownership can cause rents to be dissipated, just as they are with overgrazing, overfishing, or overpumping. Such rules create what we shall call artificial transaction costs. For example, water law often precludes the sale of water between willing buyers and willing sellers. In California today, water is still put to agricultural uses in which it is worth less than $100 per acre foot (one foot of water covering one acre), when it would be worth at least three times that much if sold to urban users.[12]

By focusing on transaction costs as they relate to different institutions, we can better understand the source of cooperation and prosperity. With property rights well defined and enforced, markets promote gains from trade and encourage more efficient resource use. On the other hand, when property rights are not well specified or protected, resource values are dissipated as people race to capture rents to unique resources.

Institutional Entrepreneurs

Our focus here is not just on how institutions promote cooperation and prosperity but on how and why those institutions change. Obviously, if rents are dissipated when property rights are not well defined and enforced, there is an incentive to change institutions so as to prevent squandering valuable resources. If people think they can capture the resource's rent, they will put effort into changing the rules that govern the resource, and the amount of effort devoted to establishing property rights will be influenced by the rate of return that these people perceive they can get from such investments. In short, far from being exogenous, property rights are endogenously produced.

The people who recognize potential gains from establishing property rights and act to establish rules that will allow the gains to be realized are institutional entrepreneurs. These are the people who will ultimately determine who has access to resources, who captures the rents from resources, and who bears the costs of using resources. Traditionally we think of entrepreneurs as the people who create value by introducing new goods and new methods of production, opening new markets, discovering new sources of supply, and reorganizing the production process.[13] To this list of entrepreneurship's contributions, we add the devising of new institutional arrangements. Some of these institutions will encourage productivity and cooperation, but others will redistribute wealth and encourage conflict. Understanding why the West was not so wild requires knowing under which circumstances we get the former rather than the latter.

Paths for Institutional Entrepreneurs

Institutional entrepreneurs benefit from three activities: (1) reorganizing existing property rights, (2) defining new property rights where they do not exist, and (3) redistributing existing property rights. A comparison of the three options reveals that not all institutional entrepreneurship is the same: the reallocation and definition of rights creates wealth for society while redistribution of rights reduces wealth for society.

REORGANIZING PROPERTY RIGHTS

The entrepreneur is usually thought of as the person who recognizes higher-valued uses for resources and profits from acting on this recognition. If Hoss is using his land for cattle grazing, and Tex thinks the land would be more valuable for wheat production, Tex can profit from buying the land and putting it to the higher-valued use. As explained above, this requires that the property rights to the land can be defined and enforced at a low enough cost for the exchange to remain profitable. Following this path, the institutional entrepreneur takes the existing set of property rights and rearranges them through the market process. This process manifests itself in contracts that transfer control of a property right from one individual to another.

The formation of a new firm is another example of this path. For example, suppose that Hoss believes it would be profitable to drive cattle from Texas to Montana, where they can fatten on lush grass and then be marketed to miners. He might purchase cattle from Tex in Texas, drive them to Montana, and capture the return. Alternatively, Hoss and Tex might join together in a business venture wherein Tex, who has superior knowledge about cattle in Texas, provides the cattle, and Hoss, who knows the trail, drives them to Montana and markets them in the mining camps. The firm allows its owners to take advantage of scale economies, specialization, and special knowledge they may share, but it also comes with organizational costs. Hoss and

Tex have to specify what contribution each will make to the firm and what share of the profits each partner will get. They must also monitor one another to be sure that each is living up to the terms. Incomplete contracts allow opportunistic behavior by allowing one party to the contract to capture part of the returns at the expense of the other party. That is to say, when contractual terms cannot be easily measured and monitored, the parties will compete for profits that accrue to the firm. For example, a worker may shirk on the job if he receives the same pay regardless of his effort. To overcome this, the firm might use piece-rate contracts, whereby workers are paid according to what they produce.

Hoss and Tex would only create a firm if they believed that its advantages, such as scale economies or specialization, less the costs of specifying and enforcing their contract, are greater than the advantages of acting separately, with Tex selling the cattle directly to Hoss and with Hoss acting independently thereafter. In forming a firm that integrates the control of the cattle from their initial purchase in Texas to their sale in Montana, the owners are substituting internal allocation decisions for market exchanges in which control is passed from owner to owner. Economist Oliver Williamson refers to the question of whether to exchange property rights or team up in a firm as a search for "efficient boundaries."[14] In effect, the entrepreneurial search for efficient boundaries of the firm is a search for the optimal scale of production and the optimal contractual form.

In the American West, the search for the optimal contractual form was an ongoing process because of the need to adapt to natural conditions that differed from those in the East and because of the dynamic economy, which was undergoing rapid settlement and development. Firms that arose to move cattle from Texas to railheads in Missouri and Kansas or to understocked regions further north epitomize the contractual adaptation to new opportunities (see Chapter 8). Between 1866 and 1886, some ten million longhorn cattle were driven from the Southwest to points north. Drovers moving these cattle experimented with herds that varied from 70 head to 45,000, but found the optimal size for a cattle drive to be approximately 2,500 head.[15] Because a herd of this size was larger than the herd on a typical cattle ranch, cattle had to be pooled for the long drives. When cattle drives began, it was difficult to specify the functions of the drover and to assign risks on the trails appropriately. Because Texas cattle owners did not know how best to move the large herds and what risks to expect on long drives, they were reluctant to hire others to supervise such drives. Had they done so, drovers might easily have stolen cattle while blaming the losses on unverifiable circumstances. In other words, a simple contract wherein the cattle owner paid the drovers for herding services would have left some of the profits up for grabs.

To overcome the costs of measuring and monitoring the drovers, cattle owners simply sold their cattle to the drovers. As owners, the drovers received the profits from the drive north and thus had no incentive to cheat on themselves. Over time it became possible to quantify the risks of trailing and to specify them in contracts. Thus specialized firms known as transportation agencies developed to contract for moving cattle over long distances.[16]

Labor contracts for the drovers also reflected institutional entrepreneurship. Because cattle drives required complete teams of workers the whole way, and because new workers were hard to come by along the remote trails, trail bosses resorted to signing on their crews for the entire duration of the journey. Wages were not paid until the herd was delivered to its final destination. By creating cattle-trailing firms and by paying cowboys at the end of the drive, institutional entrepreneurs prevented opportunistic behavior that would have reduced the return from reallocating resource use.

DEFINING PROPERTY RIGHTS

The rearranging of property rights assumes that property rights exist in the first place, and when they do not, the entrepreneur can gain by creating them through definition and enforcement activity. In so doing, the entrepreneur can capture the rents associated with a unique asset rather than have them dissipated through racing or fighting. For example, if the entrepreneur can define and enforce a property right to control access to the open range, he has an incentive to prevent overgrazing because he captures the land's rents. On this path, the challenge for the institutional entrepreneur is to balance the increased rents associated with preventing the tragedy of the commons with the costs of defining and enforcing property rights that limit access. Hence we would expect entrepreneurial action to increase with expectations of rising resource rents and with declining costs of definition and enforcement.[17]

Cattle ranchers on the frontier understood the tragedy of the commons and worked to eliminate it (see Chapter 8). They limited access to grazing lands by forming cattlemen's associations, which excluded nonmembers from grazing areas in the association's territory. They also sought the assistance of local, territorial, and state governments in establishing branding laws, registering brands, and inspecting the brands when cattle were sold.

Similarly, miners established mining claims. Knowing that they would capture the future rents from their investments, they were willing to incur prospecting costs and infrastructure investments, which allowed them to extract, process, and market their minerals. By establishing rules under the umbrella of their mining camps, miners were able to define and enforce rights to their claims relatively peacefully.

REDISTRIBUTING PROPERTY RIGHTS

Just because entrepreneurs wish to capture rents by establishing property rights to assets does not mean that their actions will always create net gains for society. As economist William Baumol points out,

> there are a variety of roles among which the entrepreneur's efforts can be reallocated, and some of those roles do not follow the constructive and innovative script that is conventionally attributed to that person. Indeed, at times, the entrepreneur may even lead a parasitical existence that is actually damaging to the economy. How the entrepreneur acts at a given time and place depends heavily on the rules of the game—the reward structure in the economy—that happen to prevail.[18]

In other words, the pursuit of rents by entrepreneurs is not always a positive-sum game; by channeling their efforts into redistributing existing property rights or acting opportunistically in contractual agreements, they can be playing zero- or negative-sum games. In such cases, they will make society's economic pie smaller.

To gain control of existing rights that currently belong to others, institutional entrepreneurs must expend effort to effect the redistribution, and this in turn forces the current resource owners to spend effort defending their rights.[19] This process is known to economists as rent seeking because the entrepreneur is seeking rents that others already own.[20] The entrepreneur doing the seeking must invest valuable time and effort trying to take, and existing owners must invest valuable time and effort in trying to defended from taking.

Whether the redistribution is effected through private actions such as theft or through governmental action such as taxation and regulation, the result is the same: resources are consumed, and the overall size of the economic pie is accordingly reduced. Private theft certainly redistributes rents, but political "rent seeking" does so as well.

A prime example of this in the American West was the federal subsidization of water projects under the Reclamation Act of 1902 (see Chapter 10). Empirical studies of these projects report that they fail ordinary benefit-cost tests, so we must ask why they were undertaken. The answer is that recipients of the government water largesse lobbied heavily to receive the water subsidies.[21] Another example of rent seeking was the federal seizure of land from early cattlemen who "locked up" the range. Through their private associations, cattlemen had defined and enforced property rights to the open range, but the federal government disallowed these rights and made the land available to homesteaders. Again the process was driven by political interests wanting to redistribute title to the land.[22] And, of course, Indians lost property rights as the federal government opened reservations to homesteading and mining and redistributed their wealth to settlers (see Chapter 4).

While rent seeking to influence the government to redistribute property rights might be legitimized by democracy, its impact on the incentive to make productive investments and promote prosperity differs little from that of war. Indeed, war is the ultimate form of rent seeking: one side expends effort to defend its territory and assets against the aggression of another. This form of rent seeking is the very essence of the wild West, where Indians fought the influx of whites into their territories, cattlemen fought sheepmen over grass, miners fought one another for gold claims, and farmers fought over water. In each of these cases, the game is negative-sum because only one side wins, but in the process, the winners as well as the losers expend resources and human lives. As we shall see, however, such fighting was far less prevalent than suggested by traditional historians.

One winner in this rent seeking process is the politician who can "sell" his ability to change the rules of the game. Such politicians extract some of the rents for themselves by threatening to confiscate privately owned rents through regulation or taxation.[23] The threat need not be carried out as long the owner can be forced to "purchase" back his ownership claims from political entrepreneurs with the power to make the credible threats in the first place. As with rent seeking, rent extraction is a negative-sum game in which politicians compete for the power to threaten. An obvious example of rent extraction in the American West is the unscrupulous sheriff who used his power to threaten property owners in the same way that a mafia boss might today.

What Motivates Institutional Entrepreneurs?

Like all other entrepreneurship, institutional entrepreneurship is activated by the expectation of high returns.[24] Such perceptions require that the entrepreneur establish control over productive resources such as labor, capital, and land. Thus the entrepreneur is first and foremost a contractual innovator who must find ways of capturing value generated by rearranging and creating property rights.

The most obvious motivation for institutional entrepreneurs is the rent that will accrue to the owner of a resource. For instance, when land prices were low in the West, efforts to define and enforce property rights in order to restrict entry to the land were scarcely worth undertaking because the rents were minimal. As land values rose, the return on restricting entry increased, and various property rights activities ensued. Initially, settlers simply announced their claims through newspapers and posters, but over time their efforts became more organized, and they threatened violence or legal sanctions against potential entrants. A decline in values can have the opposite effect. When the value of horses plummeted at the end of World War I, people reduced their investment in definition and enforcement activity by turning unbranded horses loose on the public domain (see Chapter 8). Like all economic decisions, the decision to invest in defining and enforcing property rights depends not only on the value of the property but also on the cost of securing ownership. The latter, in turn, depends on technology. For example, the invention of barbed wire lowered the costs of fencing individual claims to the open range and allowed cattlemen to specify their property rights more precisely and enforce them more efficiently. It was cheaper to

The Line Camp, by L. A. Huffman. "Line camps" were outposts built along the boundary lines between grazing territories. The cowboys who lived in these camps kept the cattle from wandering too far and protected them from rustlers. In effect, the cowboys shown in this photo helped form a human fence until the invention of barbed wire put them out of business. Courtesy of Coffrin's Old West Gallery, Bozeman, Montana.

build barbed-wire fences than to hire cowboys to ride the open range keeping cattle within certain territories and discouraging rustlers.

The decision about how much wire to use in fencing illustrates the nature of the decision about how much to invest in definition and enforcement activity. One strand of wire would demarcate a property boundary but would do little to keep cattle in. Two strands would better confine cattle, three would be better yet, four even better, and so on. But at some point (usually four strands in the case of cattle), a limit is reached on how secure to make the fence because the additional cost of another strand is not warranted by the additional benefit of more secure ownership.

Aridity, lack of readily available capital, and labor shortages meant that there were rewards to contractual innovators. The person who could contract with cattle owners in Texas to move their herds north and market the cows fattened on abundant grass could turn a handsome profit, but this required contracting with many property owners to facilitate the long cattle drives. Similarly, an entrepreneur who could contract with labor and capital owners to deliver water to arid agricultural lands stood to capture a substantial share of the newly created wealth. Again, however, building storage and delivery systems and negotiating long-term agreements with farmers required contracting abilities that not all possessed.

New technology often induced institutional change. Barbed wire made it cheaper for the individual rancher to demarcate his territory and confine his cattle. This, in turn, reduced the need for and cost of coordinating roundups through cattlemen's associations. When gold was discovered in California, it was panned from gravel in streams usually by one miner working alone. When this source was depleted, new technologies such as sluice boxes and hydraulic mining were used to extract the gold, and these required large amounts of water, which, in turn, required capital investment and larger organizations to capture economies of scale. Large firms arose to take advantage of these opportunities.

Another institutional response to technological change came with the introduction of the horse to the Plains Indian culture (see Chapter 3). Prior to the horse, Plains Indians were much more sedentary, and when they did hunt bison, they tended to organize into large groups in order to reap the benefits of scale economies.[25] Their hunting techniques required strong hunt chiefs supported by tribal police societies that enforced the rules of the hunt.[26] With the arrival of the horse, however, the organization of bison hunting changed significantly. A small group of equestrian hunters could kill buffalo as meat was needed for the group. There were few economies of scale with this form of hunting; indeed, too many people could scare a buffalo herd away, increase sanitary problems in the camps, and create grazing problems for horses.

In this technological setting, the importance of the hunt chief declined as the importance of the skilled horseman rose, and this in turn changed the compensation schemes. In the pedestrian communal hunt, where everyone contributed about equally to productivity, the meat was distributed evenly among the hunters, with some accord given to the number of dependents. The hunt leader and the decoyer, the brave man who draped a buffalo robe over his back and lured the herd toward the cliff, might be allotted a differential amount of meat.[27] In the horse culture, the individual who owned buffalo horses and could ride and shoot arrows received the lion's share. Each buffalo belonged to the mounted horseman who launched the lethal arrow, which was clearly marked to indicate ownership. Hence technological change altered the organization of Indian villages and the contractual arrangements among members of the group.[28]

Though technological change usually lowers the cost of establishing property rights, it can also make the institutional entrepreneur's task harder if it increases access to resources. On the open oceans, for example, improved ship technology increased the rents of fishing further from shore, making it harder to restrict entry and prevent the tragedy of the commons. As settlement in the West progressed, first wagon trains and then railroads facilitated access to unclaimed lands. In fact, much of the conflict between ranchers and homesteaders stemmed from the decreased costs for farmers to move to the West and compete with ranchers for the land (see Chapter 9). Whether such increased competition for rents will be overcome by institutional entrepreneurship depends on a myriad of factors, including the potential for collective action, to which we will soon turn.

Political access to the federal government encouraged frontier entrepreneurs to engage in rent seeking. Early irrigation projects were privately financed, but western farmers saw substantial gain from having others subsidize irrigation through the Reclamation Act of 1902. Indian lands were also redistributed as they increased in value and as the U.S. Army battled Indians for their land.

Collective Institutional Entrepreneurship

In many cases, the effectiveness of institutional entrepreneurship depends on the cost of organizing groups of individuals in order to protect rents from dissipation by outside forces. On the open range, for instance, an individual might have tried to cordon off a small section of the range, but in the absence of fencing materials or technology such as barbed wire, cattlemen had to deal with more and more competition for the open range. The choice between acting individually or acting collectively was easy. By acting collectively, they could include current range occupants and exclude newcomers.

Making the collective more inclusive meant that fewer people would be excluded, but also that each member of the collective would capture less rent. Making it less inclusive meant that more people would be excluded but also that each member of the collective would own more rents.[29]

Collectives that are too small may not be able to exclude potential entrants to the commons, but collectives that are too large will face higher organizational costs, or what economists call agency costs. Successful institutional innovation in creating property rights therefore requires a search for an appropriate governance framework. Three general factors determine the size and structure of that framework.

TERRITORIAL SIZE

The optimal size of the collective unit used for restricting access to rents will vary with the size of the territory to be protected, and this in turn can vary considerably depending on the nature of the resource and the production process.[30] The optimal collective organization for restricting entry to a small fishing lake will be smaller than the optimal collective for restricting entry to the ocean within 200 miles of the shore, which will in turn be smaller than the optimal collective for restricting entry to the open ocean. Similarly, a small mining camp could effectively limit entry to ore bodies that were relatively confined and not well known, but an Indian tribe was too small to restrict entry to the buffalo herds that migrated across large territories.[31] A cattlemen's association with a dozen members could control access to an unfenced grazing territory by excluding nonmembers from collective roundups. But the same association had to rely on territorial or state governments to enforce brand registration because cattle were traded across much larger territories than they grazed. Therefore, *ceteris paribus*, the larger the geographic area to be protected, the larger the optimal size of the collective unit.[32]

DIFFERENTIAL ADVANTAGE IN THE USE OF FORCE

One of the important economic reasons for collective action is the enforcement of territorial boundaries against entry by people who are not members of the collective. Preventing entry into this territory requires that members of the collective exert force both against trespassers and against members of the collective to ensure that they help pay for preventing trespass by outsiders.[33]

A determining factor in the optimal size of the collective is the extent to which having a larger force lowers the average costs of defense. In other words, are there scale economies in the production of force? If there are few economies of scale, small collectives can adequately enforce property rights, but if costs decrease with the size of the enforcement unit, larger collectives will be preferred.

Scale economies in the use of force generate pressure for people to form larger collective units. Generally on the western frontier, the six-gun was the technology that gave equal power to nearly everyone and therefore kept the collective units small.[34] Vigilante groups could and did provide greater collective power over individuals or gangs, but the fact that they were not permanent and addressed mainly local problems suggests that they had no particular cost advantage.

The national military organized to protect the nation's boarders from external threats was necessary to capture scale economies, but those large-scale economies also created the potential for using the collective coercive power to redistribute rights. Local militias were the primary military unit throughout early American history, but they were replaced by a large standing army after the Civil War. For settlers, the existence of the standing army altered the calculus of negotiating versus fighting by lowering the costs to individuals of calling upon force to take land from the Indians. Since the army was a special interest group that had an incentive to engage in warfare, it is not surprising that data on the ratio of battles to treaties show that raiding replaced trading after the Civil War.[35]

AGENCY COSTS

As benefits increase with the size of the collective unit—either because the larger unit can encompass a larger geographic territory with greater rents or because it can capture scale economies in the use of force—those benefits are offset by costs associated with the failure of governmental representatives to do what the citizens desire. For example, suppose that a group of cattlemen hires Wyatt to help defend against rustling. This extra defense will increase land rents, but there is a risk that Wyatt might act opportunistically to capture part of these increased rents. He might hold out for a higher salary, arguing that his job is dangerous or that he cannot do his job without putting in considerably more effort. He might let some rustlers get away, contending that he needs more resources under his control to do his job. More generally in the political arena, agents have the potential to extract rents through regulation and taxation. If measuring his productivity and verifying his arguments is hard, Wyatt will be able to capture more of the rents, especially if he has special law-enforcement talents. It is always costly to ensure that agents act on behalf of the citizens and that they do not use their power to extract rents from their constituents. Citizens will have to incur costs to constrain their agents (politicians, bureaucrats, police, and so on) from acting opportunistically.

These agency costs are especially evident when the collective unit is geographically large enough to make it difficult for members to exit. This situation gives agents more power over the collective's members. It is one thing to move from one municipality to another or one county to another, but it is much more costly to migrate between countries. This cost rises even more if the boundary is fenced and mined, as it was between East and West Berlin. If it is easier for people to vote with their feet, agents of the government will have less ability to extract rents, and vice versa.

The costs of monitoring agents increase not only with the geographic size of the collective but also with the number of people in the collective. This is because in a larger collective each member captures a smaller share of the rents created by collective enforcement and therefore has less incentive to monitor the agent. The result is that, as the size of the group increases, it becomes cheaper for each individual to free-ride on the monitoring efforts of others. In a smaller group, each member has a bigger stake in protecting the rents they have created and therefore has more incentive to monitor agents. With the stake in the collective inversely related to group size, we can expect less monitoring and more rent seeking and rent extraction as group size increases.

It follows that if agents design rules governing the formation of property rights for a smaller collective group, the group will more efficiently monitor the agents to ensure that the rules they design do not cause wasted effort in the property-rights formation process. Conversely, if the agents are not so closely monitored because agency costs are high, the rules they design are more likely to encourage rent dissipation.

To fully understand this point, consider the rule for establishing property rights to land with a time path of rents like that shown in Figure 2.1. The optimal time to settle and produce from this piece of land is t^*, when the rents turn positive. Premature settlement to capture the rents before they are claimed by others is likely to occur and could totally dissipate the rents unless the collective group agrees to limit racing and exclude outsiders who might not abide by their rules.[36] This was the case with land-claims clubs organized by people with a stake in reducing rent dissipation caused by racing (see Chapter 9). On the other hand, if the rules for establishing property rights are set by agents with little or no claim on the rents that are not dissipated, wasteful rent dissipation is more likely to occur. An extreme case of this was the Oklahoma land rush, in which "sooners" raced to get the land sooner than others. Similarly, to the extent that the homestead acts encouraged premature settlement (settlement prior to t^*) and required investments that would not otherwise have been made, they dissipated potential land rents on the frontier.

Other factors in addition to smaller-sized groups and competition from other collective units can help reduce agency costs. First, group homogeneity (which can be inversely related to group size) can lower the costs of monitoring agents. In relatively stable societies with numerous repeat dealings, it may be cheaper to rely on norms and moral constraints rather than on formal laws enforced by official government agencies. Such social and cultural norms develop over time as efficiency-enhancing norms replace efficiency-reducing ones and as those who disagree with norms move to other homogeneous groups where the norms better fit their preferences.[37] Cultural homogeneity also reduces transaction costs through common language and understandings that can lower the costs of specifying property rights and negotiating over their use.[38]

Maintenance of cultural homogeneity requires excluding outsiders from collective action and may help explain limits on transferability of property rights. Use rights that cannot be bought by or sold to people outside the group can be rationalized in this context. In a society that depends upon shared values and repeated interactions as the mechanism for enforcement, it would be damaging to allow a member of that society to transfer rights to outsiders. Such a transfer could allow new people to become members of the group without appropriate social conditioning and could break down social consensus regarding the distribution of rights.[39]

Water law in the West provides an example. As water rights in remote mining camps and irrigation projects evolved, the rules often followed custom and seldom had much formal codification. Even when states did begin codifying the rights, local water users relied on informal structures to determine allocation. For example, if a junior water-rights appropriator did not have sufficient water in a drought year, informal mechanisms among irrigators could reallocate water without formal contracting. Moreover, when formal legal disputes did occur, involvement in the dispute was limited to those who actually held water rights on the stream in question. By not allowing the transfer of rights outside traditional uses such as irrigation, laws may thwart allocation to higher-valued uses such as maintaining environmental amenities, but they help sustain the cultural homogeneity that can reduce transaction costs.

When norms and customs are not sufficient to control agents for the collective, formal rules offer a way of constraining agents. These rules can range from constitutional rules to statutes. Such rules serve to constrain the coercive power of the agents so that rents will not be dissipated through the redistribution of property rights. The takings clause in the U.S. Constitution is an obvious example. It specifies that property cannot be taken by government without compensation and due process. If such rules are binding on governmental action, the options for redistributing property rights are reduced; if the rules are not binding, redistribution with its negative-sum results may supplant positive-sum games. This explains why wagon trains established constitution-like contracts before heading across the plains (see Chapter 7). The wagon-train constitutions specified obligations and rights and were designed to limit the use of coercive power by the wagon master. In summary, we can expect more constitutional limits on agents as the size of the collective increases, as competition between collectives decreases, and as homogeneity decreases.

)ed above, several hypotheses follow regarding the
;hts on the American frontier.

ncrease, institutional entrepreneurs will respond by
)rt to creating, rearranging, and redistributing prop-
:e versa.

:hange lowers the costs of defining and enforcing
1ore effort will be devoted to definition and enforce-

change alters the way in which goods are produced,
new contractual arrangements will evolve to organize production and
measure and monitor input use.

4. If resources are mobile over large territories, if the production process
requires control of large areas, or if there are scale economies in the
use of force, the size of the collective unit will be larger.

5. Because each member of a smaller collective unit has a greater stake in
the residual rents (that is, rents remaining after transaction costs are
subtracted), smaller units are more likely to reduce transaction costs,
while larger units are more likely to increase them.

6. Larger collective units are more likely to create differential advantages
in the use of force and hence are more likely to be used for redistributing rights.

7. Because agency costs increase with the size of the collective, with het-
erogeneity of members, and with difficulty of exiting from the collective, larger collective units are more likely to engage in redistribution
of rights.

Let us see how these predictions square with the history of the West.

THREE

Property Rights in Indian Country

There is no better place to begin examining why the American West was not so wild than with the "red man's law."[1] American Indians as they lived prior to European contact are portrayed as the role model for human co-existence with nature. "How can you buy or sell the sky, the warmth of the land?" asked Chief Seattle in a speech supposedly delivered by him in the 1850s.[2] This speech gives the impression that property rights and markets were inimical to an Indian culture that revered nature and her bounty. It is now well known, however, that the words in the oft-quoted speech are not actually those of Chief Seattle but rather those of Ted Perry, who paraphrased classicist William Arrowsmith's translation of the speech, adding "a good deal more, particularly modern ecological imagery."[3] Though Perry, not Chief Seattle, wrote, "Every part of the Earth is sacred to my people," that underlying philosophy has been accepted as the explanation for why Indians did not despoil nature and foul their environment. As Boyce Timmons put it, "because of their cultural heritage,

American Indians have a special relationship to all things, a oneness or unity of body and spirit that has made it possible for them to endure unbelievable hardships and oppression."[4]

This simplistic view misses important responses that Indian cultures would have had to scarcity and changing competition for resources. Indeed, "long before Darwin and Wallace brought biological evolution to the attention of the world in 1858, observers of the American Indian had recognized that evolution occurs in cultures."[5] This evolution produced an array of institutional arrangements as varied as any found elsewhere in human history.

Necessity was often the mother of institutional invention for American Indians. All societies must adjust to changing resource endowments, but the evolution of culture and institutions was particularly important for those societies that "lived at the margin of subsistence. In more developed societies, departures from optimality mean lower living standards and lower growth rates—luxuries these societies can afford. By contrast, in societies near the margin of subsistence, with populations under Malthusian control, such departures had harsher effects. . . . Unsound rights structures generally implied lower population size and, perhaps, the disappearance of the society."[6] Certainly not all North American Indians were living at the margin of subsistence, but all had to adapt. If they could not or did not, they would either starve or be conquered.

The language of property as we know it generally did not exist in American Indian societies, but the lack of formal laws and modern property-rights terms does not mean they lacked rules that paid attention to incentives. To the extent that resources were scarce, survival depended on rules or customs that determined who had access to and use of resources. Personal ethics worked alongside private and communal property rights to limit access to scarce resources. As law professor James Huffman concludes:

> it is not entirely true that Native Americans knew nothing of ownership. The language of the common law of property, like all of the English language, was unfamiliar to them. But the concepts of the tenancy in common was not foreign to bands and tribes who claimed and defended entitlements to hunting and fishing grounds. Nor was the concept of fee simple title alien to Native American individuals who possessed implements of war and peace, and even lands from which others could be excluded.[7]

MAP 1. Native American Tribes, 1850

Furthermore, institutional change among American Indians was just as endogenous to their societies as it was to Europeans who confronted vastly different resource constraints when they arrived on the American frontier.

Who Really Owned the Earth and Sky?

It is difficult to fit pre-Columbian Indian institutions into the modern context of law, government, and property rights. Though today we talk of "Indian nations," few tribes had formal governing structures that extended beyond local bands. Describing the Yurok Indians who lived on the Klamath River in the Pacific Northwest, Goldsmidt finds that "we may dismiss the village and tribe with a word. Though persons were identified by their village of residence and their tribe of origin, neither of these groups had any direct claim upon the action of the individual. There was no village or national government, no village or tribal action in wars."[8] Moreover, modern notions of private property rights, as well as defined ownership enforced by governmental institutions and traded in the marketplace, had little application in Indian societies.

Nonetheless, the lack of centralized, formal governing structures does not mean pre-Columbian Indians lacked rules that prevented the tragedy of the commons. As anthropologist Adamson Hoebel put it, "primitive anarchy does not mean disorder."[9] Over long periods, customs evolved that allowed Indians to survive and prosper from the resource-rich Pacific Northwest to the desert environs of the Southwest.

Law professor and judge Richard Posner summarizes why we might expect Indian institutions that evolved at the local level to minimize transaction costs and promote wealth creation:

> It is actually easier to explain why efficiency would have great social survival value in the primitive world than to explain this for our world. The efficient society is wealthier than the inefficient—that is what efficiency means—and a wealthier society will support a larger population. This effect of greater wealth can be decisive in the competition among primitive societies, where the methods of warfare are simple and numbers of people count for much more than in modern warfare. Archaic societies sufficiently durable to have left substantial literary or archaeological remains and primitive societies sufficiently durable to have survived into the nineteenth century . . . are likely, therefore, to be societies whose customs are efficient.[10]

Efficiency in this context means two things. First, it implies that people strive to change institutions only when the net benefits are positive. Therefore we would not expect people to waste time and energy defining and enforcing property rights for resources that are not scarce. Second, it means that societies develop institutions that align individual incentives so that people bear the costs and reap the benefits of their actions. Pre-Columbian Indians of the America West were efficient on both counts.

Because Indians invested in establishing property rights when it was economical to do so, Indian land tenure varied from tribe to tribe and location to location, "ranging from completely or almost completely communal systems to systems hardly less individualistic than our own with its core of fee simple tenure."[11] Referring to the migratory tribes of the Basin-Plateau, anthropologist Julian Steward concludes that Indians did not bother defining and enforcing property rights to resources that had no or low value: "All natural resources, with the sole exception of privately owned eagle nests, were free to anyone. This was not communal ownership; it was not ownership at all because no groups whatever claimed natural resources. Water, seed, and hunting areas, mineral and salt deposits, etc., were freely utilized by anyone."[12] On the other hand, where resources were scarce or where investments were required to make land productive, "truly communal property was scant. Tenancy in common as well as fee simple ownership were found among most agricultural tribes. Especially in cases where capital investment was required for irrigation, cultivation, or husbanding, Indians defined and enforced individual or family property rights to land."[13]

The Pueblo Indians living in the Upper Colorado Basin were typical of such agricultural tribes. Because crop production required considerable investment in clearing and leveling land, farmland was owned by the clan that made these investments. "Through assignment by the Isleta governor, an individual usually obtained a single acre of land [and the necessary water rights], but if the governor or his captains found that the assignee left the land within a year or did not farm it, the plot and accompanying water rights were returned to Pueblo possession and reassigned."[14] The Havasupai also recognized private ownership of farmland as long as the land was in use. As Edward Kennard observes, the Hopi Indians assigned the various matrilineal clans of the village exclusive rights to the fields: "Each clan allotment was marked by boundary stones, set up at the corners of the fields, with symbols of the clans painted on them."[15] Daryll Forde also notes that Hopi clan lands were marked "by numerous boundary stones . . . placed at the corners and junctions points" and "engraved on their faces with symbols of the appropriate clan."[16] The clan allotments were usually assigned to the women and became associated with a specific household through inheritance.

In contrast to land, flood control dams and irrigation canals built by the Pueblo Indians were communally owned. Communal ownership was more efficient than individual ownership because these systems required considerable investment not available to individuals and because construction involved significant scale economies. The transaction costs of continually negotiating agreements among private owners for maintenance of these systems would thus have been prohibitive.

Further evidence of the efficiency of institutions among the Pueblo Indians is found in the way they dealt with the risk of crop failure in an arid environment. "Dispersal of the lands of each clan over a number of sites is of very great practical importance since it reduces the risk of crop failure; where one group of fields may be washed out there remains the chance that the others may be spared."[17] The success of the Hopi institutional structure is summarized by Forde: "Hopi agriculture thus presents a number of remarkable characteristics which serve to mitigate the severity of an arid environment. By careful adaptation to local conditions and by the use of ingenious but unelaborate devices all the characteristic plants of the American maize-squash complex are successfully cultivated on a considerable scale. Agriculture is not, as often in marginal regions, auxiliary to hunting and collecting, but basic in the economy."[18]

Numerous Indian cultures evolved well-defined private rights to resources that were unique or that required long-term investment and care, and these rights were usually inherited.[19] "So important were the piñon resources that groves of trees were considered family property in several locations" within the Great Basin.[20] In one case a Northern Paiute reflected that his father "paid a horse for a certain piñon-nut range,"[21] suggesting that the property rights were valuable and could be traded. Grazing rights, on the other hand, were usually held in common because of the cost of containing livestock and the variation in fodder over the range.

The more sedentary California Indians also enforced property rights to valuable fixed assets that required investments. "Land, among Owens Valley Paiute and, to a lesser extent, among Salinas Valley Shoshoni, was band-owned and defended against trespass."[22] Compared to Plains tribes, California Indians had land that was more fertile, providing conditions for productive agriculture and resulting in denser populations usually organized in permanent villages. Steward reports that among Paiute Indians of the

Owens Valley, "communal groups stayed within their district territory" bounded by natural features such as mountains, ridges, and streams.[23] The result was a system of enforceable private property rights supported by a degree of organized tribal control. "Ecology thus permitted, if it did not cause, band development."[24] Landowning bands with specific names lived under the direction of chiefs with well-defined authority. Communal sweat houses and mourning ceremonies reinforced band unity. Families owned piñon, mesquite, screw-bean trees, and a few wild-seed patches, with ownership "being marked off by lines of rocks."[25] Though permission to gather food was sometimes given during times of abundance, trespass was not tolerated, with "the owner rebuking him [the trespasser] with such words as, 'Don't pick pine nuts here! They are not yours, but mine.'"[26] In an extreme case reported by John Muir, the owner of a piñon tree killed a white man for felling the tree.[27]

Steward summarizes the impact of long-term investment on property rights:

> Water, seed, and hunting areas, minerals and salt deposits, etc., were freely utilized by anyone. But once work had been done upon the products of natural resources (mixed labor with them) they became the property of the person or family doing the work. Willow groves could be used by anyone, but baskets made of willows belonged to their makers. Wild seeds could be gathered by anyone, but once harvested, they belonged strictly to the family doing the task.[28]

If property rights to Indian lands evolved when defining and enforcing those rights became economical, what about property rights to other resources, such as fish and wildlife, for which definition and enforcement might have been much more costly? We would expect that, as long as game was plentiful, little effort would be put into definition and enforcement activities, but if abundance declined because of natural conditions or competition from other users, property rights would evolve. Harold Demsetz found this to be the case in the Northeast as well as the West, where communal use-rights for hunting, fishing, gathering, or agriculture were common.[29] Among the Apache, each group "had its own hunting grounds and, except when pressed by starvation, was reluctant to encroach upon those of a neighbor. . . . Each local group had exclusive rights to certain farm sites and hunting localities, and each was headed by a chief who directed collective enterprises."[30]

Thus even though rights were communal, access was not open to all members of the larger community. Boundaries were drawn that reflected both the value of the resource and the costs of defining and enforcing rights. Some tribes established rights to "bear- and goat-hunting areas, berry and root patches, hot springs, sea otter grounds, seal and seal lion rocks, shellfish beds, cedar stands and trade routes."[31]

Perhaps the best example of territorial fishing rights comes from the Pacific Northwest, where Indians had well-defined fishing sites along the Columbia River.[32] Because fish were naturally channeled at falls or shoals, Indians built fish wheels, weirs, and other fixed appliances at those places and easily harvested salmon returning from the ocean to spawn in freshwater streams. "The red man had studied carefully the habits and movements of the salmon and knew that the places to trap them were at the mouths of the tributaries and churning cascades and waterfalls."[33] Property rights to these locations and to the fixed appliances were clearly enforced by the coastal Indians. Access to these locations was limited to the clan or house group. Robert Higgs notes that sites for "the fishing stands at the great Cleilo Falls of the Columbia, and the reef locations of the Lummi tribe in the northern Puget Sound . . . were heritable individual properties passed down from father to son."[34]

The management units could exclude other clans or houses from their fishing territories. When a territory was infringed upon, the trespasser was required to indemnify the owning group or potentially face violent consequences.[35] Management decisions were generally made by the *yitsati*, the "keeper of the house," who had the power to make and enforce decisions regarding harvest levels, escapement, fishing seasons, and harvest methods. This eldest male of the clan possessed superior knowledge about salmon runs, escapement, and fishing technology and therefore was in the best position to be the "custodian or trustee of the hunting and fishing territories."[36] Though anthropologists debate just how powerful the *yitsati* was, it is clear that salmon runs were sustained over long periods by site-specific rules that evolved in small groups with a large stake in the results.[37]

Though the Indians' technology used to catch spawning salmon was so

efficient that it could have depleted salmon stocks, they realized the importance of allowing some of the spawning fish to escape upstream. Higgs
quotes a Quileute Indian born about 1852: "When the Indians had obtained
enough fish they would remove the weirs from the river in order that the
fish they did not need could go upstream and lay their eggs so that there
would be a supply of fish for future years."[38] In an important case regarding
Indian fishing rights in the Pacific Northwest, the Boldt decision (named for
Judge George Boldt) summarized historic Indian fishing rights:

> Generally, individual Indians had primary use rights in the territory where
> they resided and permissive use rights in the natal territory (if this was dif-
> ferent) or in territories where they had consanguineal kin. Subject to such
> individual claims, most groups claimed autumn fishing use rights in the wa-
> ters near to their winter villages. Spring and summer fishing areas were of-
> ten more distantly located and often were shared with other groups from
> other villages. . . . Certain types [of fishing gear] required cooperative effort
> in their construction and/or handling. Weirs were classed as cooperative
> property but the component fishing stations on the weir were individually
> controlled.[39]

Anthropologist Frank Speck summarizes why he believes Indians were
what he called "aboriginal conservators":

> [They] carried on their hunting in restricted, family hunting territories de-
> scending from generation to generation in the male line. It was in these
> family tracts that the supply of game animals was maintained by deliberate
> systems of rotation in hunting and gathering, and defended by the family
> groups as a heritage from some remote time when the country had been
> given to their ancestors by the Creator.[40]

What Speck called "naked possession" led to "the maintenance of a supply
of animal and vegetable life, methods of insuring its propagation to provide
sources of life for posterity, the permanent family residence within well-
known and oftentimes blazed property boundaries, and resentment against
trespass by the family groups surrounding them who possessed districts of
their own."[41]

Personal property was nearly always privately owned because it required a significant investment of time to produce and maintain. Clothes, weapons, utensils, and housing were often the property of the women who made them. The tepee, for example, was owned by the women who collected the hides (usually between eight and twenty hides), tanned and scraped them, and sewed them together in a collective effort. Because considerable time was spent chipping arrowheads and constructing bows and arrows, these objects were also privately owned. High-quality stone for arrowheads and knives was also privately owned, as was wood for bows that came from distant locations and could be obtained only through long-distance trade.

In some areas, "rabbits were hunted by a communal drive under the leadership of a secular rabbit chief. The officer was distinct from both the leader of the deer hunt and the antelope charmer."[42] However, the nets into which the rabbits were driven were privately owned and maintained. "The catch of these large drives was usually divided equally among those who participated, but sometimes a larger share was offered to the hunt's organizer and leader or to the owners of the nets."[43]

The Impact of the Horse

Economist Martin Bailey lists five attributes of resources or technology that determine when common property prevails over private property in the evolutionary process in tribal societies:

1. Low predictability of prey or plant location within the tribal territory;
2. The public-good aspect of information about the location of this kind of unpredictable food resource;
3. High variability of the individual's success because of attribute 1, attribute 2, or other circumstances beyond the individual's control;
4. The superior productivity of group hunting techniques, such as driving prey into ambush or over a cliff; and
5. Safety from large predators, especially when bringing home the product of a successful trip.[44]

These attributes suggest a trade-off between the superior incentive effects inherent in private property and the advantages from scale economies captured through communal activities. In a hunting and gathering society, low predictability of prey and plant locations explains why cooperation was a necessary condition for survival. Similarly, what Bailey calls the "public-good aspect of information" can be more appropriately understood as economies of scale in information collection.[45] This encouraged coordination of searching because coordination would "produce better total results for the group than would an individual's solitary tracking."[46] High variability of success at hunting and gathering meant that individual efforts could result in starvation. And finally, just as a modern business firm must trade off the gains from scale economies against the costs of monitoring the assembly line, so Indian tribes had to weigh the superior productivity of communal hunting against the potential for shirking by individual members.[47]

European contact changed several of these variables, putting pressure on American Indians to change their institutions. In some cases, the changes were more revolutionary than evolutionary, for two reasons. First, trade with Europeans dramatically altered relative prices. As already mentioned, the demand for beaver pelts induced northeastern Indians to establish property rights to trapping territories. The same thing happened with buffalo. As tribes became more mobile, the potential for the tragedy of the commons increased. At the same time, European demand for hides increased the potential rents from access to the resource. Plains Indians responded by patrolling their hunting territories.[48]

Second, European technology, especially the introduction of the horse, dramatically altered production processes. The horse "was one of the most dramatic and one of the most momentous transformations that ever took place in any land under the sun. The bare facts of the coming of the horse and the transformation thus wrought constitute the greatest animal epic ever enacted in the world."[49] The Indians' response to the revolutionary impact of the horse was to devise new, efficient institutions and property rights because the evolutionary process took place in small groups in which people had a stake in the outcome.

Applying Bailey's theory to the Indian horse culture reveals three factors that conditioned the choice between uncoordinated individual activities and collective enterprises. First, scale economies in gathering information about the location of migratory species such as the buffalo and in hunting those buffalo encouraged coordinated hunting. Second, communal organizations enabled subsistence societies to share risk in the face of variability in game location, weather, or other biological factors. Third, the gains from scale economies and risk sharing had to be traded off against the costs of collective organization. The central hypothesis that follows from this framework is that horses changed the way Indians hunted buffalo. By reducing scale economies, decreasing variability in the access to buffalo, and changing the relative value of hunting inputs, the optimal size of social organizations declined.

PEDESTRIAN HUNTING ORGANIZATION

Before the horse, hunting buffalo was a communal exercise that took place in the summer, bringing together groups that were dispersed in smaller bands throughout the rest of the year. Pedestrian hunting required larger groups for driving herds of animals (sometimes with the aid of fire) into surrounds (semicircular arrangements of women interspersed with upended travois) or over cliffs known as jumps or *piskuns*. A hunt leader coordinated activities by appointing guards "who prevented the disruption of the communal effort by attempts to hunt alone in advance of the village. These guards punished offenders through destruction of their property 'without the man or woman saying a word.'"[50] Indians chased the animals, closed in on them, and killed them. In the end, the meat was carved up and distributed approximately equally among all participants.

Three general methods of hunting bison prevailed in pre-equestrian times: the stalk, the surround, and the drive. The stalk provided the fewest scale economies of any of the pedestrian techniques and therefore allowed larger groups to disband.[51] The stalk was most successful in winter, because the bison were mired in deep snowdrifts. If the snow thawed during a warm day or two and then refroze, the hardened surface might support a human on snowshoes but collapse under a buffalo's hooves. The disparity in ground speed would then be narrowed, because the Indians with snowshoes could dart across the snow surface to great advantage. Sometimes the buffalo could be run down to the point where they became so helpless they might be killed with a dagger or spear.[52] Even after the arrival of the horse, deep snows might preclude its use, thus necessitating the pedestrian stalk even in equestrian times.[53]

The surround incorporated elements of both the stalk and the drive and therefore entailed scale economies and communal organization costs. In one version of the surround, a make-shift fence was constructed by tying dog travois together. A group of swift-footed men would rouse the herd and drive it toward the fence while others stood alongside the drive route and closed in behind the herd. When the surround was complete, the herd would run in a circle while hunters slaughtered them with arrows. Though coordination could be costly and the setup time lengthy, the economies of scale made it the choice when terrain was suitable and buffalo were available.

The pedestrian drive promised the wholesale slaughter of an entire herd, but at the greatest expense of planning, labor, coordination, and care. The drive involved corralling a herd of bison in a natural topographical pit or trap, or in a permanent man-made pound. The most famous variant of the drive was the buffalo jump, in which a herd was stampeded over a cliff. Unlike the pedestrian stalk, the successful drive had little chance of startling neighboring herds since the selected herd could be directed to the place of the killing. Thus many tribes could conduct drives all season long, until there were no longer sufficient bison in the vicinity.[54]

The surround and the drive both posed a difficulty: they required drawing the herd over great distances to the specific location of the surround or the jump. Most jumps or traps lay within an area where bison naturally gathered, often a basin or valley floor. From this area, the herds would slowly be led into the drive lines, which were made of stone, buffalo chips, or other available materials and were split into a "V" shape with the apex at the trap. The herd was thus funneled toward the trap as Indians stood at the sidelines beating their robes to prevent the bison from testing the durability of the drive lines. At one site, the drive lines extended at least 2.5 miles to the west, and bison may have been driven a considerable distance before even arriving at the opening of the drive.[55] Often the herd was led by a "runner" or "decoy"—an Indian who dressed like a buffalo and imitated its movements and calls. By bleating like a stray calf or attracting the curiosity of the herd in some fashion, the decoy could start the herd moving toward him and then ever closer to the drive lines.

If the herds had been found grazing far from the pound, a herder, an aide to the decoyer, would have gone for them, ten, twenty, as far as fifty miles away, to work them toward the pound, again using smoke and available wind, or showing himself at strategic moments, or running at top speeds to turn the herd when necessary, or sitting for hours to wait for a "convenient season." At night he might nudge them along by slapping his robe on the ground to startle them into movement. When the herder had brought the herd close, the decoyer took over.[56]

A group of people walking behind a herd could direct it by cutting back and forth as need be.[57]

The drive required a great deal of time, patience, and buffalo savvy. Though bison were considered most manageable in the fall, the drive was a difficult operation in all seasons. The slightest disturbance might set the buffalo off in a stampede, ruining the opportunity to get any animals from the herd. The greatest danger occurred just before the bison reached the edge of the cliff or the pound opening. If the lead animal was strong and wily or was not pushed forward by the press of stampeding bison behind, it might turn back, leading the whole herd back with it.[58] Success also depended on topographical features of the cliff and surrounding area.

Because the availability of buffalo fluctuated throughout the seasons, Indian bands aggregated and disaggregated in response to the supply. As Sarah Carter puts it, "[pedestrian] Indian life on the prairie followed a pattern of concentration and dispersal that paralleled that of the buffalo."[59] George Bird Grinnell describes the seasonal use of buffalo jumps and surrounds:

> As spring opened, the buffalo would move down to the more flat prairie country away from the pis'kuns. Then the Blackfeet would also move away. As winter drew near, the buffalo would again move up close to the mountains, and the Indians, as food began to become scarce, would follow them toward the pis'kuns. In the last of the summer and early autumn, they always had runners out, looking for the buffalo, to find where they were, and which way they were moving. In the early autumn, all the pis'kuns were repaired and strengthened, so as to be in good order for winter.[60]

When the Indians knew that the buffalo were nearby, they formed into their hunting groups and partook of the bounty; when the buffalo were distant, the Indians dispersed. Smaller groups would come together seasonally in groups of approximately 150 persons[61] to hunt bison.[62] When a group got larger than this, it would peaceably divide, apparently because the agency costs rose significantly.[63]

THE EQUESTRIAN REVOLUTION

The use of the horse spread northward from Mexico, passing from tribe to tribe during the period 1600–1740.[64] This spread of the horse during the eighteenth and nineteenth centuries changed the Indians' lives by increasing mobility and reducing transportation costs. "The immediate effect upon the Indians of the acquisition of a few Spanish horses by trade or theft was to discourage what little agricultural work they did, and cause them to rely upon the buffalo more than ever before. . . . With the horse they roamed for miles, encroached upon others' hunting grounds, went to war, and otherwise became marauders of the plains."[65]

Indians changed their diet from one of gathered seeds and roots, a few cultivated plants, and limited meat to one dominated by protein from buffalo meat.[66] Moreover, they used the animals they killed much less intensively:

> The abundance of buffalo in the Blackfoot Country, the relative ease with which they could be killed by mounted hunters, the limited facilities of the average family for transporting meat surpluses, and the demands of the fur trade for buffalo robes encouraged the wasteful slaughter of these animals during the 19th century. . . . As early as 1754, Anthony Hendry observed that when buffalo were plentiful the "Archithinue" [tribe] of the Saskatchewan Plains took only the tongues and other choice pieces, leaving the rest to the wolves. . . . These factors encouraged "Light butchering" and use of only the choice parts of the buffalo in good times.[67]

The horse also changed the Indians' housing from permanent or semi-permanent lodges to the large tepees that now symbolize Plains life. In the "dog days," when canines were used for transportation, Indians used tepees, but the size averaged approximately 12 feet in diameter. "Once the horse was introduced, the tepee became larger (the horse could carry the longer poles required of a larger tepee) and its territory expanded. The tepee spread so far because there was always a ready supply of buffalo skins for the cover and because it could be used in just about any terrain or climate."[68] In fact, tepee rings on the plains indicated that after the introduction of the horse, tepees 18 feet to 21 feet in diameter were common.

The optimal size of socioeconomic groups and seasonal economic patterns shifted dramatically with adaptation to the horse culture. The mobility gained with the horse immediately made the bison more available, even as the bison population declined. "With dogs, five or six miles had been a good day's journey; with the horse, ten, fifteen, or even twenty miles could be traversed."[69] Before the horse, a tribe could scarcely move 50 miles in an entire season, whereas in equestrian days, the same tribe could cover 500 miles.[70] While the horse allowed tribes to move greater distances, it also permitted them to move less frequently by enabling foraging parties to travel far from a permanent hub camp to gather meat.[71] With the horse, tribes suddenly found themselves able to undertake expeditions lasting several months or even several years, ranging across the Rocky Mountains to partake of the numerous buffalo herds in the Yellowstone region.[72] Even when the horse could not make fresh meat available, it did allow the Indians to transport more stored provisions as insurance against hard times.[73]

Acquisition of the horse reduced the scale economies in hunting, making it easier for bands to be independent of one another. On horseback, individuals could more easily track and kill game. Moreover, with greater individual ability to follow and harvest game, the need for communal insurance schemes declined.

It was the chase on horseback that fully exploited the horse's ability to run faster than the swiftest buffalo. This new hunting technique was more efficient and adaptable than any method previously employed. Not only did it require a fraction of the time and energy but it was less dangerous and more certain of success than other methods. It could be employed by a single hunter or the men of an entire village. Within a few minutes a skilled hunter, mounted on a fleet, intelligent, buffalo horse could kill at close range enough buffalo to supply his family with meat for months.[74]

Because horses required adequate pasturage and water, Indians had to move their camps to accommodate the animals' needs.[75] With the number of horses per lodge averaging between fifteen and twenty,[76] campsites always "had to be chosen with a view to adequate pasturage."[77]

If the horse eliminated economies of scale in hunting and thus the need for centralized hunting institutions, it increased the need for military institutions and their inherent scale economies. "It was . . . leisure time, the rise of the pony as a measure of wealth, and the infringement upon one another's buffalo range that was a cause of intertribal war."[78] Increased mobility brought more conflict between tribes for larger hunting territories and more raids to steal horses. As a result, Plains Indians had to "construct new trade and military patterns to replace those that had collapsed."[79]

To organize for intertribal warfare, new, more centralized political structures evolved to capture the scale economies. Demitri Shimkin described this transition for the Eastern Shoshoni: "With the acquisition of horses came . . . widespread raiding throughout the Plains, 1700–1780. In this period, it is certain that strong chiefly leadership and considerable protocol and sumptuary rights prevailed."[80] Prior to the horse, there was little intertribal warfare. For the Blackfoot, one of the fiercest Plains tribes, "traditions claim that the Shoshoni were their only enemies in pre-horse times."[81] After the acquisition of the horse, however, alliances were few and intertribal warfare was common. "Throughout the century prior to 1885, peace between the Blackfoot tribes and their neighbors (other than Sarsi and Gros Ventres) was the exception, war the rule. Peaceful periods were brief interludes between hostilities."[82]

The enhanced mobility introduced with the horse meant that tribes would encounter one another more frequently and potentially fight over common herds of buffalo. In view of the heightened danger of encroachment by other tribes, the greater dependence on the buffalo, and the ability to patrol an area on horseback, tribes everywhere laid claim to private tribal hunting grounds. Tribes drew boundary lines and signed treaties to defend them. If no clear topographic features existed to delineate the boundary, boulders wrapped in buffalo hides substituted.[83]

On the heels of intertribal warfare came conflicts with whites and an even greater demand for institutional change to accommodate warfare. During the nineteenth century, institutions with strong tribal chiefs evolved for organizing warriors. As Steward explains, "The institution of the band chief

The Buffalo Hunt, by C. M. Russell. Plains Indians had many adjustments to make when the horse entered the culture. Hunting buffalo from horseback took courage and skill and therefore required rewarding the hunter appropriately. By marking their arrows, riders such as those depicted in this painting established property rights to their kill and to a claim on the best cuts of meat. Courtesy of the Sid Richardson Collection of Western Art, Fort Worth, Texas.

was novel and hence provided opportunity for influential personalities to assert themselves" and to unite independent villages into "military bands under high commands."[84]

Because the horse had such profound impacts on Indian life, it is not surprising that ownership of horses became a symbol of wealth and prestige. Horses were always considered personal property with full rights of inheritance and trade. James Willard Schultz, who lived with the Blackfeet, remarked of them in the 1870s that "Horses were the tribal wealth, and one who owned a large herd of them held a position only to be compared to that of our multi-millionaires. These were individuals who owned from one hundred to three and four hundred."[85] Tribes living west of the Rockies, where they were somewhat immune from horse raids by Plains Indians and where grazing conditions were more favorable than on the plains, became "noted for their attention to and skill in breeding horses."[86]

Conclusion

When Hollywood's stereotype of the wild Indian (like its general stereotype of the wild West) and the popular vision of Indians as America's first environmentalists are reconsidered in an institutional context, romance gives way to reality. The Indian frontier was not so wild, for their law evolved in accordance with customs, culture, and resource scarcity. American Indians understood the importance of using rules to limit access to the commons, but devoted resources to the definition and enforcement process only when it was economical to do so. Property rights did not exist everywhere; they were created only where and when Indians could capture economic rents by going to the effort of defining and enforcing such rights. These rights evolved in small group settings where each member benefited from institutions that economized on transaction costs and reduced rent dissipation.

And when American Indians acquired the horse, they devised not only revolutionary new technologies for hunting, housing, and transportation but also institutions consistent with wealth creation, except insofar as horses increased competition for the commons. Increased mobility brought increased competition for resources—especially the bison that roamed over wide territories—and incited conflict between Indian tribes. Unable to establish property rights to mobile resources, Indians warred with Indians before they warred with whites. In fact, had the Indians not developed their military institutions in response to the intertribal conflict, they might not have been able to resist the onslaught of whites for as long as they did. In any case, both the intertribal wars and the Indian-white wars were rent seeking that resulted from incomplete property rights.

FOUR

Might Takes Rights in Indian Country

From initial contact to the present time, the history of Indian-white relations largely revolves around property rights, since the structure of those
rights determined who could claim the rents from the resources in question.
That history is basically characterized by three distinct periods. First, from
initial contact to the middle of the nineteenth century, white individuals and
colonial and U.S. governments in the main honored Indian property and
territorial rights. Second, from the middle until nearly the end of the nineteenth century, the national government used military power to take Indian
rights by force. Third, from the late nineteenth century until the present,
federal agencies have controlled the formation of property rights on reservations in ways that have ensured the survival of the bureaucracy rather than
allowing tribal sovereignty.[1]

To understand the transition in Indian-white relations, consider the relative values of land to the two groups.[2] When Pilgrims first arrived at Ply-
mouth Rock looking for terra firma, the value of a little land to the settlers

would have been quite high, while the value of an extra few acres to Indians would have been quite low.[3] Under these circumstances, the potential gains from trade must have been large, with Indians willing to accept trinkets of high value to them (but of low value to the Europeans) in exchange for land of high value to the Europeans (but of low value to the Indians).

Pushing the frontier westward, however, would have changed these values for the two groups. The value of additional land to Europeans surely declined as more land was acquired, and the value of additional land to the Indians surely rose as more and more was transferred to Europeans. At some point, the price that Indians would demand for an additional acre would exceed the price that Europeans would pay. Hence the potential gains from trade would diminish and eventually disappear as Europeans pushed the frontier westward. If the two groups had engaged in peaceful exchange of land under these conditions, the distribution of land would have reached an equilibrium, with neither group controlling all.

But Europeans could acquire land by other means than trade; they could take it without compensation. By threatening or exercising force, Europeans might have been able to acquire the land at a cost below market price. In other words, forcible redistribution of property rights (raiding) can dominate the voluntary transfer of property rights (trading). If there are differential advantages in the use of force, forcible redistribution rather than trade is more likely to occur (see Chapter 2). Of course, the cost of taking land would depend on whether Indians would respond to force with force and whether such a response would effectively counter the European threat. Again one can imagine a stalemate wherein the threat from each side is sufficiently balanced to render trading a better option than raiding. The calculus of the choice between trading and raiding can help us understand the shifts in Indian-white relations during the nineteenth century.

Trading Rather Than Raiding

The history of Indian-white relations is often portrayed as one in which whites ran roughshod over the rights of Indians. As economist J. R. T. Hughes put it, "from beginning to end primary title was deemed to come by right of conquest, Indian title being inferior in the views of the crown [and] the settlers."[4] Historian Don Russell characterizes the conventional tale as one long episode of "'massacre,' 'extermination,' and 'annihilation,' both 'utter' and 'complete,'" recounted "with overtones of racism, genocide, and other shibboleths."[5] Teddy Roosevelt believed the European settlers "had justice on their side; this great continent could not have been kept as nothing but a game preserve for squalid savages."[6]

But the following letter from Thomas Jefferson to David Campbell regarding the cost of war relative to the cost of peace more appropriately describes the 100 years of Indian-white relations after the American Revolution:

> I hope too that your admonitions against encroachments on the Indian lands will have a beneficial effect—the U.S. finds an Indian war too serious a thing, to risk incurring one merely to gratify a few intruders with settlements which are to cost the other inhabitants of the U.S. a thousand times their value in taxes for carrying on the war they produce. I am satisfied it will ever be preferred to send armed force and make war against the intruders (the white settlers) as being more just & less expensive.[7]

The legal doctrine that guided U.S. policy toward Indians in the late eighteenth and early nineteenth centuries "recognized the Indians' right to use and occupy land. Under this title, the United States is liable to pay the tribe when it decides to extinguish the Indian use and occupancy."[8] In supporting Indian land rights, Thomas Jefferson asserted that the United States had a "sole and exclusive right to purchasing from them whenever they should be willing to sell."[9] Even though this preemption theory adhered to by Jefferson gave the United States the sole right to negotiate with the Indians, it did not provide "any dominion, or jurisdiction, or paramountship whatever, but merely in the nature of a remainder after the extinguishment of the present right, which gave us no present right whatever, but of preventing other nations from taking possession, and so defeating our expectancy; that the Indians had the full, undivided and independent sovereignty as long as they chose to keep it, and that this might be forever."[10] Jefferson believed land acquisition by negotiation had been the norm, and land takings not extensive, noting "that the lands of this country were taken from them (Indians) by conquest, is not so general a truth as is supposed. I find in our historians and records, repeated proofs of purchase, which cover a considerable part of the lower country; and many more would doubtless be found on further search. The upper country we know has been acquired altogether by purchases made in the most unexceptionable form."[11]

Historians generally agree that negotiated settlements predominated over war in the early history of Indian-white relations. Economist Jennifer Roback summarizes Indian-white relations in colonial times: "Europeans generally acknowledged that the Indians retained possessory rights to their lands. More importantly, the English recognized the advantage of being on friendly terms with the Indians. Trade with the Indians, especially the fur trade, was profitable. War was costly."[12] Even after the French and Indian War, by which the English deemed themselves to have won French rights to land in the New World, "there was no assumption that Indian rights in the lands claimed by France had been extinguished. Although Indian rights were less formal and less fundamental in European eyes than European claims, they nevertheless did exist as the subject for purchase, for negotiation, for retention."[13] "More than [is] generally appreciated, the contact (between Indians and whites) was even friendly, or at least peaceful."[14]

Where trespass onto Indian lands did occur during the late eighteenth and early nineteenth centuries, it was official government policy to protect Indian rights and to expel white intruders. A memo of January 27, 1816, from Secretary of War William H. Crawford to Military Commanders bears this out:

> Intrusions upon the lands of the friendly Indian tribes is not only a violation of the laws, but in direct opposition to the policy of the government towards its savage neighbors. Upon application of any Indian Agent, stating that intrusions of this nature have been committed, and are continued, the President requires, that they [whites] shall be equally removed, and their house and improvements destroyed by military force; and that every attempt to return, shall be repressed in the same manner.[15]

During these early years, U.S. troops were respected by the Indians, who saw them not as aggressors but as protectors of Indian rights. Francis Prucha disagrees with "the widely held opinion that the Indians were ruthlessly dispossessed with nothing done to protect their rights. On the contrary, the In-

Toll Collectors, by C. M. Russell. Until the U.S. Army changed the balance of power, it was more common for whites to negotiate with Indians than to fight them. When cattle drovers took their cattle into well-defined Indian territories, they traded cattle for safe passage. Russell illustrates this trading system by showing one Indian brave negotiating the number of steers while another cuts them from the herd. Courtesy of the Montana Historical Society, Mackay Collection.

dians were not completely deserted. Explicit treaties were made guaranteeing their rights, and stringent laws were enacted to ensure respect for the treaties."[16] During the early years, what military forces there were in Indian Country were seen more as a force for protection of Indian rights than as "a wedge for whites to intrude into forbidden lands."[17]

Table 4.1 shows the number of battles and treaties between Indians and whites for the period from 1790 to 1897. At the end of the eighteenth century and for the first four decades of the nineteenth century, peacefully negotiated treaties significantly outnumbered battles. Felix Cohen, one of the most respected legal scholars of Indian property rights, referred to the early period of Indian-white relations as one of "fair dealing."[18] Unfortunately something changed at mid-century to encouraging taking rather than trading by whites.

TABLE 4.1

Indian-White Battles and Treaties, 1790–1897

	Battles	Treaties
1790–1799	7	10
1800–1809	0	30
1810–1819	33	35
1820–1829	1	51
1830–1839	63	84
1840–1849	53	18
1850–1859	190	58
1860–1869	786	61
1870–1879	530	0
1880–1889	131	0
1890–1897	13	0

SOURCE: T. Anderson and McChesney 1994, 58.

From Trading to Raiding

As described above, the amount of conflict between Indians and whites depended on the costs of defending and taking land relative to the value of that land to each side. If the parties could bargain costlessly and if each party knew precisely the military strength of its opponent and the value the opponent placed on the land, few disputes would result in fights. After all, war is a negative-sum game, and if both parties knew the outcome in advance, they would avoid this result. But bargaining is not costless, and parties do not have perfect information about military strength. Ultimately the decision about whether to raid or trade depended on many factors, including

1. The transaction costs of defining and exchanging property rights;
2. The military technology available to each side;
3. Information asymmetries; and
4. The rise of the standing army, especially following the Civil War.

TRANSACTION COSTS OF DEFINING AND EXCHANGING PROPERTY RIGHTS

If ownership rights to property are well defined and can be exchanged, the costs of negotiations decline relative to the costs of taking. If whites knew which tribe "owned" a parcel of land and knew with whom to bargain, the costs of negotiated settlements were lower and the likelihood of settlements higher.

In this regard, there was an important difference between property rights to Indian land in the East and those in the West, a difference that raised the transaction costs associated with trading as the frontier pushed westward. In the East, where sedentary agriculture was the principal activity for both Indians and whites, private property was more common. In sedentary agricultural societies, ownership claims to parcels of land were clearer, and Indian political institutions made negotiations easier. Under these circumstances, the federal government defended the property rights of Indians and negotiated trades for the rights to Indian lands.

Not surprisingly, in the absence of clearly defined property rights that could be bought and sold, armed conflict replaced negotiation. And as we saw in Chapter 3, the mobility afforded by the horse made property rights to land west of the Mississippi quite different. The horse dislodged Indians from centuries-old ancestral territories.

> As life on the Plains became more inviting with the use of horses, more
> tribes moved out there, the Sioux and Cheyennes, and Arapahos from the
> east, the Comanches and Kiowas from the west. Some abandoned their
> agriculture entirely and based their economy on the buffalo herds—"We
> lost the Corn," say the Cheyennes. Others like the Osages maintained their
> fixed residences, where they planted their crops, rode out to the Plains for
> their supply of meat, and returned to harvest their corn and settle down for
> the winter.[19]

This new way of life on the plains created conflict among Indians even before the whites arrived on the scene. As one Sioux chief declared to his white conquerors, "You have split my land and I don't like it. These lands once belonged to the Kiowas and the Crows, but we whipped these nations out of them, and in this we did what the white men do when they want the lands of the Indians."[20] In other words, white migration did not intrude on an equilibrium system of aboriginal rights respected by the various tribes, "but rather broke over a congeries of scattered groups that had been fighting one another for generations and would continue to fight one another to the day of final conquest by the whites."[21]

High transaction costs for negotiations also resulted from the inability of the governments of both sides to prevent their citizens from violating terms of agreements. Most treaty violations were committed "not by leaders of the United States or of the Indian tribes but rather by members of these groups who could not be controlled by the leadership."[22] Indeed chiefs could seldom constrain individual warriors. The Nez Perce warrior was typical, as he

> accorded his loyalty and allegiance first to his family, then to his band, and finally to his tribe, but rarely beyond. . . . The autonomous bands looked to chiefs and headmen who counseled but did not command. . . . [Warriors] obeyed or disobeyed as personal inclination dictated, and combat usually took the form of the explosion of personal encounters rather than a collision of organized units.[23]

And "chiefs rarely represented their people as fully as white officials assumed, nor could they enforce compliance if the people did not want to comply."[24] Individual warriors frequently ignored the treaties that their chiefs had signed, bringing retribution by whites onto the whole tribe or band. The bloody Sioux uprising in Minnesota and the massacre of Black Kettle's Cheyenne on the Washita River are two infamous examples.[25]

On the white side, similar problems of controlling citizens complicated the interaction with Indians. Treaties signed in good faith by white politicians proved to be unenforceable, as individual whites violated them with impunity. The problem lay with the national government's inability to defend Indian property rights against white citizens. This problem was recognized by Secretary of War Henry Knox, who wrote to President Washington: "The desires of too many frontier white people, to seize, by force or fraud, upon the neighboring Indian lands has been, and still continues to be, an unceasing cause of jealousy and hatred on the part of the Indians. . . . Revenge is sought, and the innocent frontier people are too frequently involved as victims in the cruel contest. This appears to be the principal cause of the Indian wars."[26] Thus it appears that transaction costs weighted the decision calculus toward conflict as the nineteenth century wore on.

MILITARY TECHNOLOGY AVAILABLE TO EACH SIDE

To choose conflict over negotiation requires that at least one side feels it has superior military force over the other. Though it might appear that the whites' guns would be superior to the Indians' bows, this was not necessarily the case prior to breech-loading and repeating rifles. In the early years, for example, the Indians' bows and arrows were a match for the whites' muzzle loaders. Walter Prescott Webb compares the two in the case of Texans and Comanches:

> In most respects the Indian had the best of it. In the first place, the Texan carried at most three shots; the Comanche carried twoscore or more arrows. It took the Texan a minute to reload his weapon; the Indian could in that time ride three hundred yards and discharge twenty arrows. The Texan had to dismount in order to use his rifle effectively at all, and it was his most reliable weapon; the Indian remained mounted throughout the combat. Apparently the one advantage possessed by the white man was a weapon of longer range and more deadly accuracy than the Indian's bow, but the agility of the Indian and the rapidity of his movements did much to offset this advantage.[27]

General Sherman stated that "fifty Indians could checkmate three thousand troops,"[28] and "frontier army officers often called the horse warriors the finest light cavalry in the world, and historians have repeated the judgment ever since."[29] Even when gun technology improved with fast-loading rifles and revolvers, white superiority in weaponry was often short-lived because Indians quickly obtained the new weapons from traders and trappers. Therefore the lack of clear military superiority by either side contributed to ongoing conflict.

INFORMATION ASYMMETRIES

While better military technology alone may not have increased warfare, disparities in information about that technology certainly helped tip the balance toward conflict. To understand the importance of informational asymmetries, we must recognize that there would be no fighting if both sides knew what the outcome would be in advance. The side that knew it would win would only have to threaten to fight, and the side that knew it would lose would immediately give up. When one side or the other is misinformed about the probability of victory, however, the odds of fighting relative to negotiating increase.

From the beginning of contact with Indians, whites understood the importance of providing their opponents with accurate information about white military superiority. Whites continually shipped Indians back to Europe to impress them with the extent of white technology, "with the expectation that upon their return they would spread the gospel of European superiority throughout their native villages."[30]

As the frontier moved west, however, informational asymmetries increased for several reasons. Because western Indians were more nomadic, it was more difficult for whites to communicate with an entire tribe. To be sure, nomadic Plains Indians regularly were taken to Washington to be impressed by the power of the federal government and the growing white population, but the information did not always filter down to wandering bands, and even when it did, it was not always believed.

On the white side, the different landscape and climate on the plains resulted in Indian warfare tactics different from what whites had encountered previously. The Plains Indians "greatly favored the decoy tactic,"[31] in which a small party went out from the camp to encounter a white detachment, seemingly by mistake, and then ran from it to lure pursuing whites into a trap where far more numerous Indian warriors lay hidden.

In fact, faulty information on the part of one side or the other seems to have been an important factor in just about all the bloody fighting in the West. In the notorious Fetterman Massacre in 1866, the decoy tactic enticed 81 bluecoats into a fatal encounter with some 2,000 Sioux. Custer's apparent foolhardiness in attacking over 3,000 Sioux and Cheyenne with just a few hundred men at the Little Bighorn in 1876 might attest to his arrogance but also certainly reflects his ignorance of the true number of Indians opposing him.[32]

The Wagon Box Fight in 1867, in which Sioux suffered extraordinarily heavy losses, illustrates how changing military technology contributed to the informational asymmetry. "One chief placed them [Sioux losses] at 1,137, and called the battle a 'medicine fight'—meaning that the soldiers had supernatural help. What the soldiers had were new Springfield breech-loading

rifles and plenty of ammunition, while the Indians were using the old muz-
zle-loaders."[33] When the revolver was first used by the Texas Rangers in the
1840s, the Indians were shocked by its effect. After being attacked by a nu-
merically superior band of Comanches in Nueces Canyon, the Texas
Rangers pursued the Indians on horseback, firing their pistols. "Never was a
band of Indians more surprised than at this charge," said one of the
Rangers.[34] After a chase that covered 300 miles and resulted in more than
100 Indian deaths, "a Comanche chief who was in this fight said he never
wanted to fight Jack Hays and his Rangers again" because "they had a shot
for every finger on the hand."[35] Hence, it was not just new military technology but the element of surprise in the introduction of that technology that
contributed to fighting instead of negotiation. Once it was clear that one
side had superior military power, however, those like the Comanche chief
would have little taste for another fight.

THE RISE OF THE STANDING ARMY

Arguably the most important factor contributing to increased fighting between whites and Indians was the rise of the standing U.S. Army, which created a differential advantage in the use of force and changed the benefits and
costs of fighting (see Chapter 2, hypothesis 6). In the first years of the new
republic, the militia system was common: "individual colonies, and more often the frontiersmen themselves, had to protect the frontier."[36] This meant
that the costs of fighting rather than negotiating redounded closer to home,
where individuals had to consider the prospect of losing their own or their
family's lives.

Maintaining a standing army, as opposed to raising a local militia, shifted
the cost of fighting to others and predictably increased the number of battles. The establishment of a standing army during the Mexican-American
War and the subsequent buildup of that army for the Civil War meant there
were full-time officers and, behind them, military bureaucrats, all of whose
careers and budgets were advanced by fighting. When the fighting ended in
both of these wars, the size of the peacetime army was bound to shrink, but
the "Indian problem" provided a way for military special interests to slow
the rate of decline. "Protection of the frontier population and travel routes
from hostile Indians placed the largest demand on the Army. . . . For [the

latter half of the nineteenth century], the U.S. Army would find its primary mission and its main reason for existence in the requirements of the westward movement beyond the Mississippi."[37]

The individuals involved understood the benefits of fighting. Civil War officers retained their brevet ranks and pay as long as they were fighting Indians. For example, General Custer held that rank only when he fought; otherwise he was a lieutenant colonel. For enlisted men as well as officers, peace meant ennui and lost chances for advancement.

> A soldier's duty on the frontier was dismal and frustrating. Boredom, low pay, coarse food and shabby quarters, harsh discipline and cruel punishment, constant labor of an unmilitary character, field service marked by heat and cold, rain and snow, mud and dust, hunger and thirst, deadening fatigue—these were to be expected. But they were unaccompanied by the prospect of meaningful combat and the opportunity for distinction that ordinarily make the terms of military life more endurable.[38]

The antidote for boredom was battle, but the excuse for battle was not necessarily easy to come by. After inspecting the Smoky Hill stage line that ran through the Cheyenne and Arapaho hunting grounds, General Sherman remarked, "God only knows when, and I do not see how, we can make a decent excuse for an Indian war."[39] But he also "made cynical reference to the local hunger for army contracts. Usually citizens were happy to call on the regular army to do the shooting, especially as federal troops required supplies bought locally. This factor often caused citizens to holler loudly before they were hurt."[40] Politicians also were quick to recognize that fighting meant increased federal revenues in their districts.[41] In short, the Indian wars stemmed in large part from a strong coalition of professional soldiers, politicians, suppliers, and citizens.

The anecdotal evidence that the rise of a standing army increased the number of battles with Indians is supported by empirical data. Table 4.2 confirms that the mean number of battles in the five years following the Mexican and Civil Wars was significantly higher than in the five years preceding each war.[42] A regression analysis of these data by Terry Anderson and Fred McChesney, including other variables that might explain the increase in the number of battles (for example population density and army size), shows that

TABLE 4.2

Indian Battles Before and After the Mexican and Civil Wars

	Years	Mean Annual Number of Battles
Before the Mexican War	1841–1845	2.8*
After the Mexican War	1849–1854	8.4*
Before the Civil War	1856–1860	31.6**
After the Civil War	1865–1869	110.4**

SOURCE: T. Anderson and McChesney 1994, 69.
 * Means are significantly different at .01 level ($t = 2.61$).
 ** Means are significantly different at .01 level ($t = 4.09$).

the independent effect of the Mexican War was a discontinuous increase of almost 12 battles per year, and the Civil War caused an increase of approximately 25 battles per year.[43] Clearly the rise of the standing army reduced the incentive for whites to negotiate with Indians and increased the tendency to take property and territories.

The Battlefield Moves to Washington

Once relegated to reservations, Indians struggled to adjust to their new constraints; it was either adapt or perish. Indeed, many Indians died from white man's diseases and from starvation, but others adapted. Having lived their own lives for generations before the bureaucracy caught up with the frontier, tribes now built upon what they knew best. Familiar with owning and herding horses, the Blackfeet, for example, began accumulating individually owned but communally herded cattle. When the federal bureaucracy did finally begin to try to control reservation life, "the tradition of individual ownership was so well established that Indians resisted government efforts to establish common [commonly owned] herds from 1910 to 1920."[44] The more sedentary tribes such as the Cherokee "showed much aptitude and success in farming."[45] Among tribes with an agricultural tradition, "the Indian concept of land tenure enabled various villages to make the best possible use of the land in order to meet their own specific needs."[46]

Institutional autonomy, however, was short-lived. Instead, Congress and federal agencies began molding property rights from the top down. With the Dawes Act, or Allotment Act, of 1887, the government made its first major attempt at bureaucratic control over the allocation of reservation land. Under this act, reservation land was to be allotted to individual Indians in much the same way that the federal domain was to be transferred to individual non-Indians under the homestead acts. Backers of the Allotment Act touted it as a necessary step for improving the welfare of Indians. As Senator Dawes himself stated, "Till this people will consent to give up their lands, and divide them among their citizens so that each can own the land he cultivates, they will not make much progress."[47]

Given the prominent place that private ownership holds in theories of economic development,[48] one might think that economists would cheer the goals of the Allotment Act. But doing so would ignore the lessons from public choice economics which call for closer scrutiny of the interest groups backing the legislation.[49] At least two important interest groups involved in the allotment process must be mentioned.

The first interest group consisted of the non-Indian settlers who wanted access to reservations. The Allotment Act allowed this access. Once all eligible tribal members received their parcels, any remaining lands were declared "surplus." These lands were then opened to "secure homes for actual settlers."[50] Prior to 1900 these "surplus" lands were purchased from the tribe by the federal government, and settlers were allowed to homestead on them. After the turn of the century, the government sold the lands to whites on behalf of the tribes. The result, as Leonard Carlson observed, was "one of the largest real estate transfers in history."[51]

If land-hungry settlers were the main beneficiaries of federal allotment policy, a question immediately arises: why didn't the federal government either declare all reservation land surplus and open it to homesteading, or grant the Indians full land title without trusteeship so that whites could simply buy the Indian land and gain control more rapidly?

The answer lies in the second interest group, the Office of Indian Affairs (later renamed the Bureau of Indian Affairs, or BIA), and its desire for increased budget and authority. Had the lands been given directly to Indians or whites, what role would have remained for the Office of Indian Affairs beyond supplying Indians with agricultural technology and advice? The allotment system allowed the office to increase its administrative costs by supervising each allotted parcel. "One sign of these increased administrative costs was the rapid growth of the number of clerks needed in Washington. From 1900 to 1920, the number of employees in the Office of Indian Affairs in Washington increased from 101 to 262."[52] By amending the Allotment Act in 1891 to allow for the leasing of allotments that had not been released from trusteeship, Congress allowed whites access to the lands while preserving an important role for the bureaucracy. In fact, this gave Indian agents even more power because it was up to them to determine and enforce the terms of leases. Hence, Carlson concludes, "No student of property-rights literature or, indeed, economic theory will be surprised that the complicated and heavily supervised property right that emerged from allotment led to inefficiencies, corruption, and losses for both Indians and society."[53]

From this special-interest theory of allotment, two important hypotheses follow:

1. Allotment would occur first in those areas where whites placed a higher value on the land held by Indians.
2. As the allotment process transferred millions of acres out of the control of the Office of Indian Affairs, the bureaucracy would have lost nearly all of its power had it not halted the process by retaining trust authority under the Indian Reorganization Act of 1934.

Whether and when allotment began varied across reservations, but because allotment gave access to non-Indians settlers, we would expect the reservations that were more desirable for settlement to be allotted sooner than less desirable ones.[54] To test this hypothesis, Carlson estimated the date of allotment as a function of a number of variables that would reflect a larger demand for allotment.[55] These variables included rainfall, percentage of improved land in the state in which the reservation is located, and population density of the state in which the reservation is located. He concludes:

A reservation in a region with less than 20 inches of rainfall per year was allotted 12.3 years later than a reservation located in the same state having

more than 20 inches of rainfall. . . . For the sample, the mean percentage of
land improved was 43.44 percent, ranging from 1.7 percent in Arizona to
78.6 percent in Nebraska. The model predicts that . . . a reservation in a
state like Arizona would be allotted 10.2 years later than a reservation in a
state like Nebraska. The population density had a mean of 16.25, with a
range from 1.5 in Wyoming to 48.9 in Michigan. The model predicts that a
reservation in Michigan would be allotted 14.0 years earlier than a reservation in Wyoming.[56]

These results support the theory that Indian policy was heavily dominated
by non-Indian interest groups. Just as the standing army was used to redistribute property rights away from Indians, the Office of Indian Affairs also
served to redistribute Indian land. In both cases, what made the effort to
capture the relevant agency worthwhile was superiority in the use of force.
The fact that coercive power was used to redistribute rights also means that
transaction costs of defining and exchanging property rights were increased.
Self-seeking bureaucrats and land-hungry settlers were able to mold the Office of Indian Affairs to their own purposes through the attenuation of Indian rights.

Though land-hungry farmers influenced the timing of allotment, imple-
mentation was basically up to the Office of Indian Affairs, whose job it was
to survey reservation land, assign parcels to individual Indians, and teach the
Indians to become independent farmers. As Prucha notes, if the Office did
its job, "when the process was complete there would be no more need for an
Indian Office to manage relations with the Indians, for there would be no
more identifiable Indians."[57]

From the speed with which allotment proceeded in the early years, it appeared that the Office of Indian Affairs was doing its job. In particular, surplus lands were being sold off so rapidly that tribal lands declined from
119,375,930 acres in 1887 to 52,455,827 acres by 1900. "Year by year, in fact,
the process of allotment was stepped up, and the surplus lands were rapidly
transferred to the whites. . . . So successful did the process seem that the re-
formers looked forward to the day when government supervision over the
Indians would disappear entirely and the Indians would all be absorbed into
American Society."[58] Economist Fred McChesney summarizes the effects of
the speed with which the Office of Indian Affairs gave individual Indians pri-

vate ownership unencumbered by federal trusteeship (otherwise know as fee-patent ownership or fee-simple title):

> First, as always, the aim of the new policy was an end to any federal role in Indian affairs. In its "Declaration of Policy in the Administration of Indian Affairs" of April 1917, the Indian Office declared that the fee patent system "means the dawn of a new era in Indian Administration. . . . It means re-duced appropriations by the Government and more self-respect and indep-endence for the Indian. . . . It means in short, the beginning of the end of the Indian problem." Second, as Indian population declined and lands be-came privately owned and then were sold, Indian population and lands un-der the BIA administration began to decline.[59]

Given the rapidity of allotment, the Office of Indian Affairs was working itself out of a job, but the tenacity of bureaucracies ensured that this did not happen. Indeed, growth rather than death has characterized the office throughout its history. This result is hardly surprising when we consider that bureaucrats are highly unlikely to let their mission and jobs wither.[60] In the words of the commissioner of Indian affairs in 1906, "The grand total of the nation's wards will be diminished and at a growing ratio."[61] But "instead of withering away according to the blueprint, the Indian Office vastly increased its involvement; it became a sort of real estate agent, handling a multitude of land transactions for individual Indians."[62] Laurence Schemeckebier con-cluded, "While the issuance of fee patents to allottees had decreased the number of Indians under the supervision of the Office of Indian Affairs, the control over the property and the fiscal affairs of individuals has resulted in an increase in the actual volume of work."[63]

Passage of the Indian Reorganization Act (IRA) in 1934 provided the life-sustaining rationale for what was by then called the Bureau of Indian Affairs. The act set up a process for establishing tribal governments and gave the BIA authority over this process. It also ended the allotment process and froze most allotments for which fee patents had not been issued into perpetual trusteeship. McChesney explains the bureaucratic interest in the new policy.

> In its initial phases, allotment would serve bureaucrats' interest in greater budgets because it necessitated a growing Indian Office to administer the

Dawes [Allotment] Act. . . . Ending allotments and freezing ownership for
allottees still under federal trusteeship guaranteed that bureaucratic control
would continue. Further, it meant that work would increase as the number
of Indians on the reservation . . . would begin to increase—as in fact it did.
. . . In short, one hypothesis that explains the entire allotment episode is
growth in agency budgets. . . . Every change in the sequence of allotment
events from 1887 to 1934 led to an increase in the involvement of the federal government in Indian affairs, and each change can be explained by its
ability to generate more work for the Indian bureaucracy.[64]

If, as argued above, the Allotment Act gave non-Indians access to Indian
lands, then why did non-Indian citizens and their representatives not oppose
the IRA? After all, the act halted the issuance of fee-simple title unencumbered BIA trust control, making it impossible for settlers to purchase land
directly from Indians. McChesney explains that white opposition to the IRA
did not materialize because "the value of Western land fell with the steep decline in livestock and agricultural prices [in the 1920s]" and because "the
best Indian lands would already have been allotted."[65] This took some pressure off Congress to leave reservation lands open for non-Indian acquisition
and therefore increased the relative influence of the bureaucracy.

The budgetary evidence mustered by McChesney is convincing. Not
only did BIA budgets grow, but the growth was significantly increased by
both the number of allotments and the acreage allotted. The rate of budget
increase attributable to allotments declined over time, however, giving the
BIA an incentive to find an alternative policy that would sustain its momen-
tum. The IRA, which began during the New Deal, provided the policy
change that has driven agency growth to the present. McChesney summarizes his findings by noting that an explanation

> consistent with the entire allotment episode is that its real beneficiaries were
> Eastern and Western whites, politicians, and the Indian Office. By 1920,
> however, only the Indian bureaucrats [the Indian Office] had interests
> strongly affected by allotment, and those interests dictated an end to privati-
> zation. Initial allotment and subsequent changes that augmented Indian
> ownership worked to the benefit of the bureaucrats by enlarging their budg-
> ets. But as the amount of privatized land increased, these budget gains could

not continue. Eventually privatization was stopped—which caused budgets to increase further.[66]

Whether the allotment experiment succeeded or failed depends on the goals and evaluation criteria. Measured from the Indians' perspective regarding the millions of acres transferred to non-Indians, the allotment most certainly was a disaster. But viewed from the perspective of groups wanting institutional change that redistributed property rights to themselves, namely non-Indian settlers and Washington bureaucrats, allotment was a resounding success. Non-Indians ended up owning or leasing substantial amounts of many reservations, and the BIA flourished, by operating first as a real estate agent for Indian lands and then as the trustee overseeing Indian land management. Unfortunately, the bureaucratic quagmire created by the IRA attenuated Indian property rights to land, significantly reducing productivity and wealth for Indians themselves.

Trust the Government

When allotment ended in 1934, those lands that had not been released from trusteeship remained under the trust authority of the BIA. Hence, reservations were left with a mosaic of land tenure.[67] Owners of fee-simple lands have complete autonomy over their land-use decisions. Production decisions regarding these lands are controlled by the owner, and the land can be sold or encumbered as collateral in the capital market. In the set of 39 large reservations discussed below, 47 percent of reservation acreage is in fee-simple ownership (owned by either Indians or non-Indians).

In contrast to lands under fee-simple tenure, reservation lands under the trust authority of the U.S. government are subject to regulation by the BIA even though they are owned by individual Indians or by the tribe. Under the trust authority, the BIA has no claim on improved productivity, has little responsibility for reduced productivity, and has the potential for larger budgets if Indians are less autonomous. It grants or denies permission to change land use, approves lease arrangements, and agrees to capital improvements. When held in trust, land cannot be sold and cannot be encumbered as collateral for loans. Making matters worse, individual-trust lands have often been inherited many times over, leaving multiple owners, all of whom must agree on land-management decisions. This "fractionation" or "heirship" problem increases the costs of establishing a clear owner and manager who can control land-use decisions and reap the benefits of good management. In the case of tribal-trust land, management decisions are made by tribal governance institutions, which further reduce any individual decision maker's incentive to maximize the net value of production. For example, Gary Libecap and Ronald Johnson conclude that the politics of the Navajo Tribal Council and its grazing committees have essentially legislated "a common property condition for the range" wherein access is open to all tribal members and overuse occurs. Given these constraints, we would expect the higher transaction costs associated with management decisions to thwart optimal use of the land.[68]

This three-part tenure system—fee simple, individual trust, and tribal trust—yields very different productivity for several reasons. First, because the costs of organizing production under fee-simple tenure are lower than under individual or tribal-trust tenure, the fee-simple owner's choice of a mix of land, labor, and capital should be approximately optimal. Second, because trust constraints raise the cost of capital by restricting the ability of owners to transfer land title, productivity should be lower on trust lands. Third, because the returns from individual and tribal-trust lands are distributed among many owners, each owner has less incentive to monitor land management, thus making output lower. Finally, because trust land cannot be freely alienated, farms and ranches remain too small to be optimally productive.[69]

The data confirm these predictions. Table 4.3 reports the output values for fee-simple and trust land and the ratio of the two for 39 large reservations. The ratio of the value of trust land output to the value of fee-simple land output shows that trust lands produce only about half the value of fee-simple lands per acre, and the difference is statistically significant.[70]

Terry Anderson and Dean Lueck estimated the impact of tenure on a cross section of reservations using the total value of reservation output per acre.[71] The latter value was derived from the sum of the value of output from individual- and tribal-trust land and the value of output from fee-simple land on reservations divided by Indian acres with agricultural potential plus all fee-simple acres. Using regression analysis to control for a number of other variables that might affect productivity, they found that the per-acre value of agricultural output was 85 to 90 percent lower on tribal-trust land than on fee-simple land and 30 to 40 percent lower on individual-trust land than on fee-simple land.[72] The magnitude of these numbers supports the contention that bureaucratic constraints on trust land reduce agricultural productivity. The inability to transfer title of trust lands, the difficulty in using trust land as collateral, and the transaction costs resulting from multiple ownership of small parcels all make it difficult to maximize productivity. The results are especially significant on tribal-trust land and suggest that tribal governance institutions have not significantly offset the difficulties of making collective decisions that promote productivity.

Conclusion

The interaction between Indians and Europeans on the frontier can best be understood in the context of the definition and enforcement of property rights. Initially, the two groups mostly traded rather than raided. The transaction costs for trade were lowered by the fact that eastern tribes had property rights to land more closely in line with what the whites needed and understood. Moreover, war is a negative-sum game, and during the early years of interaction, the parties choosing warfare had to bear the costs of war directly.

Several factors, however, led to a predominance of raiding rather than trading during the last half of the nineteenth century. First, transaction costs were higher because nomadic tribes of the plains did not have property rights that were compatible with what white settlers needed for settled agriculture. Second, the establishment of a standing U.S. Army following the Mexican-American War and the Civil War led to differential advantage in the use of force and allowed frontier settlers to call on the general taxpayer to bear the costs of war. And finally, the Indian wars gave the standing army a raison d'être that allowed it to maintain budget and numbers.

Raiding to take Indian lands did not end with the Indian wars but rather continued with bureaucratic reallocation of Indian property rights. From the Allotment Act of 1887 to the Indian Reorganization Act of 1934 to the

TABLE 4.3

Average Value of Agricultural Output per Acre, 1987

Reservation	Fee-Simple Lands (in dollars)	Trust Lands (in dollars)	Ratio of Trust to Fee Simple
Washington			
Colville	292.19	7.15	0.02
Yakima	857.45	24.72	0.03
Oregon			
Umatilla	143.36	43.06	0.30
Warm Springs	174.36	2.01	0.01
Idaho			
Fort Hall	132.64	102.79	0.77
Coeur d'Alene	115.80	203.05	1.75
Nez Perce	101.53	87.40	0.79
Montana			
Blackfeet	45.10	11.61	0.26
Crow	46.17	22.06	0.48
Flathead	44.69	9.46	0.21
Rocky Boys	39.54	19.64	0.50
Fort Peck	27.33	13.80	0.50
Northern Cheyenne	40.41	7.50	0.19
Wyoming			
Wind River	54.80	3.76	0.07
North Dakota			
Fort Berthold	28.83	16.52	0.57
Standing Rock	18.49	19.86	1.07
Fort Totten	41.00	15.22	0.37
South Dakota			
Cheyenne River	21.21	0.00	0.00
Crow Creek	39.35	39.68	1.01
Lower Brule	38.80	39.26	1.01
Pine Ridge	28.32	10.12	0.36
Rosebud Sioux	24.92	11.19	0.45
Yankton	45.50	42.93	0.94
Sisseton	53.01	37.22	0.70

TABLE 4.3 *(continued)*

Reservation	Fee-Simple Lands (in dollars)	Trust Lands (in dollars)	Ratio of Trust to Fee Simple
Nebraska			
Omaha	100.23	156.34	1.55
Santee	38.99	35.73	0.92
Winnebago	97.79	154.86	1.58
Kansas			
Kickapoo	98.16	47.75	0.49
Arizona			
Colorado River	1,152.61	266.83	0.23
Gila River	577.00	239.90	0.42
Nevada			
Duck Valley	95.09	6.06	0.06
Walker River	94.18	3.77	0.04
Utah			
Goshute	37.39	1.71	0.05
Uintah-Ouray	24.04	8.02	0.33
New Mexico			
Isleto Pueblo	163.94	4.85	0.03
Colorado			
Southern Ute	21.02	17.72	0.84
Oklahoma			
Osage	18.47	30.63	1.66
Minnesota			
Fond du Lac	25.99	12.58	0.48
n	39	39	39
Mean	130.18	45.57	0.54
Standard Deviation	230.83	67.29	0.49

SOURCE: T. Anderson 1995, 128–29.

present, property rights on reservations mainly have been determined from the top down, that is, not by the landowners themselves but by bureaucratic decision makers who do not bear the direct costs of their decisions. Not only are the property rights to Indian lands generally inconsistent with the time- and place-specific constraints of each reservation and tribe, but they are also held at the mercy of the federal government and therefore are always up for grabs. Not surprisingly, reservations have remained third-world islands in a sea of wealth.

FIVE

Soft Gold: Traders, Trappers, and Hunters

When it comes to the tragedy of the commons, perhaps the most often cited example is the extermination of wildlife. From millions of bison blanketing the Great Plains when Lewis and Clark embarked on their adventure, populations had plummeted to scores by the end of the nineteenth century. Economists argue that wildlife in general and bison in particular were subject to this tragedy because no one owned them; if someone refrains from harvesting a wild animal or fish, it will be harvested by someone else. That is why whalers overharvested whales, shooters killing birds for plumage markets in the early twentieth century nearly exterminated many species, and fishers overharvested salmon runs on the Columbia River. In the absence of property rights, there is no incentive to conserve.

The question here is why institutional entrepreneurs did not establish property rights to prevent these tragedies, especially for the beaver and the buffalo, two animal stocks that were rapidly depleted in the nineteenth-century American West. Most obviously the answer has to do with the benefits and costs of establishing ownership institutions. As economist Dean Lueck has pointed out, establishing property rights to wildlife depends on controlling the land that the wildlife inhabit.[1] The decision to manage land for wildlife will depend on the value of land in wildlife, the value of land in alternative uses, and the cost of consolidating sufficient land holdings to accommodate the migratory nature of the wildlife in question. Therefore if the value of land used for wildlife habitat is low compared to its value if it were used for agriculture, and if agricultural use dictates parcels too small for free-roaming wildlife, then property rights and contractual arrangements governing wildlife are unlikely to evolve. But if the comparative values are reversed, and if the parcels are large enough for wildlife, such rights and arrangements are likely to evolve. Hence media mogul Ted Turner can effectively manage wild elk and bison on his 100,000-acre and larger ranches because the value of land used for animal habitat exceeds the value in alternative uses and because the ranches were large enough for wildlife in the first place, making it unnecessary to consolidate ownership.

Of course, on the American frontier, the fate of wildlife was sealed not so much by the small size of land holdings as by the complete lack of property rights. Lacking land ownership, the institutional entrepreneur found it difficult to exclude others from access to wildlife and its habitat. The Indians had evolved reasonably effective ownership institutions for beaver-trapping territories in eastern Canada and for fishing streams in the Northwest (see Chapter 3), thus providing an incentive for individuals, families, and clans to prevent overharvesting, but even then, conflicts between tribes led to overharvesting of fugitive resources such a bison, which ranged over territories larger than individuals or tribes could control.[2]

When Europeans ventured into Indian Country, property rights to animal territories and hence sustainable wildlife management became problematic. Faced with the raid-or-trade calculus (see Chapter 4), Europeans often did not respect territorial rights of Indians. As Robert Higgs explains, well-established rights to streams and fishing locations where salmon returned to spawn led Indians in the Pacific Northwest to sustain fishing effectively.[3] Europeans, however, ignored these rights and progressively moved their nets to the mouths of rivers, where they decimated salmon runs.

When the lack of well-defined and enforced property rights was combined with the expectation of a short-term high price for the resource, the tragedy of the commons was further exacerbated. Indians had traditionally made use of beaver and buffalo, but their personal consumption of wildlife for food and clothing put little pressure on wild populations. When European traders offered what seemed like exorbitant prices for furs, robes, and hides,[4] that pressure changed as Indians and whites alike raced to capture fugitive animals. The resulting overexploitation of resources is attributed by historian David Wishart to an "attitude of rapacious, short-term exploitation,"[5] but our analytical framework suggests that property rights or lack thereof was the primary cause.

In the remainder of this chapter, we consider the institutions that governed beaver trading and trapping and those that led to the near extermination of American bison. As we shall see, neither of these cases is a quintessential example of the tragedy of the commons. Rapid depletion of beaver was a rational response to the expectation that high market values would be short-lived. Decimation of buffalo occurred because cattle could be more easily controlled and transported to market, so that it made sense to substitute cattle for buffalo as the main consumers of grass resources.

The Beaver Men

The fur trade in Canada and the United States, dominated by beaver,[6] was relatively short-lived, with its heyday from 1820 to 1840. Although English and French companies traded actively in the Canadian West throughout the eighteenth century, the American fur trade flourished only after the Louisiana Purchase and the Lewis and Clark expedition. Following on the heels of the "Corps of Discovery," Manuel Lisa took 50 to 60 men up the Missouri and Yellowstone rivers in the spring of 1807 to the place where the Bighorn River joins the Yellowstone.[7] There his party traded furs with the Crow and trapped beaver themselves. A few other expeditions continued throughout the next decade under the sponsorship of the Missouri Fur Company, but the real expansion of the beaver trade began in the 1820s and continued for two decades.[8] By 1822 at least five major fur companies engaged in trading with the Indians, trapping for themselves, or both.[9] Competition was keen, and hundreds of thousands of dollars worth of furs were removed from the Rocky Mountain West.

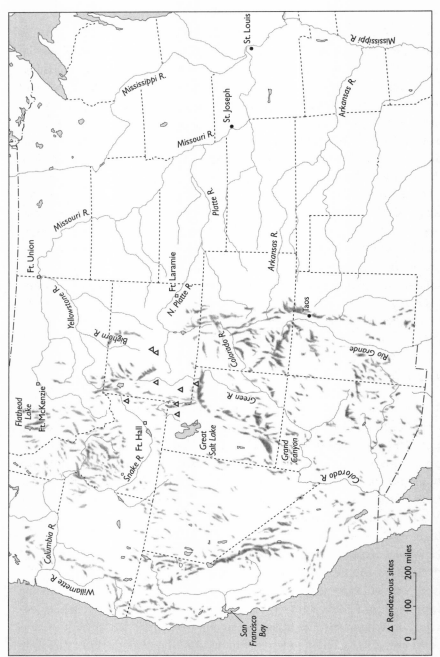

MAP 2. The West of the Mountain Men

For a variety of reasons, the fur-trading era ended in 1840 almost as fast as it had begun. From the middle of the 1830s, the demand for beaver pelts fell as silk replaced beaver fur as the fashionable material for hats in the East and in Europe. Also, the increased availability of South American nutria (an aquatic rodent) competed with what remained of the fur market. And finally, as we will see below, beaver became increasingly scarce, with the result that the cost of finding and delivering them to market rose.[10] Hence, "more trappers left the mountains in 1840 than in any other single year."[11]

Given the distance from markets, the unknown territory, and the different ways of obtaining pelts, beaver-trade entrepreneurs were challenged to establish and reconfigure property rights in that trade. They had to develop contracts for capital investment to provision expeditions that had a high risk of not returning; to recruit crews to row, push, pull, or use any other means to get boats upriver; to coordinate defense against Indians; to find and procure beavers, either by trading goods for pelts from Indians or by trapping beaver themselves; and to get the pelts to European markets.

Contracting was complicated by the cost of communication between frontier outposts and markets. It took months to communicate with Europe to determine the demand for the end product, and weeks to get that information to St. Louis, the jumping-off point for the frontier.[12] Communication with expeditions upriver from St. Louis was even more difficult. Trading and trapping expeditions could easily be out for a year or more before any news of their success trickled back. Even after steamboats came into prominent use,[13] travel times were long. In 1843 it took 40 days to get as far upriver as Fort Pierre and 49 days to get to Fort Union.

TRAP OR TRADE

The decision by Europeans to trade or trap depended on whether they believed Indians had defendable rights to the beaver. If so, trading provided a way that both parties could benefit from the asset. If not, conflict was likely, and the beaver were more likely to be subject to the tragedy of the commons.

The decision to trap or trade followed a calculus similar to the "raid or trade" calculus discussed in Chapter 4. Where Indians held clear territorial rights and where they had the upper hand in defending those rights, Euro-

peans were much more likely to trade rather than trap. Where the territorial
rights were unclear or where uncertainty about property rights prevailed,
trapping was more likely. Hence General Henry Atkinson, one of the early
western military leaders, "perceived no 'impropriety' in trapping the territory of Indians not yet brought under federal jurisdiction"[14] because independence from the government meant property rights were unclear. But Benjamin O'Fallon, an Indian agent in the region, cautioned "that once formal
relations had been established with those tribes, hunting and trapping of animals properly belong to them and should be banned."[15] And the *Niles's
Weekly Register* editorialized in 1823, "it appears to us that the lands yet un-
ceded must be regarded as their [the Indians'] own, and if so, we suppose
that a party of white persons cannot have any more right to enter upon it for
the purpose of catching and killing the wild beasts of the forests, than the Indians would have to enter our settlements and carry off whatever they
pleased."[16]

The issue of territorial control first surfaced when the beaver men ven-
turing up the Missouri encountered the Hidatsa villages. These villages controlled strategic locations for trade between Indian cultures from Hudson
Bay to the west slopes of the Rockies to the plateaus of Mexico. Mari Sandoz
describes what trading was like at these strategic locations:

> The western people brought the skins and horn of mountain sheep and
> goat, the fur of marten and lion besides the plants and herbs, obsidian for
> arrow and spear points, and sea shells and walrus ivory from their own trad-
> ing centers on the farther slopes. From the north came much dried meat,
> winter wolf, often pipestone and sometimes reindeer horn and white bear
> and fox. In exchange they took home corn and beans, the lesser products of
> the agrarian villages, their handsomely worked deerskins and buffalo robes,
> and always the memory of another pleasant visit to a place where there was
> a half moon's time of peace for all.[17]

The Hidatsas and other tribes such as the Mandans and Arikaras had a virtual monopoly on trade and "managed to keep a hand on a good share of the
trade through their favored upper-river position. . . . For years . . . the goods
had been brought right through their gates by the British and by the merchants from down the Missouri, enlarging the importance of the villages as
a trading place of peace."[18]

But the beaver-rich streams farther to the west were too tempting for the beaver men. These non-Indian traders tried to push past the trading tribes, potentially cutting the tribes out of what they considered their rightful share of trading gains. Not surprisingly, the tribes tried to persuade or physically stop traders from moving west. For example, when François Larocque tried to head west after an Indian/non-Indian trading fair, "the Mandans particularly rose in anger. They could not permit it." They feared that if western tribes got guns, "they would become independent, insolent and dangerous, too, but Larocque knew that it was the prospective independence that the Mandans feared most, independence from paying profit, paying tribute to the Five Villages for their goods."[19] As the non-Indian traders pushed upriver, tensions increased. The Indians tried to increase prices for the goods they had to offer, and the non-Indian traders tried to avoid trading at the higher prices, hoping to get better deals farther to the west. In Larocque's case, the Mandans first refused him the horses he needed for his westward journey. They eventually did agree to trade horses, but for twice the price.

The decision of whether to trap or trade was relatively easy to make for the Hudson's Bay Company. Given that its monopoly on trade with the Indians was enforced by the government, the company was able to keep other traders and trappers out and to control supply by adjusting the price it paid for pelts.[20] Hence it essentially hired Indians to do the trapping and traded with them at a price it controlled. Because the company traded, it was even able to peacefully engage the Blackfeet, who continually terrorized white trappers throughout the upper reaches of the Missouri.[21]

Other beaver men who chose trading found similar success. One of the early entrepreneurs in the beaver trade, Kenneth McKenzie, for example, "much preferred to get his pelts through trade rather than exposing men and animals to the ferocity of a people who looked on all wildlife as theirs, to exploit or not as they wished."[22] So successful was McKenzie with trading that he "achieved the incredible feat of opening negotiations with the Blackfeet and securing their sanction of a trading post [Fort Piegan, later named Fort McKenzie] high on the Missouri, near the mouth of the Marias."[23]

The dominant trading company of the era, the American Fur Company, avoided conflict where possible by honoring territorial rights of Indians. Its basic strategy was "to work within the limits of the existing patterns of Indian occupance to encourage the production of furs and robes."[24] This was especially important if the company was to protect its investments in forts and the goods stored in them. The gains from cooperation are also indicated by the fact that trading occurred for items other than furs. In 1831 one Indian agent estimated that about half of the meat consumed at trading posts was supplied by Indians. In areas where Indian farming occurred, vegetables and grains were also traded.[25]

To ward off battles by promoting trading rather than trapping by white entrepreneurs, the War Department tried to implement a licensing system. Licenses were supposed to give early companies the right to trade rather than trap. After an encounter with the Arikaras, Colonel Leavenworth wrote, "this trapping business is carried on under a license to *trade*," and therefore "this *trapping* business should be fully and completely suppressed."[26] And just as early federal land policy used the military to evict white settlers from Indian lands (see Chapter 4),[27] Leavenworth favored using military force to evict unlicensed white hunters and trappers from Indian territories.

But the licensing system proved totally ineffective, both in keeping out foreigners, especially the British to the north, and in preventing "free" white trappers (those without a long-term contract with a company) from taking beaver with no attention to Indian rights. The system did not work for two reasons. First, there were many free white trappers in the region who had no licenses and hence cared little about government policy. They trapped beavers and traded with the licensed companies. The simple fact is that these beaver men came to the mountains to make a profit from beaver, whether by trading with Indians or by trapping for themselves.

Second, the paucity of military troops in the area made it impossible to enforce the licensing scheme. One effort to reduce conflict with the Indians and limit beaver men to trading came on the heels of an 1823 encounter between William Ashley and the Arikaras.[28] Senator Thomas Hart Benton, of Missouri, wanted to station troops on the upper Missouri, but his colleagues resisted because they did not feel sufficient power could be mustered to prevent illegal hunting on Indian lands. But a compromise in May 1824 authorized treaty commissioners escorted by troops to "ascend the Missouri and make peace with the Indians." In these treaties, signed by the Poncas, Sioux, Cheyennes, Hidatsas, Mandans, and even the Arikaras, the Indians "promised to protect American Traders and turn over all foreign traders to Amer-

ican officials. Provisions dealt with regulation of trade and redress of griev-
ances. None addressed hunting or trapping on Indian land."[29] If anything,
Ashley's expedition eventually fueled the trapping conflicts because it laid
the groundwork for companies to build forts for trading with the Indians.
These forts also traded with white trappers and afforded them protection
from Indians.

Working in favor of trapping and against trading in the "trap or trade"
calculus was the fact that negotiation costs for trade deals were high. Dealing with the settled village Indians, such as the Mandans and the Hidatsas,
was relatively easy, but negotiating with the more nomadic Blackfeet,
Assiniboines, and Crow was much more difficult. Also working in favor of
trapping was the fact that the rents the Indians were capturing from the
beaver trade continually tempted entry by white trappers. Moreover, much
of the territory into which the beaver men ventured was "no man's land."
Essentially, the triangle formed by the Missouri River, the Yellowstone
River, and the Rocky Mountain front was contested by the tribes in the region. Indeed, anthropologists Paul Martin and Christine Szuter argue that
the abundance of game found by Lewis and Clark in this region can be attributed to the fact that Indians did not hunt in this triangle because it was
contested and therefore more dangerous. Given that Indians did not want to
venture here, that the area was rich in beaver, and that the beaver men
thought they could elude Indians in the area, trapping rather than trading is
understandable.[30]

Eventually, however, almost no white trapper working the streams along
the Rocky Mountain front could avoid the Blackfeet country, which "was to
stand like a wall across the path of the American fur men for a long time"[31]
American companies were able to establish forts on the Missouri as far up as
the Marias, on the Yellowstone at its confluence with the Bighorn, on the
Henry's Fork of the Snake, and throughout the Pacific Northwest, but they
could not penetrate the Blackfeet wall. Indeed, all efforts to establish a fort
at the Three Forks of the Missouri, one of the richest fur regions, failed because the Blackfeet stole supplies, pelts, and horses from the traders or killed
and mutilated the trappers they caught.[32]

Given the Blackfeet wall, it is not surprising that the bulk of the beaver
trappers rushed into other territories, because "the Blackfoot . . . repulsed
any American attempts to tap these furs, choosing instead to channel their

furs north to the Hudson's Bay Company posts in Canada. Blackfoot country remained a virtual preserve of fur-bearing animals until the 1830s," and
"even then the Blackfoot would permit only traders, not trappers, on their
turf."[33]

FUR COMPANY ORGANIZATION

Whether in trapping or in trading, numerous new combinations of property
rights were necessary in order to capture the returns from the valuable fur
resource. The beaver were located an enormous distance from market and
required a substantial investment of time and money in order to be harvested. Therefore, numerous fur companies were organized to provide capital and organizational detail to the trapping enterprise. The Hudson's Bay
Company, chartered in 1670, was the most hierarchal and, through its base
in the contested territory of Oregon, sent numerous trading and trapping
expeditions into the Rockies and beyond. The British also contested for furs,
through the North West Company until it merged with the Hudson's Bay
Company in 1821. In 1808 and 1809, Manuel Lisa managed to secure the
backing of St. Louis merchants to form the Missouri Fur Company. That
company was dissolved in January of 1812, but a new one was formed later
in the year with a capital of $50,000.[34] John Jacob Astor contested the
British influence in the Pacific Northwest with his founding of the Pacific
Fur Company in 1810. The enterprise, however, lasted only three years, until the company sold its equipment to the British.[35]

After 1820, other companies organized and competed for the fur trade.
The French Fur Company, with backing from St. Louis merchants, dominated the lower reaches of the Missouri.[36] The Columbia Fur Company was
formed in 1821 by traders and trappers who found themselves redundant after the merger of the Hudson's Bay Company and the North West Company. Astor continued to be an influential player in the fur trade through his
American Fur Company, which he formed after he sold the Pacific Fur
Company. His company organized the Western Department in 1822 to take
advantage of the Missouri River trade. Another major competitor was the
Rocky Mountain Fur Company, formed in 1830.

Each of these companies used innovative contractual arrangements to
bring to the area the capital necessary to capture beaver and move the pelts

to market. Given the long production period involved, they had to tap the financial resources of merchants in St. Louis and elsewhere to sustain them until payments could be received. Despite the problems of communication, "the system was a tightly controlled unit, carefully supervised and organized, united by a continuous movement of furs, goods, and people, and regulated by information feedback which focused on St. Louis, the main decision-making centre."[37]

The trading system was complex. The Indians would request particular items they desired in trade, and they were very specific about them.[38] For instance, they desired Brazilian tobacco over Virginia tobacco; Cree traders went so far as to reject the Virginia brand.[39] The Indians also preferred the Chinese variety of vermilion pigment, and in many cases would not accept American vermilion. In order to meet these demands, fur-trading companies contracted with suppliers for specific trade goods. These goods were usually purchased on credit, which was provided by financial companies in England.[40]

Of course a major portion of the organizational effort was devoted to the actual trapping. To protect themselves and to gain from specialization, trappers were organized into fairly large groups.

> What the trappers did between rendezvous differed from the popular understanding. They did not wander in lonely solitude through the mountains trapping beaver. That would have been suicidal, an invitation to watching Blackfeet. Instead, they traveled in brigades of 40 to 60 men, including camp tenders and meat hunters. From brigade base camps, they fanned out, usually in pairs to set their traps. Then they were the most vulnerable, and then Indian ambushes took their heaviest toll.[41]

Labor contracts varied, depending on the individual's skills. One group of workers was responsible for caring for and packing and unpacking the work animals, gathering firewood, and tending camp. Another group consisted of hired trappers, who were equipped by the company and were paid an annual salary. Other trappers worked on a share-cropping agreement in which the company provided them with supplies and in return received a share of the year's catch. Finally, the free trappers, being the most skilled, were the least likely to enter into fixed-payment contracts. They usually attached themselves to an organized group, but always retained the option to sell their furs to anyone they pleased.[42] Not surprisingly, the size of the trapping expedition, the form of the labor contracts, and the combination of trading and trapping underwent constant revision as a part of the entrepreneurial search for optimal organization.

One of the most dramatic institutional innovations of the era was the rendezvous. Supplying the trappers was a difficult process, relying upon either fixed locations in the trapping territory, which were expensive to maintain and defend, or annual trips to St. Louis, where the trappers would sell furs and replenish supplies. But in 1825, a new system was devised, when William H. Ashley, as a leader of a major trapping expedition, announced that he would reunite with his several trapping parties somewhere downriver on the Green before July 10. Other trappers heard of the gathering as well and decided to show up. This rendezvous on the Henry's Fork of the Green River was the first of a series of meetings that continued annually through 1840.

The rendezvous site would be announced a year in advance and was generally located in a wide valley with ample forage for horses and mules. Six of the rendezvous were held in the Green River Valley west of the Wind River Mountains; the Bear River and Bear Lake, north of the great Salt Lake, were also popular locations.[43] The rendezvous offered the opportunity for drinking, socializing, and contesting among the mountain men. More importantly, it was an efficient way to supply the trappers and to allow them to stay in the mountains year-round.

The supply trains for the rendezvous usually comprised 50 to 70 men and more than 100 pack horses and mules.[44] Transportation costs came down somewhat after 1832, when wagons were introduced to the supply train. These supply expeditions usually left Missouri in late April and generally followed the Platte River for much of their journey, crossing the Continental Divide at South Pass, which had been rediscovered by Jedediah Smith in 1824.[45] In 1833, a supply train led by Nathaniel Wyeth cost $11,382 for supplies, labor, and animals.[46]

Competition to supply the rendezvous sites could be fierce, with several fur companies attempting to arrive first in order to secure the best trading opportunities. In 1834, for instance, Andrew Wyeth and William Sublette led competing supply trains to the rendezvous site in southern Wyoming, where the Ham's Fork joins the Muddy River. Sublette reached the rendezvous site on June 13, four days before Wyeth.[47]

A fascinating aspect of the rendezvous, indeed of the trapping system in general, was the lack of armed conflict among the trappers.[48] The rendezvous offered particularly ripe opportunities for theft, with all the supply goods and valuable furs concentrated in one location. But in general, these men respected property rights to the furs a trapper had harvested. Further, because all parties bore arms and knew how to use them, force was not used. Thus, even though inequalities of power undoubtedly prevailed at times, and the rendezvous occasioned heavy drinking and brawling, the records show very few instances of the use of arms or the taking of harvested furs. Both traders and trappers confidently brought their goods to the rendezvous sites with little fear that they would be stolen. Most of the violence that occurred stemmed from personal challenges and pride. In describing the period, Hiram Chittenden states: "It might be concluded . . . that, as the country was literally lawless, or without means of enforcing laws, lawlessness and disorder would be the rule. Such was not the case. . . . It will be found that life, liberty, and the right to property, were as much respected in the depths of the wilderness as within the best regulated of cities."[49]

OPEN ACCESS TO BEAVER

Throughout the fur-trapping era, mountain men and company officials generally recognized that overexploitation was a problem. In 1829, David Jackson, Jedediah Smith, and William Sublette, in a meeting at Pierre's Hole, bemoaned the trapping prospects for the next season. Historian Dale Morgan has reconstructed the tenor of the meeting from the letters and journals of Jedediah Smith: "The southern Rockies were overrun with trappers from Taos. The Utah country was trapped out. The Flathead lands were not a likely prospect for this year. The Snake Country, trapped by British and Americans alike, seemed all but exhausted."[50] In 1831, a longtime trapper, William Gordon, said, "The furs are diminishing and this diminution is general & extensive. The beaver may be considered as extirpated on this side of the Rocky Mountains."[51] Another trapper, Edwin Denig, said that there had been plentiful beaver on the upper Missouri at one time, "but in the 1830s they had become very rare, having been trapped and dug out by the Indians and the fur trappers residing with them."[52] Wishart, in describing the end of the fur era, says, "The Snake River country could no longer be relied upon because in many areas the beaver had been trapped to extinction." He continues, "The resource base had been virtually destroyed by the Euro-American excursion into the Rocky Mountains—only a change in fashion in the United States and Europe saved the beaver from extinction in extensive areas of the Trans-Missouri West."[53]

An apt description of the tragedy of the commons with regard to furs is provided by a trapper of the time:

> Indians were wont to hunt in a slovenly manner, leaving a few animals yearly for breeding. But that the White hunters were more thorough-spirited, and made root-and-branch work of it. When they settled on a district, they destroyed the old and young alike; and when they left it, they left no living thing behind them. The first party proving successful, more were fitted out, and every successive year has seen several armed and mounted bands of hunters, from 20 to 100 men and more in each, pouring into the Indian hunting grounds; and all of this has been done in open and direct violation of the law of the United States, which expressly forbids trapping and hunting in Indian lands. The consequence has been that there are now few fur-clad animals this side of the mountains.[54]

WHY NOT TERRITORIAL TRAPPING RIGHTS?

In light of the numerous concerns expressed by trappers about the beaver extinction, why were the trappers and the fur companies unable to establish and enforce property rights among themselves? As hypothesized in Chapter 2, when rule makers stand to gain substantially from efficient rules, it is more likely that rents will be created and protected, rather than dissipated, through institutional innovation. Several factors thwarted this innovation in the case of trapping.

First, the trappers were difficult to organize because there were so many of them, they were so scattered geographically, and they were always on the move. Robert Utley estimates that the number of trappers was approximately 1,000 at its peak.[55] Wishart puts the number even higher because he includes trappers from Mexico and Canada. He states:

> Altogether there may have been 1,000 American trappers in the mountains that summer (1832)—probably the highest population that the Rocky Mountain Trapping System attained. To this total should be added the 600 men that the Hudson's Bay Company employed in Oregon, and the numerous, and largely anonymous, Mexican and American trappers who worked the southern and central Rocky Mountains from bases at Taos and Santa Fe.[56]

With some 2,000 trappers spread over all of the Rocky Mountains and continually moving from place to place, it would have been difficult to come to collective agreement on what the property rights should be or how they should be enforced. And even if property rights had been agreed upon, enforcement would have been expensive. The presence of the owner (or an agent of the owner) was important for enforcement of rights to land on the frontier, and after the beaver were trapped from an area and with no other profitable alternative uses for the land, maintaining a physical presence was very costly.

The rendezvous system might have provided a way of lowering the cost of coordination, but that system was precarious, with competition even to establish rendezvous locations. As described previously, several fur companies competed to be the first to a rendezvous site, and any attempts to restrict competition to the rendezvous would simply have resulted in competing alternative sites being used.[57]

Second, competition among the companies was keen. If one trapper or group discovered fertile territory, others quickly entered. "In the Rocky Mountains the American Fur Company's operational strategy was straightforward: Henry Vanderburgh and Andrew Drips (the field captains) intended to learn the best trapping grounds by following the Rocky Mountain Fur Company brigades and to capture the trade of the free trappers by offering inflated prices for their furs."[58] Joe Meek, a trapper for the Rocky Mountain Fur Company, described the effect of this competition:

The rival company had a habit of turning up at the most unexpected places, and taking advantage of the hard-earned experience of the Rocky Mountain Company's leaders. They tampered with the trappers, and ferreted out the secret of their next rendezvous; they followed on their trail, making them pilots to the trapping grounds; they sold goods to the Indians, and what was worse, to the hired trappers.[59]

If individual trappers did not stake and defend claims to trapping territories, why did the companies not organize their trading and trapping to prevent the tragedy of the commons? There was precedent for this from the Hudson's Bay Company in Canada. Edwin Denig, the head trader at Fort Union, at the confluence of the Yellowstone and the Missouri, explained how the Hudson's Bay Company's restrictions worked: "They allow the Indian to trap certain streams at stated seasons and prohibit the successive hunting of any place for two or three years. The country in which that animal (the beaver) abounds is parceled out into hunting portions which are worked in rotation each third year leaving them the intervening two years to accumulate."[60]

Ann Carlos and Frank Lewis find that where a company had a monopoly on the fur trade (particularly at Fort Churchill) backed by a charter from the crown, it controlled Indian trapping by refusing to take small pelts and by actually burning pelts (without paying for them) if a trapper brought in more than the company thought was sustainable and profitable in the long run.[61] Carlos and Lewis show that this procedure generated a sustainable population of beavers. In contrast, where the company faced competition from the French, overexploitation occurred.

Unlike the Hudson's Bay Company, American fur companies did not have charters that gave them exclusive rights to trade and trap in a particular region. American companies did try unsuccessfully to get government regulation of entry into U.S. trapping areas. In 1816, Congress made it illegal for any foreign fur traders to operate in U.S. territory.[62] William Ashley suggested to Thomas Hart Benton in 1827, "Such is the peculiar situation of the country, that, under suitable regulations, it would probably afford a great quantity of furs for centuries to come."[63] And, as discussed earlier, the U.S. government attempted to control activity through a licensing system for trading but not trapping. Unfortunately, neither the restrictions on foreign traders nor the attempts to license trading were successful.

Policies to restrict entry to trapping and trading failed for two reasons. First, the United States lacked an adequate enforcement mechanism on the frontier. Second, although the United States had purchased much of the territory in the Louisiana Purchase in 1803, claim to much of the beaver-rich area was disputed. For example, all of the Pacific Northwest was contested by the British until 1846. In 1819, the two countries had agreed that they would jointly administer the region from the crest of the Rockies to the Pacific Ocean and north of the forty-second parallel, the present southern border of Oregon. The Hudson's Bay Company used the British claim of sovereignty over the region as a warrant for active participation in the fur trade and frequently crossed the Rockies. The company's trappers even tried to create a "fur desert" in all of Oregon west of the Continental Divide in order to prevent further American activity in the area. George Simpson, the governor of the company, said in 1827, "If the country becomes exhausted in Fur-bearing animals, Americans can have no inducement to proceed further."[64]

Much of the rest of the region was contested by Mexico until the Treaty of Guadalupe Hidalgo in 1848. Overlapping claims by the United States and Mexico meant that efforts to restrict entry were doomed to failure. In 1824, the Mexican government tried to prohibit foreign trapping, but American trappers simply evaded the restriction by declaring Mexican citizenship.[65] D. J. Weber estimates that as much as a third of the total catch from the Rocky Mountains in the early 1830s was taken out through New Mexico.[66] Sea captains also made regular calls at California ports and purchased furs from trappers.[67] Again the tragedy of the commons prevailed.

Permanent fur-trading forts did hold the potential for capturing location rents and therefore should have had an incentive to sustain beaver populations in the region from which they obtained pelts. As Wishart notes, posts such as Fort Union, Fort Tecumseh, and Fort William "served as control points for the fur trade: decision-making centres, collection foci for the furs from dependent regional posts, and major trading centers in their own right."[68]

Again, however, competition raised its ugly head. Getting the best locations required that forts be established at the time when the discounted present value of location had just become positive (see Chapter 2). This race for the best fort locations would have dissipated location rents through premature entry. William Sublette, upon his entry into the fur business in 1833, began "erecting trading houses adjacent to most of the fixed posts that the American Fur Company maintained on the upper Missouri."[69] As a result of the competition for good locations, "more and more duplicating posts stared across streams and inlets at each other."[70]

The final factor contributing to the lack of property rights to fur-trapping territories was the short life of the beaver market. The first trapping of any note in the Rocky Mountains did not occur until around 1805–6, and significant expeditions were not organized until the second and third decades. By 1840, the beaver trade was essentially over. Property rights evolve, but not immediately, especially when there are many players from different ethnic backgrounds ranging over thousands of miles.

Economic models of resource exploitation show that rational use will occur at a rate that will cause the rental value of the resource to rise at the rate of interest.[71] However, the price data in Table 5.1 show fur prices declining throughout most of the period.[72] Given falling prices, trappers and their companies had little incentive to invest in protecting trapping territories. And given the precipitous decline in demand brought on by the shift from beaver hats to silk hats in the 1840s, it appears in retrospect that their expectations were well-founded. Had they trapped less intensively and left more beaver to propagate, the forgone trapping efforts would have had a negative return. Add to falling prices the fact that beaver quickly restocked areas that were trapped out, and incentive to conserve the resource is even further undercut. One observer, writing in 1854, noted that beaver populations had rebounded quickly in the areas where, after 1840, trapping had ceased. In his words, beaver were again "tolerably plentiful in all of the small streams and in the Missouri and Yellowstone."[73] In short, investing effort into the definition and enforcement of property rights to beaver-trapping territories made little economic sense.

The Buffalo Commons

An even more dramatic allegation of the tragedy of the commons is the extermination of American buffalo. Although 30 million bison roamed the plains before extensive market hunting began,[74] bison were almost totally

TABLE 5.1

Nineteenth-Century Fur Prices

(Price adjusted, 1821–25 = 100; prices in other periods are expressed as a percentage of the 1821–25 price)

	Price for All Furs
1801–5	61.5
1806–10	63.3
1811–15	60.3
1816–20	67.0
1821–25	100.0
1826–30	105.7
1831–35	97.1
1836–40	84.3
1841–45	75.4
1846–50	72.8
1851–55	58.2
1856–61	54.5

SOURCE: Calculated from U.S. Bureau of the Census 1975, 205, Series E-97 and E-109.

exterminated by 1886, with only a few in captivity and a very small wild herd in Yellowstone National Park. Is the rapid and almost complete destruction of buffalo herds on the Great Plains another example of institutional failure? If so, why did it occur, and how could it have been prevented?

Some commentators attribute the near extinction of buffalo to competition and the capitalistic profit motive. For instance, Andrew Isenberg, a leading historian of the buffalo, argues that "the root of the failure to regulate bison hunting was a mid-century belief in economic competition. Everyone, Indian or Euroamerican included, was engaged in a race to exploit resources for individual gain. To reserve resources for anybody's exclusive use violated the competitive ideal."[75] He continues:

Although it is in the interest of all to preserve common resources such as the bison, in a competitive economy, it is in every individual's interest to ex-

haust available supplies in the pursuit of private wealth. . . . Like Euroamerican industrial society, which felled trees and mined coal and iron ore at an
alarmingly destructive pace, by the mid-nineteenth century the nomads'
economy was based on the unsustainable exploitation of the herds. . . . But
when Euroamericans slaughtered the bison to pacify the plains nomads . . .
they exposed the fragility of all societies, including their own, that rely on
the unsustainable exploitation of nature.[76]

The competition and overexploitation described by Isenberg are best an-
alyzed in an institutional context. The question is, what were the costs and
benefits of establishing property rights to bison or their territory? To set the
context, it is important to understand that buffalo numbers were large
enough initially that few people could imagine their near extermination; that
they roamed over large territories and were difficult to control; that they
were even harder to transport alive to meat markets in the East; and that
they competed with cattle for valuable forage. For these reasons, buffalo
were simply not an economically valuable resource. Open access certainly
speeded the process of extermination and probably took the numbers closer
to zero than otherwise might have been the case, but a rapid and large reduction of the buffalo herds was probably inevitable given that it was less
costly to market valuable grass through cattle rather than bison.

THE ROBE AND HIDE TRADE

On the Great Plains, most of the early market trades that affected the buffalo numbers were for their robes, that is, hides with the hair on. The buffalo were shot in the wintertime and their hides carefully tanned by Indian
women. The resulting robes were a valuable trade commodity for Indians.
In contrast to beaver, bison robes were harvested mostly by Indians rather
than whites.[77] In the 1840s, the St. Louis market averaged 90,000 robes per
year, and that grew to 100,000 during the 1850s and 1860s.[78]

The slaughter of buffalo speeded up dramatically during the last quarter
of the nineteenth century for three reasons. First, the defeat of the Sioux Indians in the battles of 1876–77 made it safer for whites to hunt buffalo. Second, extension of the Northern Pacific Railroad west of Bismarck, Dakota
Territory, reduced the cost of delivering robes to market. Third and perhaps

Five Minutes' Work, Montana, 1880, by L. A. Huffman. The near extermination of buffalo herds is often cited as an example of how white settlers exploited the natural resources of the West. Because it was not economically feasible to establish property rights to live buffalo and to get them to markets in the East, exterminating them and replacing them with cattle was the only way settlers could capture a sustainable profit from the grass resources of the Great Plains. Courtesy of Coffrin's Old West Gallery, Bozeman, Montana.

most importantly, hides as raw material for leather replaced robes as the principal product from the buffalo. Robes were mostly tanned by Indians and, to be of highest quality, had to be harvested in the fall and early winter when the hair was thickest. The switch from robes to leather from hides, mainly for belting in industrial applications, meant that hair quality did not matter and that therefore buffalo could be harvested at any time.

The hide hunters took only the skins, leaving the carcasses to rot, thus reducing the time it took to process an animal. They would kill as many as one hundred bison at a time by shooting the lead cow first, which left the rest of the herd milling around.[79] The difficulty of coordinating the shooting and skinning resulted in tremendous waste in the early part of the period, with a yield of only one marketable hide from three dead buffalo.[80] Reorganization of buffalo-hunting teams reduced the wastage, probably to a yield of one hide from 1.25 dead buffalo.

The effect of the shift to hides and the increase in demand was rapid. "The buffalo of western Kansas were destroyed in less than four years (1871–1874), those of western Texas in less than five (1875–1879), and those of eastern Montana in no more than four (1880–1883)." John Hanner estimates that between eight and ten million buffalo roamed the High Plains in 1870.[81] Once the hide trade started in 1871, the slaughter was so rapid that by 1883 the buffalo were almost completely gone.

> The extirpation of the buffalo was so rapid that it even caught the hunters by surprise. Curiously enough, not even the buffalo hunters themselves were at the time aware of the fact that the end of the hunting season of 1882–83 was also the end of the buffalo, at least as an inhabitant of the plains and as a source of revenue. In the autumn of 1883 they nearly all outfitted as usual, often at the expense of many hundreds of dollars, and blithely sought "the range" that up to that time had been so prolific in robes. The end was in nearly every case the same—total failure and bankruptcy. It was indeed hard to believe that not only the millions, but also the thousands, had actually gone, and forever.[82]

YOU CAN'T FENCE BUFFALO

Given the value of buffalo at the outset of market hunting and their increasing scarcity, our theory predicts that institutional entrepreneurs would have had an incentive to invest in the definition and enforcement of property rights to bison. But for several reasons, they were not successful.

First, property rights failed to develop because of the rapidity with which the extirpation occurred. Although hunting by the Indians significantly reduced the buffalo on the Great Plains from 1840–70, a very large herd, probably eight to ten million, still remained by the time market hunting began in earnest. But once it did start in the 1870s, it took just over a decade for buffalo to be almost completely wiped out. Given the speed with which this occurred and the fact that many buffalo hide hunters thought the herds had simply moved to different regions, most participants did not perceive the increasing scarcity.

Second, as in the fur trade, the large number of autonomous hunters raised the cost of collective action to create property rights and limit entry. William Hornaday estimates that in the northern range alone there were 5,000 white hunters and skinners.[83] Isenberg estimates that in the winter of 1872–73, between 1,000 and 2,000 hide hunters were working in western Kansas.[84]

A possible third factor was the role of the army. It is widely held that the military contributed to the extermination of the buffalo in order to help pacify the Indians by destroying their food source.[85] Although the army itself was not large enough to kill large numbers of buffalo, it did provide protection to the hide hunters and made ammunition available to them.[86] However, given the other pressures mentioned above, it is doubtful that army policy played much of a role in the demise of buffalo.[87] A particularly compelling counter to the army-policy theory is the fact that extermination of buffalo on the Canadian plains occurred just as rapidly as in the United States even though Canada did not have a military policy that favored killing buffalo to control the Indians.[88]

The fourth and perhaps most important reason that property rights to buffalo did not evolve was that bison were difficult to control and manage. Ownership and control required either that an owner control a sufficiently large amount of land over which bison could freely range or that he be able to fence them. U.S. land policy was directed toward settled agriculture with small-scale farms, and this made it difficult to establish ownership and control of large land areas (see Chapter 9). Homestead policy during the hunting era established 160 acres as the maximum size that a settler could claim. Some settlers were able to control more access through multiple claims and fraud, but rarely were property rights secure enough to establish claims to the several thousand acres needed for a viable buffalo herd. To fence buffalo in a smaller area was improbable because barbed wire was not patented and produced in commercial quantities until 1873 and because federal land laws prohibited fencing of the open range. In other words, artificially high transaction costs made it almost impossible for anyone to think of establishing ownership of a buffalo herd.

With buffalo being undomesticated, they were not suitable for any sort of settled agriculture.[89] The buffalo were difficult to handle, particularly in stressful situations, and could not be herded or driven to market like cattle.[90] Ernest Seton reports:

> The pure-blooded Buffalo has not proven a success as a domestic animal. Its obstinate and often ferocious temper remains unchanged by contact with man. The cows when with the calves, and the bulls at all times are of a fierce, combative disposition. One never knows when this may break out. A number of men have been killed by tame buffalo, and those who know them best, trust them least.[91]

Because the transportation cost for meat not on the hoof was so high, buffalo meat was left to rot. In the words of Hanner, "a buffalo carcass was valuable only if it could be transported to potential consumers at a reasonable cost. Even in cold weather when meat could easily be saved, overland carriage across the plains was so demanding of time and effort that only buffalo killed within a short distance of a rail depot were normally butchered."[92]

COMPETITION WITH COWS

To argue that bison were becoming increasingly scarce and therefore worth the investment in developing property rights requires asking: worth it compared to what? The answer is: compared to cattle. Basically, buffalo and cattle consumed the grass of the Great Plains and converted it to products in demand in the East and Europe. Hence the entrepreneur had to ask what was the most profitable way to convert the grass into marketable products. The fact that cattle could easily be trailed to a rail head or even to market meant that cattle were valuable for their meat and their hides, while the intractable buffalo were valuable only for their hides.[93] In the 1880s, a buffalo hide was worth $3.00, while a cow was worth $20 to $25, with both prices at the point of shipment, such as Miles City, Montana.[94] In view of such a price difference, it is not surprising that cattle appeared a more profitable alternative to buffalo.

Thus, simultaneously with the removal of the buffalo, cattle were being trailed into the grassland prairies to harvest grass (see Chapter 8). As discussed previously, this happened rapidly once Indian pacification occurred and buffalo were removed. By 1883, over 500,000 cattle grazed in eastern Montana.[95] In fact, the replacement of the buffalo by cattle occurred so rapidly that by 1890 there were probably more cattle on the High Plains than there were buffalo in 1870.[96]

SAVING THE BISON

Although the buffalo did not prove profitable for widespread ranching, it was private entrepreneurs that eventually prevented the complete extinction of the species. Individual entrepreneurs were more alert than the government to the near extermination and saw the importance of preserving at least a few buffalo. In 1878, Texas rancher Charles Goodnight captured a few bison calves near his ranch. In 1882, Frederick Dupree captured six calves in Montana and took them to his ranch in South Dakota. And two Montana ranchers of Indian ancestry, Charles Allard and Michael Pablo, purchased remnants of other people's captured buffalo herds and captured some of their own. Allard and Pablo went on to become two of the most successful breeders of buffalo, providing the animals for several restocking efforts in Canada.[97]

Private not-for-profit efforts also aided in the preservation of bison. In 1905 several wealthy individuals formed the American Bison Society and raised money to aid in preservation efforts. The federal government eventually provided assistance for buffalo preservation through the purchase of 21 bison to supplement the rapidly declining herd in Yellowstone National Park in 1902 and through the establishment of the National Bison Range in Montana in 1908. Except for the small resident herd in Yellowstone National Park, all the bison-preservation efforts took place through capture, a difficult and expensive procedure.

With respect to simply preserving the buffalo from absolute extinction, the efforts succeeded. By 1996 over 200,000 buffalo lived in private preserves as well as 11,000 in public herds.[98] Today, public awareness and private rights to buffalo are enough to ensure continued preservation.

All in all, perhaps the history of the American bison was close to economically optimal. They were magnificent animals that populated much of the Great Plains, and they formed an economic resource that supported Indians and early settlers. They were exploited rapidly by both the robe trade and the hide (leather) trade, perhaps more rapidly than private rights would have allowed. Nevertheless, it is likely that, given the low economic value of buffalo and the fact that they were primarily valuable as an amenity resource, the appropriate degree of preservation occurred.

Conclusion

The saga of the beaver and the buffalo are best understood in the context of institutional entrepreneurs coping with resources that were either not valuable or not likely to sustain their value, and for which the transaction costs of coming together to define and enforce property rights would have been high. As a result, beaver and buffalo were rapidly exploited, as trappers and hunters raced to capture the rents. The beaver did return to many of their original haunts once the trapping ceased in the 1840s. Buffalo, however, suffered almost complete extermination and now exist only as ecological curiosities. In both cases, several lessons can be learned from the institutional history of the era.

In organizing the trade in "soft gold," as furs were called, and in organizing the actual production of the pelts, robes, and hides, institutional entrepreneurs were quite successful. At a time when organizing team production was hard, entrepreneurs used innovative contracts that shared the risks and got the incentives right.

These entrepreneurs, however, were less successful at developing property rights to the beaver and buffalo, for two main reasons. First, federal policies made the definition and enforcement of property rights more difficult. For the beaver, the lack of any clear sovereign control of the beaver-rich mountain streams by a single nation made it hard to establish any rules that restricted entry. Government imposed artificial transaction costs on establishing property rights to the buffalo range by restricting the ability to fence and by requiring that only small parcels could be claimed under the homestead acts.

Second, and most important, values perceived with hindsight do not always coincide with the values of foresight. Hence we look back on the era and wonder why the trappers and traders did not conserve more of their prey. Quite simply, the *ex ante* expected value of the resource was not high enough to warrant postponing harvesting. And when returns were higher from alternative uses of complementary resources, it certainly made sense to deplete the wild game animals and replace them with domesticated ones. Hence what appear at first glance to be classic examples of the tragedy of the commons, on closer examination are examples of institutional entrepreneurs responding rationally to the benefit and cost constraints of the times.

SIX

There's Property Rights in Them Thar Hills

If rising resource values are a major cause of institutional change, the discovery of gold and silver had to be one of the more dramatic cases of the formation of property rights. As prospectors rushed to the hills, institutional entrepreneurs had their tasks cut out for them. In places such as California after the 1848 discovery at Sutter's Mill and Nevada after the 1859 discovery of the Comstock Lode, land went from being practically worthless to being extremely valuable in a matter of days or weeks. The rowdy mining camps that immediately sprang up create images of thievery and violence among miners fighting over claims and the gold from them.

In reality, however, miners avoided the negative-sum game of violence, opting instead for establishing and enforcing property rights. To be sure, violence did occur in the mining camps, but it was "generally confined to a few special categories and did not affect all activities or all people," specifically not children, women, and law-abiding citizens. Despite the frontier's reputation for violence, "crimes most common today—robbery, theft, burglary, and rape—were of no great significance."[1]

In the absence of formal government, miners in a particular location would gather and hammer out rules for peacefully establishing claims and resolving disputes over them. Since the streams they panned and the veins they mined had not previously been owned, their task was all the more difficult. Nevertheless, from the mining camps came rules for mineral and water allocation that exist to this day. Moreover, these rules follow closely the predictions of our theory, varying with the types and locations of precious metals and with the technology used to extract them. This property-rights activity was economic in nature, responding to the benefits and costs of definition and enforcement.

When territorial and state governments were formed, they codified the rules from mining camps, but the federal government did not get into the act until 1866. Until then, federal land law made no provision for mineral exploration or establishment of mineral rights in the West. Antecedents for regulating mining existed in the Land Ordinance of 1785, which specified that one-third of all gold, silver, lead, and copper found on public lands belonged to the government.[2] This provision lasted only until 1807, after which the national government experimented with a leasing program (primarily for lead mines) designed to generate revenue for the government.[3] Difficulties in enforcement, however, doomed the leasing policy, so that in 1846 Congress authorized the sale of lead mines and in effect ended attempts at leasing. Then, in 1866, Congress passed the Mining Law, which to this day governs mineral exploration and development on public lands and generates endless controversy about who owns minerals thereunder.

The rules that govern western mining and mineral rights evolved literally from the ground up. It was up to the miner with specific knowledge of the resources and the mining technology to devise the rules for mining. Not only did the miners pave the way for mineral rights throughout the West, but they laid the foundation for western water law. In this context it is not surprising that the rules varied considerably, according to whether the precious metals were found in streams, surface gravel, or underground veins.

All that Glitters Could Be Gold in California

Early mining law in California was rooted in Spanish law. This law, while well developed, was complex in nature and consisted of a set of centralized regulations designed primarily to generate revenue for the government. According to Charles Shinn, "the mining laws of New Spain, more particularly of Mexico . . . constitute the most unique, laborious, and complicated system of special jurisprudence ever developed on this continent."[4]

After Mexico secured its independence from Spain in 1821, Spanish institutional influence declined rapidly, especially after the United States declared war on Mexico in 1846. The peace treaty signed at Guadalupe Hidalgo in 1848 ceded California to the United States, but specified that Mexican property rights in land and other resources were to be honored as long as they did not conflict with the United States Constitution.[5] Of the fourteen million acres granted by the Mexican government to individuals prior to the 1848 treaty, nine million acres were actually confirmed by the United States.[6] These grants, however, had little impact on California mining because they were primarily in coastal areas rather than in the foothills of the Sierras, where gold was discovered. Moreover, just ten days after the treaty was signed, the military governor of California, Colonel Richard Mason, abolished Mexican laws and customs governing the acquisition of mining rights on public lands.[7] In their place he proposed a leasing system or auction of mineral lands, but neither was adopted.

Perhaps the main reason that Mexican laws were abandoned and a leasing system never put in their place was that gold was discovered at Sutter's Mill near present-day Sacramento on January 24, 1848, just nine days prior to the signing of the treaty of Guadalupe Hidalgo. Without a strong formal government to replace the top-down Mexican government, miners were free to develop their own mining institutions from the ground up. Colonel Mason formally ended any chance that Mexican mining laws would govern the new discoveries, and even if a territorial legislature had tried to pass mining statutes, they would have been ignored since most of the discoveries took place on federal lands. Hence the miners started with a clean slate on which to write their new rules.

No alcalde, no counsel, no justice of the peace, was ever forced upon a district by an outside power. The district was the unit of political organization, in many regions, long after the creation of the state; and delegates from adjoining districts often met in consultation regarding boundaries, or matters of local government, and reported to their respective constituency in open-air meeting, on hillside or river-bank.[8]

With the discovery of gold in 1848, the rush was on. By the end of 1848, four-fifths of California's males were gold miners.[9] California's population grew from 14,000 in 1848 to 100,000 by the end of 1849, and to 223,000 by the latter part of 1852.[10] Forty thousand of the 100,000 in 1849 were miners, and by 1850, their numbers had grown to 50,000.[11]

The rapid influx of miners is even more impressive when one considers what immigrants had to go through to get to California in the mid-1800s. Americans from anywhere east of the Mississippi who wished to travel to the gold fields had three choices: they could take a four- to eight-month voyage around Cape Horn in South America; they could travel by ship to Panama, by land across the Isthmus of Panama, and by another ship to San Francisco, a total of thirty-five days; or they could trek for several months across the country from various embarkation points in Missouri. All three alternatives were arduous, expensive, and risky, and many who started never finished.

A race for gold in the California foothills with over 100,000 entrants would seem the perfect recipe for conflict, violence, and disaster, as a newspaper of the time predicted:

> The gold regions of California will be a theater of tragic events—the scene of bloodshed and strife. The Sun never yet shone on a more motley crowd than will be assembled there. We tremble for the result upon the morals of the people and the peace of the country. In the confusion which must prevail there for the next 12 months, the law will be powerless, rights will be disregarded, reason dethroned and brute force will reign triumphant.[12]

The "theater of tragic events" proved far less violent than the newspaper predicted, because institutional entrepreneurs with a stake in defining and enforcing property rights developed effective rules for governance and order. To be sure, some miners entered a classic race for property rights, enduring great hardships to discover the mother lode before others could beat them to it. But the race remained relatively peaceful. In 1849, one observer noted that the mining camps rapidly developed a set of rules that "placed the strong and the weak upon a footing of equality, defined the claims that might be set apart, protected the tools left on the ground as evidence of proprietorship, and permitted the adventurers to hold their rights as securely as if they were guaranteed by a charter from the government."[13] As outlined above in Chapter 2, a rapid increase in the value of a resource tends to increase efforts to define and enforce property rights to that resource,[14] but this still leaves the question of whether conflicting ownership claims will be settled peacefully or violently. A large body of literature has developed examining this question in the context of whether conflicting parties litigate or negotiate.[15] From this literature, it is clear that the decision depends on the expected cost of negotiating relative to the expected cost of litigating.

John Umbeck applied this general framework to California mining camps, where residual claimants had an incentive to conserve on resources consumed in the definition and enforcement process.[16] Importantly, he considered the productivity of claims, the potential for scale economies in mining those claims, and the ability of miners to use force against one another. Because the expected productivity of claims was relatively equal; because there were few scale economies in placer mining, especially prior to the use of hydraulic techniques; and because the six-shooter gave everyone a nearly equal ability to exercise force, miners had every incentive to settle disputes peacefully (negotiate) rather than to fight (litigate). "Contrary to the television westerns which claim to depict this period of American history, the reported incidence of violence was remarkably low. Instead of fighting over the rights to mineral land, the miners entered into contractual arrangements which assigned mineral rights in an orderly and . . . predictable fashion."[17]

Cultural norms enhanced the tendency to seek positive-sum solutions. As Richard Zerbe and C. Leigh Anderson put it, "Culturally derived norms of fairness embodied in familiar institutions helped to facilitate collective action and produce order among the California gold miners, by acting as focal points to solve the initial coordination problem. By embodying familiar and fair principles these institutions provided for cooperation in the gold fields."[18] These cultural norms included a strong commitment to the princi-

California Mining Camp. Miners who rushed to get rich in the gold fields of California and Nevada came from a variety of backgrounds and ethnicities. To reduce
claim jumping and encourage investment, miners established clear and enforceable
rules regarding what constituted a mining claim, how large it could be, and what
was necessary to maintain ownership. Disputes were adjudicated in miner courts,
local extralegal bodies usually made up of all the miners in a particular location.
Kern Co.: Randsburg; courtesy of the California History Room, California State
Library, Sacramento, California.

ple of first possession,[19] to justice provided through majority rule, and to
trial by jury for the resolution of disputes. These norms assured that miners
resorted to force primarily to enforce agreed-upon rights rather than redistribute them.

Even so, an initial agreement on rights was still needed to prevent rent
dissipation, and some miners contracted with one another before coming to
the gold fields in order to clarify who would own what. These early contracts involving 40 or 50 miners specified joint production with a required
amount of daily work hours by the parties and an equal sharing of the gold
found.[20] However, these contracts seldom worked.

This ability for self-organization showed itself in California in hundreds of mining companies. The first of these were formed in 1849 before the Argonauts left their homes in the East. It was customary for groups of intending gold seekers to unite their efforts in joint-stock associations, for mutual protection in the wild country to which they were going and to facilitate a sharing of expenses. Eastern investors often furnished capital to such companies in return for shares of stock.

Almost all of these companies disintegrated soon after reaching California. The elaborate charters and constitutions under which most of them were supposed to operate had been drawn up by persons ignorant of California conditions. They generally proved unworkable when put into force.[21]

Not surprisingly, the incentive to shirk in the joint-ownership system led to the dissolution of these companies and the creation of new contracts. When conflicts arose among miners in a camp, a meeting was called and a contract drawn up that specified how property rights would be defined and enforced. The contract specified the boundaries of the district, the size of the allowed claims, and the methods by which claims would be enforced. It also provided for registration of claims, usually with one of the more respected miners in the camp.[22] Typical contracts specified that, by occupation, each miner could hold only one claim not to exceed 100 square feet; that purchased claims required a bill of sale certified by two disinterested persons regarding the validity of the signature and the consideration; that a five-person jury would decide disputes regarding sales; that a claim could be made by posting a notice of intent to be renewed every ten days until water was available to work the claim; and that claims were considered abandoned and forfeited if the miner was absent from the claim for five days for reasons other than sickness or injury.[23]

These contracts reflected the special characteristics of the mining districts and were often reformulated as new information and new conditions arose. According to Theodore Hittell, a nineteenth-century historian of California mining: "Nearly every bar, flat and gulch had separate rules. Their jurisdictions were frequently changed, some consolidating into larger districts and others dividing into smaller ones—the change being dependent chiefly upon the character as to homogeneousness or otherwise of the mining region embraced and the convenience for the miners of access to a common place of meeting."[24]

One of the most complete studies of the contracts is provided by Umbeck, who assembled nearly 200 of the original contracts that governed early mining camps.[25] These contracts generally created property rights through the principle of first possession and also often granted a double claim to the initial discoverer of a strike. For reasons of both efficiency and equity, the contracts limited the size of the claim, with the average being the size that could productively be worked by a miner. Umbeck found that larger claims were allowed when the expected productivity per acre was less.[26] Although limits on the size of claims were based on equality of opportunity, the limit sizes were not so small as to impair productivity. Moreover, equality of opportunity did not allow unlimited entry; once a district was fully allocated, further subdivision and entry were prohibited.

Once a claim was registered with the local recorder and the corners were staked (sometimes with a written notice including the name of the claimant), other indications of use were required. In some cases, property rights could be maintained by leaving tools on the claim, but more often, districts specified the minimum number of days per month that a claim had to be worked for title to be maintained. Exceptions were made for illness, and requirements were either reduced or removed altogether during the winter months, when water was often not available.[27] Minimum workday requirements entailed an expenditure of resources but provided an inexpensive way of determining if a claim was still active and of enforcing rights by ensuring that enough miners were present to defend claims against outsiders.[28]

Dispute resolution was rapid and effective under the rules of mining camps. In 1849, a participant noted, "Judgment and sentences and justice are too speedily executed here to make stealing profitable."[29] Shinn provides a description of such proceedings:

> When acting as tribunals of life and death, all who appeared were entitled to a vote and to be heard; but when deciding laws concerning claims and local government, members of other camps could not vote. The accused—camp thief, sluice-robber, horse stealer, or murderer—was guarded by men with revolvers or was tied to a tree. The miners' court was in such cases assembled at once, not by formal notices, but by a cry running from claim to claim, from height to height, proclaiming, for instance, that "they've caught the fellow that robbed John Smiley's sluice-boxes last night." Nearly every-

one then came into camp, and the case was usually brought to trial within half an hour. . . . If there was no jury, the case was submitted to the decision of the miners present, who also fixed the punishment. In small camps, where only 30 or 40 men assembled, this was perhaps the usual system; but in larger camps, the jury system prevailed.[30]

Because incarceration required scarce resources to build a jail and guard it, punishment usually consisted of whippings, banishment from camp, and, in the most severe cases, hanging.[31]

With property rights to claims defined and enforced, miners formed efficient capital and labor contracts to exploit the resources.

> The exigencies of the work of mining claims required two or three persons to labor together if they would utilize their strength to the best advantage. The legal contract of partnership, common in settled communities, became under these circumstances, the brother-like tie "*pard*"-nership, sacred by camp custom, protected by camp law; and its few infringements were treated as crimes against every other miner. . . . There soon were larger associations to work deep claims, or turn the channels of rivers; but each such association came into existence when it was needed, not a moment sooner.[32]

The rules governing mining claims in California successfully established secure property rights to encourage efficient and orderly extraction of the gold, as the production figures in Table 6.1 indicate. The effectiveness of the bottom-up system of property rights hammered out in California is confirmed by the fact that an active market in claims soon developed and by the fact that federal legislation formalizing this system of property rights had no discernable impact on gold extraction.[33]

Bringing Water to the Gold

In California, placer mining dominated. In placers, gold was mainly found mixed with gravel and soil and therefore had to be separated from its medium by using water. Water requirements varied with the technology employed. Panning separated gold from streamed gravel through the use of

TABLE 6.1

California Gold Production, 1864–1870

Fiscal Year	Gold Produced ($)
1864	24,071,423
1865	17,930,858
1866	17,123,867
1867	18,265,452
1868	17,555,867
1869	18,229,044
1870	17,458,133

SOURCE: Paul 1947, Appendix A.

readily available water, but it could process only small amounts of material. Sluices, in which water ran through a rocker box to separate out the gold, could process more gravel but required larger amounts of water and hence additional investment for water diversion. And hydraulic mining, which used pressurized water to dislodge gold from soil, required even more water and investment.

To secure the water and encourage investment in storage and diversion, institutional entrepreneurs hammered out the prior-appropriation system that dominates western water law to this day. Under this system, water rights were granted to a person or company when they diverted the water from its source; and when not all water claims could be met, the priority of rights was determined by the first-in-time-first-in-right rule. Under this rule, claims were adjudicated on the basis of the date filed. In years of low water flow, that meant that late claims might not have a right to water, but water owners had a secure right and a reasonable expectation about how much water they could claim under what circumstances.

Under this institution, water companies organized to dig ditches, construct dams, and build flumes. Sometimes the flumes ran as high as 35 feet above the ground and were several thousand feet long.[34] By 1857, over 4,000 miles of canals, ditches, and flumes had been built, at a cost of nearly twelve million dollars.[35] Securing such investment required security of water rights, which the prior-appropriation system provided.

Because water could flow between districts, the local nature of district rules caused some problems for water development. Because of the lack of coordination among the districts, duplicate dams and diversions were built along streams. Water would be stored once, diverted to a hydraulic mining site, returned to the river, dammed and diverted again, and so on.[36] According to Umbeck, "There was apparently no technological reason why these groups could not have constructed just one dam up river from the area to be mined, dug 1 long ditch equal in length to the sum of the separate ditches, and saved all the costs of constructing separate dams. However, this was not observed."[37]

Although the original mining-district rules evolved with little or no formal legal control from either the state or the federal government, statute law did have an influence on the mining camps over time. In 1851, California passed the Civil Practice Act, which established a judicial system and basically codified the agreements that had been reached in the mining camps. The justices, in deciding mining cases, were to admit as evidence "the customs, usages, or regulations established or enforced at the bar or diggings embracing such claims, and such customs, usages and regulations, when not in conflict with the Constitution and laws of this State, shall govern the decision of the action."[38]

The national government also became involved, but, like the state laws, most of its early intervention simply codified and recognized customary rules. In *Sparrow v. Strong* (1865), the Supreme Court ruled that the local rule had the implied sanction of the federal government.[39] In 1866 Congress passed the first mining legislation governing mineral extraction in the West. It recognized the right of entry onto public lands to explore for minerals and provided for patenting of those claims through occupation and improvements.[40] The Mining Law of 1872 clarified the provisions of the 1866 law.[41]

The central codification of the miners' customary rules may have lowered the transaction costs of defining and enforcing property rights by providing specific rules applicable to all camps, but it also opened the possibility of using larger units of government to redistribute wealth. Larger collective-action units have the potential for lowering the costs of transacting across jurisdictions, but they also raise the cost of exiting jurisdictions that redistribute rights (see Chapter 2). An example of this redistribution was the Foreign Miners' Tax, passed by the California state government in 1850. This tax was designed to limit entry by foreign miners by taxing them at a rate of $20 per month. Local mining camps certainly tried to discriminate against foreigners too,[42] but foreigners could escape such local discrimination by moving to other camps or establishing their own camps. "There were many villages peopled nearly all together by Mexicans, others by Frenchmen; some places there were parties of two or three hundred Chileans forming a community of their own. The Chinese camps were very numerous; and besides all such distinct colonies of foreigners, every town of the southern mines contained a very large foreign population."[43] And in the words of Philip Choy,[44] "in 1852 the formation of Chinese camps along rivers and canyons [was] noticeable throughout the entire gold region." Under a single statewide law, however, such options were eliminated.[45]

Far from being a "theater of tragic events—the scene of bloodshed and strife," mining camps in California were a crucible for institutional evolution. Miners recognized violence as a negative-sum game and devised efficient methods for defining and enforcing property rights. Shinn concludes, "Everywhere we find, among the observers of mining-life, testimony to the success of the system of self-government adopted in the camps."[46] Similarly, Zerbe and Anderson find that "the prediction that the mines would be the scene of chaotic violence was wrong. Rather than anarchy or violent gang rule, what quickly emerged in the California goldfields were social institutions and rules for gold mining that relied upon a system of norms without unusual violence. Each mining camp drew up an explicit contract, usually in writing."[47]

There's Gold Under Them Thar Hills

Mining in Nevada provides another example of rapid development in an institutional vacuum. Gold mining had occurred in western Nevada throughout the 1850s, but yielded too little to cause significant conflicts. Only about a hundred miners worked in an area of 40 square miles; hence competition for the resource was minimal and incentive to define and enforce property rights lacking.[48] This changed rapidly in January 1859, when two Irishmen discovered the Comstock Lode, one of the richest finds in the West.[49] The Comstock Lode was so rich that, by 1889, it had produced over 12 percent of all of the gold and silver ever mined in the United States.[50] Between 1859 and 1861, the mining population rose from 100 to 20,000.

California and Nevada mining camps had many institutional similarities but also substantial differences. Like the discovery of gold at Sutter's Mill in California, the discovery of the Comstock Lode sharply increased the benefits of engaging in definition and enforcement activity, and as our theory predicts, institutional entrepreneurs immediately responded with a wide variety of institutional innovations. Also, like that in California, the early institutional development in Nevada flourished independently of local, state, or national mining laws. The various national land laws, such as the Preemption Acts[51] and the homestead acts, applied to nonmineral lands, with the federal government retaining ownership of all mineral lands,[52] but otherwise these laws did not deal with minerals. In the absence of formal mining laws in the face of rapidly rising resource values, spontaneous action was required to prevent anarchy and to establish extralegal procedures for creating property rights.

The first efforts to create property rights in Nevada closely followed those of the mining camps in California.

> Within five months of the Comstock ore strike, a formal mining camp government, Gold Hill, was established by prospectors at the site of the earliest discoveries. The Gold Hill District had written rules regarding the establishment and maintenance of private holdings, and the rules were enforced by a permanent claim recorder and an ad hoc miners' court. Three months later a similar government was organized in Virginia City, and the Devil's Gate District followed in early 1860. . . . In general, the mining camp regulations described the recording requirements for locating a claim, the size of individual allotments, the procedures for marking claim boundaries, and the work requirements necessary for maintaining ownership. By following the rules of the mining district, claimants were granted locally recognized possessory rights to mineral ground.[53]

One of the substantial differences between the early California gold discoveries and those in Nevada was the location of the resource. Unlike placer claims, which could be defined with surface boundaries, quartz claims such as the Comstock Lode were deep veins, requiring different mining techniques and organizational forms. Because the gold was subsurface, the rights structure chosen by the miners separated surface claims from subsurface rights. For instance, the original rules in the Gold Hill District allowed a claimant to have mining rights for 200 linear feet along the vein.[54] The miner established rights by discovery of the vein and then could pursue it underground, even if it passed beneath someone else's surface rights. "Under this theory, the lode was the property, and the surface became a mere easement."[55] Fewer work requirements were imposed on quartz claims because those claims were easier to enforce. Unlike a placer claim, where a claim jumper could simply start panning or sluicing, a quartz claim jumper had to invest significant capital in tunneling to the vein.

Disputes over quartz claims broke out more frequently than disputes in placer mining because the paths of veins were less obvious, especially if tributary veins existed that could be accessed from different surface locations.

> Mining camp rules clearly defined subsurface claim boundaries between mines along the same vein, and they were not subject to much dispute. Those rules, however, were less definite regarding boundaries between mines on *different* veins. This lack of precision for side boundaries was due to the practice of granting extralateral rights which allowed miners to follow their section of a vein wherever it traveled beneath the earth. Those rights . . . made it possible for a mine to run under a claim of another as long as the two mines were accessing separate veins. Because of their indefinite side boundaries, rich Comstock mines were open to competition from "vampire" claims which tapped the same ore deposit while asserting that it was in a separate vein.[56]

Because of the difficulties in clearly establishing rights to a valuable mineral, the task of developing greater precision in property rights received renewed attention. Specialization in the definition and enforcement process again made sense, superannuating the early method of simply calling miners together to resolve conflicts. The need for information about subsurface geology and the direction of veins made permanent institutions and records more valuable. Experts were necessary to resolve disputes, and central recording of their finds had benefits beyond the local level.

All of this created strong pressures for more formal and permanent arrangements for the definition of rights and the resolution of disputes.[57] In 1861, pressed by the local mining community, the federal government granted Nevada territorial status. The Nevada legislature (territorial until 1864, when statehood was granted) devoted its attention to the questions of mineral rights. Between 1861 and 1866, it passed 47 mineral-rights laws. These laws focused mainly on resolving the issue of who had the right to follow extra lateral veins branching from a main vein, on the procedures for arbitrating disputes, and on the evidence that the courts should use in defending property rights from trespass.

Because of the difficulties in solving disputes over underground rights, territorial courts were "overwhelmed by the massive case load."[58] Indeed, miners' litigation costs amounted to 11 percent of their total costs. Leshy reports that in 1865 "the surveyor-general for Nevada estimated that one-fifth of the 45-million-dollar output of the Comstock Lode was spent in litigation."[59]

The costs of deciding cases individually rose so high, Gary Libecap argues, that state statutes lowered these transaction costs:

> By 1868 Comstock mining rights were well established. . . . While during the six-year period 1863–1868, the [Nevada Supreme Court] had thirty-two mineral rights cases (60 percent of the total considered through 1895), there were only seven cases in the following six years; after 1880 Supreme Court rulings on Comstock mining rights almost ceased. . . . Mineral rights law became highly defined through the enactment of 178 statutes and Supreme Court verdicts by 1895—the situation stood in sharp contrast to the general, unwritten rules that had existed in 1858.[60]

Using regression analysis, Libecap shows that the demand for state statutes and court rulings to resolve disputes was driven by the value of mining claims; that is, people responded to the higher benefits of defining and enforcing property rights. "The pattern of legal change in Nevada from the mining camp through the state government was largely determined by efficiency needs—the need to reduce ownership uncertainty as competition for mine income grew." He concludes that, by 1868, "private mineral rights were relatively secure, reducing the need for further legal adjustments, even though deeper shafts led to new bonanzas with output peaking in 1876."[61]

Conclusion

Mining in the West offers an interesting test of the hypothesis that property rights develop in response to shifts in benefits and costs. Because gold and silver strikes occurred so rapidly, sorting out the influence of increases in value from other factors is relatively easy. In both California and Nevada, miners quickly found effective ways of defining and enforcing property rights. Miners' groups were small enough that resource savings in designing and adjudicating rules were obvious. Thus most of the institutional change took the form not of redistribution but of creating property rights and repackaging them in new contractual forms for production. In California most of the definition and enforcement activity took place at the local, extralegal level, although it was eventually ratified and codified through statute and court action. Because of the complexity of establishing property rights to underground veins and because of the returns to specialization in definition and in enforcement, Nevada moved more quickly to a formal legal system. Even there, though, the heavy influence of mining in the state economy led to rules that were focused on the creation and defense of property rights rather than their redistribution.[62]

SEVEN

Wagon-Train Governments

Like the mining camps of the West, the mobile groups of people crossing the Great Plains in search of riches from the land faced an institutional vacuum that had to be filled if they were to complete the arduous trip. Once they rolled out of Independence, St. Joseph, or any other major departure point, they left behind the institutional infrastructure known as formal government. It was up to each group to develop its own rules necessary to police its members and provide protections from outsiders (mainly Indians), to resolve disputes among group members, and to organize production of public goods that required teamwork, such as crossing streams, hunting, and fighting Indians. In short, these migrant societies had to form their own governments.

Indeed hundreds of institutional experiments were tried by the 300,000 emigrants (see Table 7.1) who braved the perilous crossing of the Great Plains and Rocky and Sierra mountains between 1840 and 1860. From 1841 through 1848, an overland journey to California or Oregon took an average of 164 days.[1] Accordingly, travelers had to leave as soon as possible in the

TABLE 7.1

Overland Emigration to Oregon, California, and Utah, 1840–1860
(numbers of people)

Year	Oregon	California	Yearly West Coast Total	Cumula- tive West Coast Total	Utah	Cumula- tive Grand Total
1840	13	—	13	13	—	13
1841	24	34	58	71	—	71
1842	125	—	125	196	—	196
1843	875	38	913	1,109	—	1,109
1844	1,475	53	1,528	2,637	—	2,637
1845	2,500	260	2,760	5,397	—	5,397
1846	1,200	1,500	2,700	8,097	—	8,097
1847	4,000	450	4,450	12,547	2,200	14,747
1848	1,300	400	1,700	14,247	2,400	18,847
1849	450	25,000	25,450	39,697	1,500	45,797
1850	6,000	44,000	50,000	89,697	2,500	98,297
1851	3,600	1,100	4,700	94,397	1,500	104,497
1852	10,000	50,000	60,000	154,397	10,000	174,497
1853	7,500	20,000	27,500	181,897	8,000	209,997
1854	6,000	12,000	18,000	199,897	3,167	231,164
1855	500	1,500	2,000	201,897	4,684	237,848
1856	1,000	8,000	9,000	210,897	2,400	249,248
1857	1,500	4,000	5,500	216,397	1,300	256,048
1858	1,500	6,000	7,500	223,897	150	263,698
1859	2,000	17,000	19,000	242,897	1,431	284,129
1860	1,500	9,000	10,500	253,397	1,630	296,259
Total	53,062	200,335	253,397	253,397	42,862	296,259

SOURCE: Unruh 1979, 119–20.

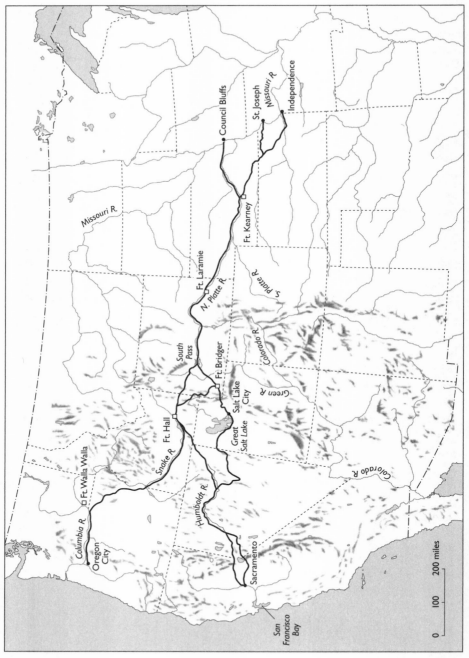

MAP 3. Emigrant Trails

| 0 | 100 | 200 miles |

spring to reach their destination before the onset of winter. For the period 1850 through 1860, travel time fell to 116 days because of improved services on the trail, better ferries and bridges, and shortcuts that shortened the distance. Nevertheless, the trip continued to be hazardous and arduous, taxing the emigrants to their limits.

Why did so many people undertake this perilous journey? The answer, of course, is that they saw potential rents from western resources. The first wave of overland travelers consisted of settlers wanting to claim land in the Willamette Valley in Oregon. Prior to 1840, several Protestant missionaries from New England traveled around Oregon with fur trade caravans.[2] Their reports encouraged a trickle of settlers to head west in 1840, and that trickle soon grew to a flood. The second major wave of travelers comprised miners rushing to the gold fields of California in 1848. During the spring and summer of that year, news spread rapidly about the discovery of gold at Sutter's Mill, and by 1849, thousands were crossing the Great Plains to stake their claims. The final wave, following closely on the heels of the "49ers," consisted of Mormons escaping religious persecution in the Midwest.

The expected riches must have been great given the high costs of making the trip. Indeed, first beholding the immensity of the Great Plains and realizing the hardships that lay ahead was referred to as "seeing the elephant."[3] Diseases, particularly cholera, mountain fever, and scurvy, inflicted great suffering along the trail. Drownings occurred with some frequency at river crossings. Firearm accidents were also a risk. Broken limbs and other injuries resulted from working with draft and riding animals. John Unruh estimates trail mortality at 4 percent, somewhat higher than the 2.5 percent mortality that he claims the overlanders would have faced if they had stayed at home.[4]

Though important, the death rate among the overland migrants gives an incomplete picture of the hardships they endured. The 2,000-mile journey to the West Coast pushed people and their draft animals to their limits for four to six relentless months. Storms, wagon breakdowns, a spartan diet, and interpersonal conflicts all added to the costs of the trip. Possessions often had to be discarded along the trail to lighten the overloaded wagons. Large numbers of emigrants experienced times of near starvation. The fact that so many completed the overland migration attests to human will and cooperation.

In view of these hardships, we might ask why emigrants did not wait until information and transportation improved to make the journey less costly. Again, the answer is found in the race for property rights. The only way to obtain property rights to land was to possess the land first. Thus a person hungry for land could not wait until the net present value of the rents turned positive, because someone else would have beaten him to the resource. Combine this race with the high costs of obtaining information about the value of the land, and it is not surprising that some people underestimated the net return of the journey and failed in their enterprise. Since each land parcel had different characteristics and potential, and since communication from the new regions was sporadic, few emigrants knew, before arriving at their destination, precisely what land was available and what income could be generated from it. The additional difficulties of mustering capital for the trip and preventing shirking by members of groups crossing the plains make it surprising that rent dissipation was not greater.

On the other hand, contractual arrangements established by people with a high stake in organizing a successful trip tended to promote order on the trail and reduce rent dissipation (see Chapter 2). The rules to which they agreed before starting their journey and their adaptation to new circumstances along the way comport with our theory of institutional evolution.

Constitutions for the Elephant

Individuals or even small groups would have had little success in crossing the Great Plains. Although a few made the trip solo, in the words of John Reid, "Combining resources was the technique by which a large percentage of travelers crossing the plains obtained the means to make the trip. Many, possibly most of the single men in small groups leaving the Missouri River might never have started had they been unable to share the elephant."[5]

Because crossing the Great Plains had to be a joint effort, astute travelers developed the rules of collective action before starting their journey. Nearly every group adopted constitution-like agreements prior to embarking on the trail. A typical agreement read as follows:

> Resolved, that we as subscribers, members of the Green and Jersey County Company of emigrants to California, now rendezvoused at St. Joseph; in

view of the long and difficult journey before us, are satisfied that our own interests require for the purpose of safety, convenience, good feeling, and what is of the utmost importance, the prevention of unnecessary delay, the adoption of strict rules and regulations to govern us during our passage: and we do by our signatures to this resolution, pledge ourselves each to the other, that we will abide by all the rules and regulations that may be made by a vote of a majority of the company for its regulations during our passage.[6]

In the same manner, in 1849, the Union Emigration Company began its constitution with this statement: "We the undersigned hereby agree to form ourselves into a company for our mutual benefit and protection in emigrating to California & we pledge ourselves to protect each other in person & property in all justifiable cases and also to conform to the constitution and bye laws."[7] The constitutions typically specified a set of officers and duties for those officers. They also established eligibility for voting and decision rules for amendments. Most also delineated punishments for violation of the rules and set up guidelines for the dissolution of the company.

Just as scale economies in the modern firm make attention to contracting all the more important for the prevention of shirking, so, too, scale economies for nearly all activities made it necessary for nineteenth-century institutional entrepreneurs to establish specific rules for production. Making and breaking camp, defending against thieves and Indian attacks, crossing rivers, taking wagons up and down steep slopes, and hunting wild game were all more efficiently carried out by groups larger than the family. Returns on joint production were partly due to the indivisibility of inputs necessary for crossing the plains. For example, it made little sense for each person separately to acquire knowledge about the route when one person's knowledge could be utilized by several. Hence, wagon trains spread this cost by hiring an experienced guide to lead them on the trail. Similarly, a typical wagon equipped for the journey was too large for a single person and therefore was used and owned jointly by four or five people. The same was true for other human capital, such as medical and hunting skills, and for physical capital, such as draft animals and tools.

One contractual form that evolved to deal with the problems of joint production was the mess.[8] In this contractually governed arrangement, individuals committed their property to joint production for the purpose of crossing the plains but retained ownership of it and required that it be remitted to them at the end of the trail. These contracts typically specified the general conditions under which the property was to be used and the decision rules for governing specific unforeseen uses that might arise along the trail. A meeting of the mess could be called by a quorum, usually specified by the contract as between three and seven of the wagon-train members. Usually the captain of a wagon train operating as a mess had the power to determine start and stop times, rate of travel, posting of the guard, and other joint production activities.[9] The mess contract also established procedures for removing the captain in the event that enough members disagreed with his decision. Some contracts allowed a simple majority to remove the captain, but others required a two-thirds majority.[10]

Another form of arrangement common on the trail was a joint-stock or partnership contract, in which equipment necessary to the trip was owned by the group. In this arrangement, members either contributed an equal amount of capital to the original formation of the company or contributed draft animals or wagons that were then owned jointly. For instance, "a trio of young men arrived in Council Bluffs in 1854 with an equal amount of funds but no outfit except a yoke of oxen owned by one of the three." Pooling their money they "bought a shackly, light two-horse wagon for $45, [and] a pair of wild steers that had never been handled for $60."[11] These joint-stock agreements also specified how the partnership would be dissolved, as the following example illustrates: "We the undersigned having entered into a partnership for the better accomplishment of a trip to California do hereby agree to divide the joint stock or proceeds thereof among each other in proportion to the amount invested by each. Such division to take place as soon as convenient after our arrival at our destination."[12]

In some cases, joint-stock companies or partnerships came together to form a mess. Reid describes one example:

> Three forty-niners from Wisconsin owned a wagon in partnership. After crossing the Missouri at St. Joseph, these three "joined in a mess with four others." That made a total of seven men who remained together as a traveling group until after reaching California. They were not a partnership of seven owners of concurrent property, but two separate partnerships—one of three members, the other of four—joined in one mess of seven members.[13]

The choice of contractual form depended on the activities likely to be undertaken at the end of the trail. Most emigrants who were heading for Oregon planned to engage in farming and came from farming backgrounds. They tended to own their wagons and draft animals prior to the beginning of the journey and planned to use them at the end. Therefore they were more likely to choose a mess arrangement. On the other hand, California gold seekers who did not own equipment necessary to joint production prior to hitting the trail were more likely to form joint-stock companies or partnerships, dissolving the arrangements, selling all of their property, and dividing the proceeds when they reached the gold fields.[14]

Regardless of the general contractual arrangement chosen for organizing a wagon train, other contracts had to be negotiated to maximize cooperation and minimize conflict. For example, the most favored position in a wagon train was at the head, where dust was not a problem. Therefore, individual owners rotated in this position, with the wagon that went first one day moving to the end of the train the next, and so on. Some companies allowed an exception to this rule when an individual owned more than one wagon, in which case the rule stated that "as many as wagons as a man had, so many days he drove at the head of the train, then dropped to the back end."[15]

Wagon trains also contracted for labor from individuals who were not members of the mess or joint-stock companies. Through these contracts,

Many young men got their first view of the fabled Far West by working their way across the plains. Sometimes the employee was asked to pay something in addition, but as often as not, he simply received his meals and transportation in return for his labor.

During the gold rush, the old practice of indentured servitude was also revived. Speculators offered to pay a man's expenses to California providing he then worked in the mines for a specified period of time, often a year, with a hefty portion of his proceeds earmarked for the sponsor.[16]

It was also common for people who lacked the capital to contribute to the mess or joint-stock company or who lost equipment along the way to engage in rental contracts. As Reid describes it, "the practice was to combine sets of complementary property as, for example, Davidson hitching Mann's spare animals to his own wagons. A similar case occurred . . . when Mrs. Goltra 'joined teams with another man and threw our wagon away until we could get a lighter one.'"[17]

Conflict Resolution on the Trail

Of course, amidst this social order, conflicts inevitably flared over property rights and contractual arrangements for joint production. These occasions required procedures for dispute resolution. Unlike the violent, disorderly West of the popular imagination, the overland trail was generally a place where rights were respected and order was maintained. Miscreants went to trial, and judgment was swift. Barbara Hansen provides an example:

> A brutal murder which aroused strong reactions from the emigrants occurred near the area of LaBonte. Lafayette Tate brutally stabbed a man by the name of Miller, the leader of a section of a train. It appears that Tate's brother had defied Miller's instructions to wait further travel until the captain of the train should come along. . . . The murderer started off at an attempt to escape, but he was shortly apprehended by a group of fifteen men. Tate maintained that there was no law upon the plains and his trial should be held in organized territory. His claims were ignored and a judge, defense, and prosecuting attorneys and a jury were quickly selected from trains in the neighborhood. Justice moved rapidly and that midnight, the murderer was hanged for his crime, much to the relief of many of the emigrants. It was a relief to be assured that justice existed on the trail and that travelers were protected from those elements of the migration whose behavior was dangerous to life.[18]

The resolution of conflict and pursuit of justice were high priorities for the emigrants. Wagon trains often cooperated with each other to capture criminals, and sometimes called upon one another to help in investigations or to provide more impartial judgments as to appropriate punishments.[19] Another interesting practice for achieving justice was codified in a rule that "resolved, that in case of any dispute arising between any members of the Company, that they shall be referred to three arbiters, one chosen by each party, and one by the two chosen, whose decisions shall be final."[20] Reid summarizes the nature of justice among emigrants on the trail:

They [emigrants] were neither vigilantes nor regulators acting outside established law, for there was no sovereign command on the overland trail. They were not anonymous lynch-mobs enacting vengeance upon individuals who had transgressed some criterion of behavior offensive to part of the community. . . . Just as emigrants believed they had a right and a duty to arrest suspected wrongdoers and to determine their guilt by subjecting them to a trial judged by their peers, so they also believed they had the right to impose a sanction upon those convicted and it was their civic duty to punish certain "criminal" acts.[21]

Thus it is clear that the emigrants created and enforced contracts that allowed them to cooperate in joint-production efforts—efforts yielding returns above what would have been available to travelers acting individually or in very small groups. They maintained a reasonable degree of law and order and respect for property rights. Cooperative behavior characterized the trip West because individuals gained from it. Emigrants bore the costs of rules that did not specify property rights clearly but rather encouraged rent dissipation.

Recontracting for the Elephant

The constitutions and contracts for joint production made before emigrants left their jumping-off places along the Missouri River formed the basis for social coordination. But the emigrants could not anticipate all the conditions they would meet on the long, uncertain journey. Hence recontracting along the way often became necessary.

One of the main organizational issues at the jumping-off points was the appropriate size for a wagon train. If the train were too large, the glut of people would cause monitoring and shirking problems, the glut of wagons would create congestion at river crossings, and the glut of livestock would overtax the forage along the route. On the other hand, if the train were too small, the shortage of people would minimize the benefits of risk sharing, and the shortage of capital would put scale economies out of reach. According to Reid, companies disbanded on the trail for three reasons, all relating to optimal size: "dissatisfaction with the pace of travel; arguments over retaining property necessary for the trip; and fear animals were burdened with too much weight."[22] The rate of travel was an issue because going too fast meant more stress on the draft animals, but going too slow put the train in danger of not reaching its destination before winter. Too much equipment and personal property overloaded wagons and slowed progress, but too little meant that necessary capital would not be available along the way or at the destination.

Adjusting the size of a train on the trail often required the participation of other wagon trains, to provide additional wagons or to absorb excluded ones. Thus in the early days of the westward migration, when wagon trains on the trail were few and far between, reorganizing a train could be difficult or even impossible. After the first few years, however, this problem subsided because travel on the trail increased to the point that wagon trains were often in sight of one another.

As public-choice theory teaches, collective rules are important if orderly reorganization is to occur. Economists James Buchanan and Gordon Tullock point out the problems inherent in two forms of rules. On the one hand, decision rules that allow a small portion of a group to decide for the whole reduce decision-making costs but have the potential for imposing other costs on nondeciding members without their consent. On the other hand, decision rules that tend toward full-group unanimity reduce the potential for imposing costs on nondeciders but raise the decision-making costs.[23] The key to good collective decision making is to balance the two opposing costs.

Wagon-train constitutions reflected an understanding of the importance of establishing good rules for collective decision making prior to departure.

> The judicial institutions that they devised were intended to resolve disputes and maintain harmony between members of their own trains by mandating adjudication in place of potentially disruptive face-to-face conflict. This purpose was especially relevant to joint-stock companies which were formed by members who purchased equal shares and owned equal rights in the company's concurrent property. It was expected that once beyond the Missouri River, concurrently owned property would be divided only with difficulty, and to prevent controversy, tribunals of adjudication should be established to settle questions that might arise regarding distributions and fair shares.[24]

Because one person's decision to withdraw from a wagon train on the trail had significant implications for everyone else in the train, rules for withdrawal were clearly specified. The procedure was simpler for wagon trains organized as messes. Hansen gives the following example:

> The Sagamore Company, organized in Lynn, Massachusetts, reached its denouement on June 22, 1849, but managed to do so through democratic action. That night the first mess petitioned for withdrawal from the company. After a free discussion, the decision was reached to proceed with partitioning of the organization. The teams and other divisible goods were distributed equally among the messes, but that property difficult to divide was sold at auction and the proceeds allotted to the investors. A committee appointed to negotiate the transactions performed its functions well, inspiring an unknown diarist to comment that "all is peace and harmony."[25]

Reorganizing joint-stock companies and partnerships that held property in common was more complicated. "One of the heaviest property burdens individuals encountered as members of joint-stock companies was the rule, contained in many articles of agreement, that no one could withdraw from the association without approval of a specified percentage of the membership. The usual penalty for doing so was forfeiture of property rights."[26] Often the procedure for reorganizing a joint-stock company or partnership was to determine the value of the concurrent property and then divide it among the members. In one case, "what had been company property was redistributed in three steps. First, every member who contributed to an 'extra assessment or any part of it' was reimbursed from cash on hand. Next, 'such property as could be divided' was parceled out in individual shares. Finally, the balance was sold and the proceeds handed over to the stockholders."[27] But even in these complicated cases, Reid concludes, "at least as many dissolutions of partnerships were negotiated amicably as with rancor."[28]

The Mormon migration in the late 1840s offers an example of how group homogeneity and sense of purpose lowered transaction costs for collective action. Forced out of Nauvoo, Illinois, by religious persecution in 1846, 2,200 migrants made their way to the Great Salt Lake valley in 1847. The number of Mormon emigrants increased over the next several decades so that, by 1860, over 40,000 had made the journey.[29] Religious and cultural homogeneity and a willingness to submit to centrally organized discipline lowered agency monitoring costs.[30] This manifested itself in larger Mormon wagon trains. For instance, the 1848 migration included 566 wagons, 3,000 oxen, and approximately 2,000 emigrants,[31] whereas the typical non-Mormon wagon trains consisted of 10 to 20 wagons and 50 people.[32]

Even without the homogeneity of the Mormons, most emigrants facing new conditions and stressful circumstances on the overland journey were able to establish order in a world of anarchy. Property rights were respected, and when existing rules were inadequate, recontracting occurred to prevent dissipation of rents. Participants had good reason to search for institutions that promoted cooperation, since their groups were small enough that they could capture the gains from efficient institutional design.

One prominent exception was the race to be first on the trail. Trains would leave as early as possible from Independence or St. Joseph, Missouri, in order to secure grass for their animals along the trail. Although some entrepreneurs sold grazing rights and hay, much of the grazing was treated as an open access resource, and overexploitation resulted. Wagon trains also raced for trail position since following closely behind another wagon train or a cattle herd was dusty and unpleasant. The account of one emigrant captures the essence of the race:

> [We] had calculated to lay still to day but early in the morning we found we were camped just between two large droves of cattle. Baker a head and Pomeroy close behind. About 3 o'clock in the morning we heard pomeroys cattle comeing, and in fifteen minutes we were out of bed and underway as we were determined not to take the dust and the leavings of two droves of stock and it is almost impossible to pass a drove on the road and to be behind they raised such a dust you can hardly live and muddy every spring & branch.[33]

Entrepreneurs for the Elephant

The large number of people crossing the Great Plains created a market for goods and services on the trail. Entrepreneurs quickly filled this niche. As

Wagon Boss, by C. M. Russell. Emigrants leaving on wagon trains knew they were embarking on a perilous journey and that cooperation was essential to success. To ensure cooperation, before departing they wrote detailed contracts (constitutions) that specified responsibilities and methods for settling disputes. The agreements often also set out mechanisms by which the wagon trains could be disbanded and common property allocated. Courtesy of the Gilcrease Museum, Tulsa, Oklahoma.

explained earlier (see Chapter 4), potential gains from trade motivated more trade than fighting between Indians and whites.

That such beneficial interaction occurred, frequently and with considerable significance, contradicts the widely disseminated myth of incessant warfare between brave overlanders and treacherous Indians. . . .

While a relatively small number of overlanders relied upon Indians for route information or trail guidance, many overlanders willingly entrusted their stock, wagons, belongings, and even their families to Indian swimmers and boatmen at dangerous river crossings all along the trail. Most of this Indian assistance prevailed on the Oregon side of Fort Hall at crossings of the

Snake and Deschutes rivers, and especially in navigating down the Columbia River from The Dalles.[34]

Emigrants understood the importance of property rights for peaceful exchange and seemed to respect Indian property rights.

Emigrants knew and acted on the belief that, with the exception of stolen property, individual Indians owned what they possessed. If they wanted to own an Indian's horse, emigrants sought to buy it, if they wished to use an Indian raft, they bargained with the owners to rent it. We have already seen that there were numerous Indian traders along the trail, selling anything from products such as salmon and vegetables to their expertise as woodsman, implying that they expected Overland emigrants to understand and act on their notions of personal ownership.[35]

Closely related to trade with the Indians were the trading posts that sprang up during the fur trade years (see Chapter 5). As the fur trade diminished in importance, these outposts evolved into significant sources of supply for emigrants on the overland trail. Often, travelers stayed at these posts for a week or more, resting their animals and restocking their provisions. Three trading posts were particularly important for the Oregon Trail: Fort William, at the confluence of the Platte and Laramie Rivers; Fort Hall, near the confluence of the Snake and Portneuf Rivers; and Fort Boise, near the mouth of the Boise River.[36] The latter two were operated by the Hudson's Bay Company, which saw profitable opportunities in travelers' need for provisions and for draft and riding animals to replace those that had become trail weary.

The demand for draft animals along the trail also opened an opportunity for the many mountain men. As early as 1841, when migration was still a mere trickle, mountain man Joseph Reddeford Walker drove horses and mules to the Green River Valley, where he met and traded with wagon trains. In 1843, Jim Bridger established a trading post in the southeast corner of what is today Wyoming, saying that travelers were "well supplied with money, but by the time they get there, are in want of all kinds of supplies. Horses, Provisions, Smithwork, &c brings ready cash from them."[37]

Trading posts offered location rents as long as the overland trail was close by, but when new routes were discovered, the traders had to pursue the wagon trains. For example, when a new route bypassed Bridger's trading post, his partner, Louis Vasquez, made repeated business trips to the new trail. Unruh notes, "Mobile traders flocked to the trails . . . and new posts periodically appeared. . . . As . . . more and more travelers took to the trails, travel routes shifted and shortened at the same time that competition increased. Accordingly, traders became more and more aggressive in attempts to ensure the continuing appearance of creaking wagons at their service stations."[38]

Guide service provided another important trade opportunity for mountain men familiar with travel routes from their beaver-trade experiences. A variety of contracts were used, a common one being a per-person or per-wagon charge,[39] with the payment made after the safe arrival of the caravan at the agreed-upon destination.[40] Sometimes the guides were familiar only with the early part of the route and accordingly contracted to stay with the wagon train only to a certain point. The train then secured the services of other guides to complete the journey.

By 1850, however, the trail was well enough established and guidebooks had become sufficiently reliable and available that few emigrant trains hired guiding services.[41] The guidebooks contained useful information about river crossings, forts and trading posts, and appropriate rates of travel, as well as providing lists of supplies that would be needed. Guidebooks competed with each other, with some developing a reputation for greater accuracy and usefulness. Newspapers often endorsed certain books and also provided updated information about trail conditions.[42]

Specialized knowledge of river crossings also fostered trade. Ferry services developed rapidly at these crossings. Indians provided many of the early ferry services, but whites soon entered the market. After the 1847 migration to the Salt Lake valley, Mormons established ferries at several important river crossings. Competition prevailed at most river crossings, and if charges climbed too high, someone would start a competing ferry or the emigrants would build their own rafts. When the price charged by Indians at Wolf Creek rose to $5, four competing bridges were constructed in two days.[43]

Entrepreneurs also developed new shortcuts and charged tolls for improved roads. In 1845 and 1846, Samuel K. Barlow opened a 90-mile road in the Cascade Mountains, for passage on which he charged $5 per wagon and 10 cents per head of stock.[44]

Blacksmithing needs created another market niche that entrepreneurs raced to fill. Resetting wagon tires and shoeing draft animals were much-needed services, and numerous temporary blacksmith shops were built along the trails.[45]

After the Mormons had established themselves in the Salt Lake valley in the late 1840s, they took advantage of trading opportunities. They raised vegetables, provided short-term housing, and traded draft animals with wagon trains that stayed in the valley for a short respite. This trade helped the struggling Mormon settlement get on its feet as well as providing a much-needed source of resupply for the travelers. In 1849 alone, at least 10,000 migrants detoured to the Mormon settlements to trade.[46] The Mormons also sent scavenging parties onto the trail to pick up discarded goods, which were promptly added to their trading supplies.

Conclusion

If there was ever a time and place where chaos might have reigned, it was on the long, hard, hazardous journey across the Great Plains. People who formed wagon trains often did not know one another, did not expect to have any continuing relationship after the journey, faced unexpected challenges, and moved far beyond the pale of formal governmental institutions. Under such conditions, it would not have been surprising to find conflict.

The fact that so many emigrants successfully made the journey attests to their ability to develop innovative institutions. At the beginning of their journey, they adopted constitutions that set the overall institutional framework for making collective decisions. They hired wagon masters in competitive markets at the trail heads and bound those masters to a constitutional rule. Like a modern corporation that must agglomerate capital to take advantage of scale economies, wagon trains became firms with limited lives that shared physical and human capital inputs for the journey. The emigrants experimented with different contractual forms and new forms of property rights. As members of relatively small groups, they bore the costs and reaped the benefits of institutions that minimized transaction costs and rent seeking; thus they generally got the incentives right. Famous disasters such as the Donner party's demise crossing the Sierras contribute to the image of the wild, wild West, but for the untold numbers of farmers, miners, and entrepreneurs, crossing the plains "was a tale of sharing more than of dividing, a time of accommodation rather than discord. Far removed from lawyers and courts, the concept of concurrent ownership proved to be one of legal strength, not of legal failure, for promoting social peace, not internal disharmony. The overland trail was not a place of conflict. More accurately, it was a place of settlement."[47]

EIGHT

Cowboys and Contracts

As settlers moved west, it became evident that livestock would be a major economic resource in the region. The area where the buffalo roamed in great numbers was suited to animal grazing, and its low rainfall rendered much of the region unprofitable for farming. Hammering out the institutions necessary to make ranching feasible, however, required institutional entrepreneurs who recognized the new constraints and new opportunities.

The drovers who moved millions of cattle north on the famous trails saw the grasslands of the Great Plains as a void to be filled. In the words of historian Terry Jordan, "in all, over 5 million Texas cattle were reportedly driven north between 1866 and 1884, involving the largest short-term geographic shift of domestic herd animals in the history of the world."[1] Three economic forces combined to produce this massive movement of cattle. First, during the Civil War, many cattle herds in Texas increased rapidly, creating a surplus that could be moved to other areas where returns were higher. Second, as bison were eliminated and Indian lands were secured for settlement by whites, the net value of grazing territories on the northern plains rose dramatically. Third, the extension of the railroad into Kansas and later into the rest of the West lowered transportation costs and increased the value of grazing land by providing a ready link to eastern markets for any cattle that could reach a railhead.

Moving cattle into new territories to capture higher land rents from grazing presented many challenges for institutional entrepreneurs on the frontier. In driving the herds northward, owners of cattle and drovers on the trail had to devise efficient contracts. Cattle owners had to find ways of insuring that the drovers exercised proper care in a risky world. They had to contract with skilled cowboys to prevent the cowboys from opportunistically threatening to leave the drive unless they received higher pay. In order to drive the large herds across private land, cattle owners had to contract with landowners to compensate them for damage the herds might cause. Once the cattle were settled in the new territories, questions arose regarding who owned the cattle, how the owner's rights would be enforced, and how cattle companies would be organized. Again, the West became a crucible for institutional change.

Before Branding

Because so many cattle were abandoned as cowboys went off to fight in the Civil War, numerous longhorns were available for rounding up in Texas following the war. Ernest Staples Osgood observed that "cattle were in some sections of the state almost common property." As cowboys returned from the war and cattle became more valuable, drovers gathered the feral animals and marketed them. They "did not put the owners through the trouble of a roundup, but went out on the range and collected such cattle as appeared saleable without reference to ownership."[2]

The drovers were not rustling the cattle, since the owners were eventually compensated. Rather, the value of cattle was so low that the cost of full-fledged roundups was not justified. Thus the drovers invested only a limited amount of effort to define and enforce property rights. In 1874, *The Pleasanton Journal* described the process for enforcing property rights:

When [the feral cattle were] collected, he [the drover] would examine and make a memorandum of the brands borne by the cattle. Each year there is held a "stock meeting" at which all the stock raisers, cattle drovers and traders come together and those who have driven cattle out submit a memorandum of the brands on the cattle taken out by them and settle up with the owner of the brands. If an outsider came and wished to buy up a herd, he would hunt around for someone who would sell him two or three thousand head. . . . The terms agreed upon, the seller would go out upon the range, drive up the required number of cattle, without reference to who owned them, and turn them over to the outsider who would drive them north. At the annual meeting, the seller would report the number of cattle and the several brands and make settlement with the owners.[3]

Such informal agreements worked because the number of parties involved was small, and those parties had to live up to their word because they depended on their reputations in repeat dealings. According to Paul Wellman, whenever cattle belonging to another owner ended up in a herd going north, "careful account of such animals was kept and when they were sold it was a point of honor to 'settle up' with the owners."[4] Drover Joseph McCoy reported that

most of them [Texan drovers] are honorable men, and [regard] their pledged word of honor or their verbal contract as inviolable, sacred, and not to be broken under any circumstances whatever. Often transactions involving many thousands of dollars are made verbally only, and complied with to the letter. Indeed, if this were not so, they would often experience great hardships in transacting their business as well as getting through the country with their stock. We remember but few instances where a Texan, after selling his herd, went off home without paying all his business obligations. But one occurs to us now which we relate: A certain young drover, more youthful than honest, after selling off his herd slipped off to Texas leaving his supply bills and banker unpaid. A number of leading drovers met together and after counseling about the effect of such conduct upon the credit of drovers as a class, decided to send one of their own number to Texas after the young rascal, which was done, and in a few weeks he was brought back and compelled to settle his outstanding indebtedness, also the expense in full of his own arrest and return.[5]

As the number of cattle owners and drovers increased, more formal definition and enforcement activity was called for, and the informal customs and norms were codified by the Texas legislature. For example, in 1866 it passed a law making it a misdemeanor to drive unbranded stock from its accustomed range. This conserved on the cost of branding by granting property rights to unbranded cattle to the ranchers who controlled the particular area where those cattle ranged. This law sufficed for a period of time, but as the value of the cattle rose and the number of animals being moved north grew, the marginal benefits of definition and enforcement activity shifted again. In 1871, the Texas legislature passed another law requiring that cattle being trailed north had to have a road brand, "a large and plain mark, composed of any mark or device he may choose, which mark shall be branded on the left side of the back behind the shoulder."[6] The law also required adequate proof of ownership, and "it was the rule for the several owners of cattle making up a trail herd to give bills of sale to the drover which set forth the brand, number, ear marks, and other identifications of each contribution to the herd."[7]

On the Trail North

Because moving cattle required substantial time on the trail—at least a month for the drive from Texas to railheads in Kansas and more than three months for the drive to northern ranges in Montana and Wyoming—and because skilled cowboys were essential, cattle trailing became a separate enterprise from cattle raising. The modern theory of the firm suggests that an institutional entrepreneur will reorganize property rights so that the person or input owner whose contribution to the enterprise is the most difficult to measure will bear the profits or losses, or what is left over after all contractual obligations are met.[8] Cattle trailing involved unimaginable risks through hostile Indian territory, uncertain weather, and high information costs regarding markets for the final product. Not surprisingly under these conditions, almost all the early cattle drives were organized by a drover who purchased the cattle from their owners and hence had to bear the risks and any financial losses but also could capture any resulting profits.[9]

One of the more dramatic early drives was initiated by Nelson Story, a

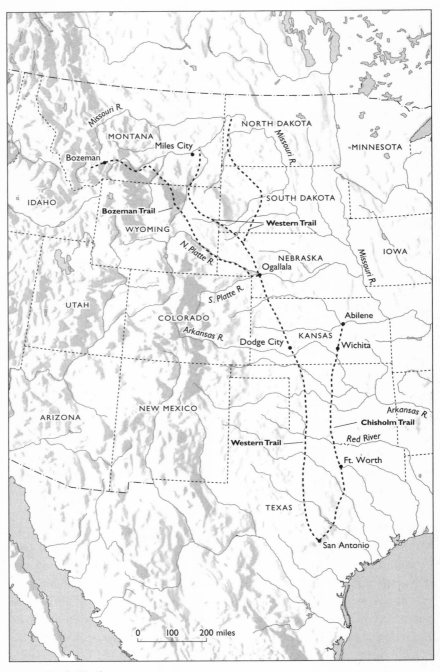

MAP 4. Cattle Trails

miner who struck it rich in 1866 on a placer claim in Montana's Alder Gulch. Believing that there were bigger profits in serving miners than in being one, Story took $30,000 from the claim and traveled to Forth Worth, Texas. There he bought 1,000 longhorns at $10 per head, hired a crew of cowboys, and started north though through uncharted territory. He even bought wagons at Fort Leavenworth, Kansas, and loaded them with provisions, intent on selling them along with his cattle to the 10,000 miners in the vicinity of Virginia City, Montana.[10]

Story followed the Oregon trail to Fort Laramie, in Wyoming Territory, and from there took the Bozeman trail to Virginia City. En route, he lost two cowboys when his party was attacked by Sioux raiders near Fort Reno. Story pushed on to Fort Phil Kearney, in northern Wyoming, but the commander of the fort refused to let him proceed further. After waiting several days and realizing that permission to proceed would probably not be forthcoming, he consulted his men about forging ahead without permission. All but one, George Dow, agreed. Dow was forced to stay with the herd, and Story and his men trailed at night and grazed the herd under guard by day. As they journeyed, Indians attacked them twice, killing one cowboy. At last, on December 9, 1866, a month and a half after leaving Fort Phil Kearney, they arrived at Virginia City.[11]

The perilous journey of Nelson Story illustrates why the drover was the residual claimant for the cattle drive. It would have been almost impossible for a cattle owner remaining in Texas to contract with a drover to move his cattle as Story did. There were simply too many unmeasurable and unmonitorable margins to specify, ranging from stampedes and treacherous river crossings to Indian raids, Indian tolls, and delays caused by unpredictable military authorities.

As the risks became better known, however, trailing firms developed which sold their services to cattle owners.[12] Ike T. Pryor, one of the entrepreneurs involved in developing these agencies, delivered as many as 45,000 Texas cattle per season to the northern ranges between 1881 and 1884.[13] The market was extremely competitive, with no one transportation agency controlling more than 15 percent of the traffic.[14] In most cases, cattle were transported for a set fee, although, in a few instances, the principals negotiated a cost-plus contract.[15]

The fee for driving cattle on the long trails depended on the size of the herd and the distance it was moved. Considerable experimentation was required to determine optimal herd size for a drive, with early drives moving from 70 to 25,000 head. Drovers settled on 3,000 head as the best herd size. A herd of 3,000 was large enough to capture some economies of scale, yet small enough to minimize the problems of managing a larger labor force and of keeping a herd together and moving at the appropriate speed. Moving 3,000 head required ten cowboys, including the trail boss, each with six to eight horses, and a cook who drove the chuck wagon and prepared the meals.[16] This operation cost approximately $1.00 per head.[17] With as much as a $10 difference between the price of cattle in Texas and the price in the northern range, it is not surprising that thousands of cattle were trailed northward.

A major problem for the trail boss was "How to get men who could live and work together, through weeks of semi-isolation, and who would 'stick' until the job was finished."[18] Indeed, since replacement workers were hard to come by on the trail, cowboys could act opportunistically to extract a larger share of the profits by threatening to leave the drive. To combat this problem, trail bosses did not pay the crew until the task was completed.[19]

Not in My Back Yard

Many of the organizational problems associated with driving cattle 1,200 miles north to Montana and Wyoming were internal, that is, they concerned the contracting parties themselves. Who owned the cattle? How would ownership disputes be resolved? Who would bear losses that occurred on the drive? How much would the cowboys be paid? When would they be paid? Each of these situations involved transaction costs, which had to be managed by the institutional entrepreneurs who stood to profit from establishing and reorganizing property rights.

But organizational problems external to the contracting parties arose as well, each with its own transaction costs. Dealing with these issues provided another niche for institutional entrepreneurs. One of the most difficult problems with which they had to deal was the impact that a herd of 3,000 cattle would have on a region where crops grew and other cattle grazed. Imagine the sight of 3,000 longhorns moving toward your farmstead's newly planted corn crop. Even if the crop were fenced, which it probably was not in most early instances, that many cattle might well leave a swath of devastation across your property. To make matters worse, the herd might well carry Texas (Spanish or splenic) fever. This cattle disease resulted from a microscopic parasite for which the cattle tick served as an intermediate host. Cattle from south Texas that were continually exposed to the parasite developed an immunity to the fever, but when they were trailed north, the infected ticks they brought with them would bite nonimmune cattle, causing rapid death.[20] Losses from Texas fever were great. Dr. John R. Mohler, chief of the Pathological Division of the Bureau of Animal Industry, estimated a total loss of $63 million in the value of cattle because of the fever between 1866 and 1889.[21]

The potential for conflict between farmers and drovers was especially prevalent near towns that were railheads. For example, when Joseph G. McCoy, a cattle trader from Springfield, Illinois, approached the residents of Salina, Kansas, with the idea of locating a railhead with the Union Pacific Railway in their town, he found the farmers unreceptive to the idea of droves of cattle descending on their area. His entrepreneurial solution was to move a little farther east from Salina, where a dozen log huts made up the fledgling town of Abilene.[22] Abilene was well clear of Salina yet still far enough west of settled country that cattle could be trailed there without interfering with existing agriculture. McCoy proceeded to erect a three-story hotel, the famous Drover's Cottage; an office with a large Fairbanks scales; and shipping pens to accommodate 3,000 head of cattle. He also negotiated a contract with the railroad in which he was to receive one-eighth of the gross amount of freight on all cattle shipped east over the line.[23]

McCoy completed his construction in time to capture only a portion of the cattle trade in 1867, but still received 35,000 head. That winter, he engaged in an extensive advertising campaign, spending $5,000 to communicate to Texas drovers that Abilene was the appropriate place to bring their cattle.[24] The advertising succeeded so well that 1868 brought many more cattle through Abilene. In fact, more than 1,000 carloads were shipped out in June alone.[25]

By providing adequate facilities, McCoy not only encouraged cattle drovers to come but also created an opportunity for a network of other services. Numerous buyers stayed at the Drover's Cottage, and other complementary business ventures grew rapidly. By 1870, the First National Bank of Kansas City opened an office in Abilene and conducted over $900,000 in business in its first two months of operation.[26]

Abilene was a place where buyers could purchase livestock not only to be shipped by rail to feedlots and slaughterhouses further east but also to be driven north and west. "The driving of herds purchased at Abilene, to the territories, became quite as common as driving from Texas to Abilene."[27] For instance, of the 190,000 cattle trailed to Abilene in 1871, only 40,000 were shipped out by rail; the balance were trailed to greener pastures.[28]

Despite McCoy's efforts to establish a trade center in a place that was sparsely settled, he still encountered some opposition to the development of a widespread cattle trade in Abilene. One group of settlers called a meeting to discuss the possibility of preventing droves of cattle from coming into the county. McCoy asked a fellow drover to speak at that meeting and discuss the potential gains from trade:

> The speaker pointed out how the immense influx of men camping on the adjacent prairies would need every aliment of life, and told them that if they taxed their little farms to the utmost in raising grain and vegetables, yet they could not furnish a tithe of the amount that would be needed, and of course if the supply was small and the demand great, the prices must and would be exorbitantly high, and that the only trouble would be that they could or would not furnish one-half the amount needed, no matter what the price might be. . . . Whilst this little talk was being made, nearly every drover present, by previous arrangement, went to bartering with the Kansans for butter, eggs, potatoes, onions, oats, corn, and such other produce as they might be able to use at camp.[29]

One settler expressed the sentiments of many when he said, "If I can make any money out of this cattle trade, I am not afraid of 'Spanish fever'; but if I can't make any money out of this cattle trade, then I am d——d afraid of 'Spanish fever.'"[30] The presence of cattle brought the settlers other positive spillovers as well. In one case where fuel was scarce, "cattlemen were asked by the settlers around Abilene to bed their cattle down for a night or two so that the dung from the cattle might be utilized for the winter's fuel."[31]

To further facilitate gains from trade, McCoy took active measures to

COWBOYS AND CONTRACTS   147

protect the local population from harmful impacts: "Every effort was made in good faith so as to arrange and conduct a cattle trade as not to work a hardship upon a few settlers and in the county, and to this end, a man was employed to work on locating eligible herding grounds, the herds as fast as they arrived."[32] McCoy also promised to indemnify any local cattle owners who suffered losses because of Texas fever. In 1868, he paid out $4,500, of which he was able to raise $1,200 from other drovers, with the rest coming from his own profits from the cattle trade.[33] In 1869 McCoy evidently posted a bond of $20,000 to assure local cattle owners that there would not be undue damages.[34] In all of these activities, McCoy was the quintessential institutional entrepreneur, seeing opportunities to internalize both costs and benefits by creating and reorganizing property rights.[35] By forming a brand-new town with few existing land claimants, he ensured that new settlers came with the understanding that Abilene was a cattle trailing town. By compensating settlers already there for losses, he created gains from trade by allowing cattle drovers to "purchase" access rights to local lands. And by purchasing land for the town site and putting up pens, he personally captured gains from cattle coming to Abilene, some of which he realized by selling lots to businesses intent on profiting from the drovers' presence.

Though McCoy succeeded at purchasing property and forming contracts to prevent negative spillovers, some problems remained unresolved, especially in other areas where Texas fever posed a threat. In response, many states passed laws regulating the importation of diseased livestock. In 1855, for instance, Missouri enacted a law prohibiting importation of cattle unless they were disease free. Kansas followed with a similar law in 1858, but in 1866 the state repealed that legislation because of the obvious economic impact on a market dependent on cattle arriving from Texas. A compromise was reached in 1867 that established a quarantine line through the middle of the state.[36] No cattle could be driven into the area east of the line unless they were quarantined or arrived during the winter months, when they supposedly were not carrying ticks. The quarantine line was continually moved westward as population density and domestic cattle herds increased in the western part of the state. Other states and territories—Arizona, Colorado, Montana, Nebraska, New Mexico, and Wyoming—passed similar laws restricting the importation of Texas cattle, and some experimented with quarantine and inspection regulations.[37]

State and national regulations governing animal health issues created even more complete property rights, but once power was concentrated in the hands of regulators, it could be captured by special interests concerned to redistribute rights.[38] Evidently that happened in this case, for producers in various parts of the country were quite willing to cite threats of disease to prevent entry and to eliminate competition.[39] Any restrictions on the movement of Texas cattle to market or to the northern ranges meant increased returns to cattle producers in Wyoming and Montana, and those producers were quite willing to use the regulations to their advantage.[40]

Ranching on the Range

Once cattle were located on their various ranges, several institutional problems became apparent. Should land be privately owned? Or was communal ownership more desirable? What mechanisms for enforcing rights were the cheapest and the most effective? How large should ranch operations be? What form should labor contracts take? How would necessary capital be obtained, and how would capital owners monitor its use? Institutional entrepreneurs turned their attention to these questions and developed solutions that promoted more efficient resource use.

THE OPEN RANGE

We provide more detail on landownership in the next chapter, but suffice it to say here that the vastness of the range and the high cost of fencing challenged the cattlemen trying to create ownership institutions for capturing the value of the grass. Because fencing land was impossible until barbed wire was invented, cattle were allowed to range widely. Cowboys formed a sort of human fence, patrolling customary range boundaries between neighboring outfits. The open-range era lasted from approximately 1870 until 1900, when a combination of homesteading and barbed wire enclosed the land and supplanted many of the functions of the open-range cowboy. In the meantime, cattle ranching required cooperation to determine and enforce the boundaries between ranges, associations to control access by newcomers, and cowboys to patrol against rustlers and to keep the cattle from straying too far from home.[41] This was truly the romantic era of the cowboy.

DEFINING RIGHTS TO LIVESTOCK

Defining property rights to livestock was easier than defining such rights to land thanks to a long history of branding, which originated in Spain and came to the Southwest with Spanish settlers. The use of these permanent marks spread rapidly throughout the West.

Initially brands were established by custom, but as the number of herds increased and as markets widened, owners banded together in cattlemen's associations to acknowledge their unique marks, to register those brands to particular owners, and to adjudicate disputes. Indeed, one of the first actions of the Montana Stockgrowers Association at its meeting in Miles City, Montana, in 1885, was to publish a brand registration book, recording their brands for all to see.

As the number of associations grew, they banded together to lobby territorial or state legislatures to record and enforce brands. In Montana and Wyoming, such a registration system was established in the first territorial legislative sessions. The brand-registration system required that both a brand and a description of where it would be placed on the animal had to be agreed upon by other ranchers and recorded with the territorial or state government.

Not only did brand laws establish ownership, they also laid out clear rules for ownership transfer. Without a registered brand, ownership of cattle could not be legally transferred.[42] If someone other than the registered owner had possession of a branded animal, that person had to have an appropriate bill of sale. The brand-registration system also provided for the sale of the brand itself.[43]

For a brand system to enforce property rights effectively, brands had to be inspected at the point of sale of cattle. Both the Wyoming and the Montana stockmen's associations paid for inspectors within their regions and paid for inspectors at distant points such as St. Paul, Chicago, Council Bluffs, and Omaha, where cattle were shipped for sale. The Wyoming and Montana associations cooperated to reduce the costs of inspection, with Montana paying for an inspector in St. Paul and Wyoming for one in Chicago. In each case the inspector maintained a book of current registrations of brands for both states and examined each animal as it was unloaded to ensure proof of ownership.[44]

The brand-registration system also facilitated the sale of cattle that strayed far from their customary range:

> In the open range days, a beef roundup inevitably included cattle from out-fits that had no rep with the crew. If these critters were far from their home range—some of them did wander an astonishing distance—and were in shipping condition, it would have been a disservice to their owners to have left them behind, eventually to die of old age. Moreover, they would eat grass that would support some marketable steer who knew enough to stay on his accustomed range. So they were deliberately included in the beef shipment as a "courtesy of the range," with the assurance that an alert brand inspector would spot them and the owners would receive payment. Such cattle were sold on the same basis as those with which they were shipped, and the sales money remitted directly to the owner of the estray when in-structions were on the file for such disposition of the funds.
>
> In case the owners could not be determined, the sales price was sent to the secretary of the Association, before it became a state responsibility, with a report of marks and brands for each estray. The Association staff searched the records and made inquiries in a thorough effort to locate the owner. As soon as ownership was established beyond a doubt, the money was remitted to him. By this system, close to $625,000 had been recovered for owners during the year 1898 alone.[45]

Brand-registration rules also dealt with unbranded cattle, known as mav-ericks. An unbranded calf in the company of an obvious mother cow with a brand was assumed to belong to the cow's owner. But an unbranded calf that was lost or whose mother had died could not be paired with a branded ani-mal. If this happened on a customary range where only one herd grazed, the calf was assumed to belong to the cattleman with the rights to that range. If a maverick became mixed with cows bearing other brands, as was common in large roundups, ownership could not be determined. To solve this prob-lem, ranchers in Montana decided that mavericks in a common herd would be sold to the highest bidder and branded with his brand. "Only cattle owners on the range could purchase these calves. The money received from the sale of mavericks shall be turned into the roundup fund."[46] In 1884 the Wyoming Territory dealt with the problem by passing a law requiring that all mavericks be offered for sale at auction on the range every ten days during the roundup. The money from the sale of mavericks went to the treasury of the stockgrowers' association to be used for the payment of inspectors and for other enforcement activities.[47]

Cattlemen's associations provided effective enforcement against rustlers by patrolling the range and hiring stock detectives who tracked down thieves. Rancher Granville Stuart reported:

> The civil laws in courts had been tried and found wanting. The Montana cattlemen were as peaceful and law-abiding a body of men as could be found anywhere but they had $35,000,000 worth of property scattered over seventy-five thousand square miles of practically uninhabited country and it must be protected from thieves. The only way to do it was to make the penalty for stealing so severe that it would lose its attraction.[48]

The perceived inadequacy of legal enforcement led to a general recognition that cooperative action among stock owners was necessary. Bob Ford, a prominent Montana rancher, said:

> The stealing of cattle and horses is becoming a common occurrence and by organizing and all of us becoming detectives as it were, we can the easier put a stop to this thieving business. As it is now, if a man steals thirty or forty head of cattle from you or me and gets off with them, the chances are we will never exert ourselves to catch him because the cost is too great and we will say, "Let him go." But if we organize and bear our pro rata of the expense, the thief will be hunted down and punished and it will cost each of us but little.[49]

In 1884 the Montana Stockgrowers Association organized a posse of armed detectives. Over the next eighteen months, this vigilante committee of the stockgrowers made several raids upon dens of rustlers. Stuart argued that the posse did not act arbitrarily but represented a reasonable enforcement of rules against stealing:

There were but fourteen members of the vigilance committee and they were all men who had stock on the range and who had suffered at the hands of the thieves. There was not one man taken on suspicion and not one was hanged for a first offense. The men that were taken were members of an organized band of thieves that for more than two years had evaded the law and robbed the range at will. The fact that the stock men loaned milch cows, horses, and farm machinery to settlers on small ranches, branded their calves for them at roundup prices, established schools for them, bought their butter and vegetables at high prices and in every way helped them to get a start is proof that any law-abiding person was welcome in this country.[50]

However, ranchers weren't always interested in just enforcing their rights. In some areas where there was a strong government, cattlemen were able to capture its coercive power and use it to their advantage by redistributing range rights in their favor. Wyoming's famous Johnson County War in 1892 provides a case in point. With the implicit sanction of the state, a group of leading members of the Stock Growers' Association entered Johnson County with the express purpose of wiping out a supposed den of rustlers living there. Local citizens, however, believed they were being invaded by a foreign army and organized a response that erupted in a battle between the two factions. Under siege, the stockgrowers used their political influence to oblige Wyoming governor Amos Barber to telegraph President William Henry Harrison, asking him to order federal troops in to restore order and rescue the invaders.[51]

Though cattlemen during the last quarter of the nineteenth century most often sought to define and enforce property rights as suggested by our theory in Chapter 2, they did not always do so. As mentioned above, during the Civil War, when labor was not available to enforce property rights to cattle, thousands of head were allowed to become feral in Texas. Union troops also tried to prevent cattle marketing so that the Confederates would not have food supplies. So successful were they, as Ernest Staples Osgood tells us, that "cattle were almost worthless. In the central portions of the state, they roamed at will, their owners scarcely knowing where their property was nor particularly interested in its increase."[52]

Perhaps horses offer the best example of reduced definition and enforce-

TABLE 8.1

Real Price of Horses in Montana, 1918–1926

	Price per Head ($)
1918	145
1919	132
1920	77
1921	99
1922	84
1923	75
1924	65
1925	60
1926	56

SOURCE: U.S. Department of Agriculture 1938, 117.
NOTE: Nominal prices converted to real using wholesale price index, 1967 = 100.

ment activity resulting from declining livestock values. As shown in Table 8.1, the real price of horses fell by 61 percent from 1918 to 1926. This decline in price resulted from the reduced demand for horses, which was caused by the introduction of tractors on farms and by the downsizing and mechanization of the U.S. Cavalry following World War I. Because of the lower prices, the expense of feeding horses and enforcing property rights to them was no longer worth bearing. Hence hundreds of horses were turned loose on the public lands and became an ongoing problem for ranchers trying to control overgrazing.[53]

WORKING TOGETHER ON THE OPEN RANGE

Even with property rights to cattle well defined by the branding system, cattlemen still had to learn how best to organize ranching operations. Generally cattle were not supervised day to day, nor were they fed in the winter, but they had to be rounded up twice each year, once in the spring for branding and once in the fall for marketing. Recognizing that the roundup on the open range afforded economies, ranchers developed norms of cooperation with neighbors. One contemporary cowhand commented on what led to a joint roundup rather than separate roundups conducted by individual ranchers:

> When a stock owner wished to work his cattle, he would send word to his neighbors and all would round up, get their stock, brand calves, turn loose and drive home. But so many outfits had come in and rounded up the stock, and ginned them over so much, that they could never get fat.[54] This continual working over and over of cattle was detrimental to the business, and those interested . . . wanted some plan or system laid down.[55]

As mentioned above and in Chapter 9, stockgrowers formally organized associations in the 1870s and early 1880s to register their brands, and they used these organizations to coordinate the roundups. Teddy Blue, an early cowboy, recalls how the roundups worked:

> The whole thing was run according to a system. By '84, the range in southern Montana and Wyoming was all organized into roundup districts, bounded by certain mountain ranges and streams. There were no fences, and while each outfit would have a line it would call the boundary of its own range, the cattle drifted, and they all ran together more or less. All the outfits belonging to any one roundup would get together in the spring with their wagons and work through the territory, creek by creek. Ownership of a calf was determined by the brand on the cow.[56]

The roundup districts were carefully laid out, with considerable attention to detail. In 1886, the *Weekly Yellowstone Journal and Livestock Reporter* described a district that serves as an example:

> District #4 commences at Hocket's ranch, May 25, 1886, works down Powder River to the mouth of the Mizpah and splits. The first division works up Mizpah to its head then meets the Tongue River roundup at the mouth of Pumpkin Creek and works back up Pumpkin Creek to its head. Second division works down Powder River to its mouth and then down the Yellowstone to Cabin Creek, up Cabin Creek to its head, then to the head of Little

The Roundup #2, by C. M. Russell. Cattle were sorted by brand in the spring roundup, then the calves were roped and branded according to the brand on their mother. Cooperative roundups by several ranches made more sense than individual roundups conducted by each ranch separately. The roundups also served as an exclusionary mechanism to prevent overgrazing of the open range.

Beaver and down Little Beaver to the lower Hashknife Ranch. E. P. Fletcher, foreman.[57]

Roundup rules provided detailed instructions regarding the contribution of each participant. In 1884, *The Cow Boy*, a paper published in Medora, North Dakota Territory, said:

The cattlemen are all supposed to know that the roundup for this section of the Bad Lands begins May 25, at the Beaver Creek crossing of the N. P. R. R. Every stock owner will send enough cowboys to look after his interests, who will be under orders of and subject to dismissal by the foreman, John Goodall. Each cattle owner will provide a mess-wagon or make arrangements with someone else. At least six good horses will be needed by every man. There will be day and night herding, where each man must take a part. Branding will be done every day. Every man who wishes his cattle taken care of, must be represented on the roundup. The time taken by the roundup will be six weeks to two months and the extent of the territory is about one hundred by fifty miles. In this district there are about 40,000 cattle.[58]

To enforce the start dates and the contribution of all to the roundup, cattle-men's associations refused to cooperate with those who might have tried to be free riders.

The stockgrowers' associations coordinated other activities besides the roundups. Glanders, a contagious disease in horses, was controlled through the Wyoming Stock Growers' Association, which used its powers of sanction to force horse owners to allow inspections and to destroy infected animals.[59]

Associations also regulated the quality of bulls that each member pro-vided on the open range. Without fences, cattle mingled, with the result that one owner could free ride on the high-quality bulls provided by others. If a rancher provided low-quality bulls or too few bulls, he did not bear the full costs of such an action because a portion of his herd would be bred by the bulls of another ranch. Local and state associations attempted to overcome the free-rider problem by specifying both the bull-to-cow ratio on the open range and the quality of bulls.[60]

ORGANIZING THE LABOR AND CAPITAL INPUTS

Managing labor on the open range, where labor demands were quite uneven from season to season, was another challenge for ranch owners. Peak de-mands for skilled cowboys who could ride, rope, and handle cattle occurred during the spring and fall roundups.[61] During the winter, many cowboys were unemployed. Although the ranches usually did not pay wages during the winter, they did offer room and board to cowboys who stayed around and became part of the labor pool the next spring.[62]

To meet the capital requirements of ranches with herds running between 10,000 and 100,000 head on the open range,[63] cattlemen secured investors from the eastern United States and from England and Scotland.[64] In the 1870s investors realized good returns from investing in livestock operations in the Southwest, and by the 1880s, Colorado, Dakota Territory, Montana, and Wyoming were considered attractive locations for cattle ranches. U.S. investors lived primarily in New York and Boston; they even hired the firm of Dun and Bradstreet to investigate and rate investment opportunities in different locations in the West.[65] Gene Gressley reports that during the boom cattle years of 1882 through 1886, 93 cattle companies incorporated in Wyoming, with a total capitalization of $51 million; 66 in Montana, with a capitalization of $19 million; 104 in New Mexico, with a capitalization of $24 million; and 176 in Colorado, with a capitalization of $74 million.[66]

More common than loans were direct investments by investors who owned the cattle and hired a resident manager to direct the operation. This arrangement required the owner to monitor the manager, a difficult task at a time when communication channels were so poor. To overcome the monitoring problems, entrepreneurs experimented with a wide range of ownership arrangements. Both partnerships and joint-stock corporations were used. In some cases the managers became partial claimants on any profits through ownership of stock in the corporation. To reduce the problem of managers branding ranch cattle for themselves, many investors stipulated that the ranch foreman could not personally own cattle.[67]

The difficulties of monitoring managers combined with the problems caused by the closing of the range by homesteaders. As more homesteaders fenced off small parcels, open-range ranching became less profitable over time. The problems grew more obvious in the disastrous winter of 1886–87. That winter convinced many operators that the absentee-owner, large-scale firm was not an appropriate form of organization. It became apparent that ranching required much closer attention and that putting up hay in the summer to be fed in the winter was crucial to a successful operation.[68] In 1889, the Miles City correspondent of the *Montana Livestock Journal* described the change in the scope and type of operation:

> I can prove [that such changes have occurred] by citing the operations of several large owners in Custer County who have for two or three years past, been preparing themselves for this change by the purchase of land, the erection of substantial and commodious buildings, the taking out of water for irrigation purposes, and the shrinkage of their range herds down to a 1,000 or 2,000 well-bred cows, to be close herded, served with a bull at the proper time, and fed and protected during the few weeks of severe winter when they cannot take care of themselves.[69]

By 1900 much of the outside capital had been withdrawn and financing came from local or regional banks.[70] The last big roundup in Montana, consisting of 150 men and 9 wagons, occurred in 1903.[71] The era of the open range, with all of its unique organizational problems, had ended. In the more arid parts of the West, some range remained unfenced as late as 1940, but no longer did vast herds graze thousands of acres with no human intervention beyond the spring and fall roundups.

Conclusion

The romantic era of open-range cattle ranching required tremendous institutional entrepreneurship. Organizing cattle drives to move several thousand cattle 1,500 miles to northern ranges, enforcing property rights to those cattle on the drive and on the range, and marketing the cattle once they had fattened presented contracting challenges for creating new property rights and reorganizing existing ones. Amassing capital from across the continent to fund ranching operations posed challenges as great if not greater. Despite these tremendous obstacles, millions of cattle were moved from Texas onto the western plains, and an effective combination of private and communal rights evolved to produce beef for eastern markets. The fact that many of the institutional innovations, such as branding and brand registration, continue to this day attests to the innovation of cattlemen on the frontier.

NINE

Home on the Range

Once the question of ownership between American Indians and the settlers was resolved (see Chapter 4), land became available simply for the taking. With open access for all comers, a race for property rights seemed inevitable. At least two factors contributed to the potential for a race. First, new systems of property rights had to be invented to accommodate resource endowments on the frontier, especially climate and topography. Because natural boundaries differed from those in the East, watersheds were larger, and fencing materials were not available, settlers had to find new ways of specifying and enforcing boundaries to land. Second, local initiative had to substitute for formal government because settlement preceded legislative bodies, governing statutes, and the judicial system. Aside from the U.S. Army, there were no legally sanctioned governmental organizations with the power to limit entry.

Lacking formal systems for establishing and adjudicating property rights, institutional entrepreneurs had a blank slate on which to establish property rights, but this endeavor required restricting entry to the land. Settlers responded to these opportunities by forming voluntary associations, by developing specific rules for restricting one another's access to the land, and by restricting entry by outsiders. The success of these voluntary associations ultimately was undermined by governmental rules that trumped customary land rights and reopened the land for a homesteading race.

This Land Is Whose Land?

Even before cattlemen drove their herds to the northern Great Plains, farmers on the frontier of Ohio, Indiana, and Illinois confronted the problem of creating property rights in the absence of formal legal institutions. To limit entry onto the land, they formed land-claims clubs or associations that registered the settlers' claims to land and ensured that those claims would be honored when the land was formally opened for settlement under the various federal land laws.[1] These clubs established their own constitutions and bylaws, developed rules for adjudicating disputes, and devised procedures for registering claims. One purpose of the clubs was to assure that squatters could buy the land at the minimum price when it was put up for sale by the government.

Because members of the land-claims clubs had a direct stake in the outcome, they had an incentive to develop an orderly process that minimized the expenditure of resources in establishing property rights. Defining and enforcing property rights took some effort, but to the extent possible the effort was focused on productivity. For example, the club in Webster County, Iowa, required claimants to perform $10 worth of labor on their land for each month they owned the property after the first month, while the club in Poweshiek County required claimants to perform only $30 worth of labor on their land during the first six months of property ownership and $30 for each succeeding six months. The club in Johnson County did not require resident members to invest any resources in their land until they so desired; nonresidents, however, did have to perform $50 worth of labor on their land for each six months the claim was held.[2] The local land-claims clubs' specification of claimants' expenditures in terms of labor allowed the farmer a great deal of latitude as to what work to do, and did not require continual residence on the land. This stands in sharp contrast to the federal homestead acts, which specified claimants' investments in terms of cabin size, irrigation ditches, amount of land to be plowed, and acreage to be planted with trees, most of which added little to the productive value of the land.[3]

Like members of the land-claims clubs, cattlemen economized on their efforts to define and enforce property rights. When the first drovers brought their cattle to fatten on the northern plains of Montana and Wyoming, the abundance of land enabled new arrivals to avoid the tragedy of the commons by simply moving onto unoccupied land. In the words of historian Ernest Staples Osgood, "There was room enough for all, and when a cattleman rode up some likely valley or across some well-grassed divide and found cattle thereon, he looked elsewhere for range."[4]

But settlement took place quickly as more and more cattlemen sought to capture a share of the grass on the northern plains. Granville Stuart reported:

> In the summer of 1883, Conrad Kohrs drove in three thousand cattle and placed them on the Sun River range, and D. A. G. Floweree drove three thousand Texas cattle in and threw them on the Sun River range. The Green Mountain Cattle company drove in twenty-two hundred and located on Emmel's Creek. The Dehart Land and Cattle Company came in with two herds of three thousand each and located on the Rosebud. Griffin Brothers and Ward drove in three thousand head and located on the Yellowstone. J. M. Holt came in with three thousand head and located on Cabin Creek. Tussler and Kempton brought in three herds of twenty-five hundred each and located on Tongue River. Ryan brothers brought in three herds of three thousand each and located on the Musselshell. . . . These cattle were nearly all Texas cattle and came up over the Texas trail. By the first of October, there were six hundred thousand head of range cattle in the territory, and these together with the horses and sheep was as much stock as the range could safely carry.
>
> It would be impossible to make persons not present on the Montana cattle ranges realize the rapid change that took place on those ranges in two years. In 1880, the country was practically uninhabited. One could travel for miles without seeing so much as a trapper's bivouac. Thousands of buffalo darkened the rolling plains. There were deer, antelope, elk, wolves and coyotes on every hill and in every ravine and thicket. In the whole territory of

Montana, there were but two hundred and fifty thousand head of cattle, including dairy cattle and work oxen.

In the fall of 1883 there was not one buffalo remaining on the range and the antelope, elk and deer were scarce. In 1880, no one ever had heard tell of a cowboy in "this niche of the woods" and Charlie Russell had made no pictures of them; but in the fall of 1883, there were six hundred thousand head of cattle on the range.[5]

Similarly, Osgood reported, "With a rapidity that could almost be measured in months rather than years, every available bit of range in north and central Wyoming was occupied; the country in eastern Montana, north of the Yellowstone to the southern boundary of the Indian reservation was filled up, and herds began to look for favorable locations beyond the international boundary along the Saskatchewan River."[6]

In this setting of rapid settlement, first possession became the accepted way of establishing property rights. According to Osgood, "by grazing a certain area the stockgrower was in the way of gaining a kind of prescriptive right to the same as over against a newcomer who should attempt to drive off the stock thereon."[7] This right was generally recognized by custom and even came to be respected by law enforcement officers.[8]

To notify others that land was already claimed, cattlemen advertised in local papers outlining the areas they were claiming. For instance, on April 12, 1884, Charles S. Johnston announced in the *Glendive Times*, published in Glendive, Montana, "I, the undersigned, do hereby notify the public that I claim the valley, branching off the Glendive Creek, four miles east of Allard, and extending to its source on the Southside of the Northern Pacific Railroad as a stock range."[9] As more and more people came to the Great Plains (see Table 9.1), however, competition for the land intensified and more effort had to be put into the definition and enforcement of property rights.

To better define and enforce property rights to land in the face of rising land values, cattlemen established line camps along their customary range boundaries. From those camps, cowboys rode along the boundaries, driving cattle back to their customary ranges and guarding against cattle rustling.[10] Line camps were especially important in the winter, when snow storms could compel cattle to drift long distances. Without line camps, neighboring ranchers and farmers would have had to leave the comfort of their "homes

TABLE 9.1

Population of the Great Plains, 1850–1900

	Population
1850	274,139
1860	872,892
1870	1,481,603
1880	3,549,264
1890	6,044,884
1900	7,377,091

SOURCE: U.S. Bureau of the Census 1960, 12–13.
NOTE: This series includes the states and territories of
North Dakota, South Dakota, Kansas, Nebraska, Texas,
Montana, Wyoming, Colorado, and New Mexico. For the
years 1850, 1860, 1870, and 1880 the Indian population
living in Indian Territory and on Indian Reservations is
excluded. Indians living in the general population are included. For 1890 and 1900 population figures include all
Indians.

on the range" in rough weather to drive stray cattle off their land and back
to their accustomed ranges.[11] Hence, the line camps effectively enforced
customary rights to the open range, enforced property rights to cattle, and
provided employment for cowboys when they were not involved in
roundups.

CATTLEMEN'S ASSOCIATIONS

To develop the branding system, to adjudicate conflicts between first-posses-
sion claimants, to help exclude newcomers once the range was claimed, and
to perform other definitional and enforcement activities, cattlemen formed
local associations, as discussed in Chapter 8. In 1871 Wyoming stockmen
organized the Wyoming Stock Graziers' Association, which changed its
name to the Wyoming Stock Growers' Association in 1879. In 1873 two
stockgrowers' associations were organized in Colorado. Many other local associations followed in each of the states. For example, in 1873 a group of
ranchers in western Montana met to form the first organization in that ter-

ritory. In 1885 the Eastern Montana Stockgrowers Association merged with the group from western Montana to form the Montana Stockgrowers Association. These associations provide strong counterevidence to the claim that the early settlers in the West were highly individualistic, operating in an atomistic fashion without relations with other settlers. The cattlemen's associations had three aims: "first, to preserve the individual's ownership in his herd and his increase; second, to afford protection to the individual's herds; and third, to control the grazing of the public domain or to prevent overcrowding. These aims, which might have been achieved by an individual in the earlier days of comparative isolation, could now only be realized through group effort."[12]

PREVENTING OVERLOAD ON THE RANGE

To limit access to the grazing commons, the associations had to find cost-effective ways of excluding outsiders. Contrary to the image of range wars as the norm, the cattlemen recognized the negative-sum nature of such conflict and therefore opted for a more efficient enforcement mechanism. The roundup, described in Chapter 8 as a contract among producers intended to realize economies of scale in joint production, provided that mechanism. Starting in 1874, Wyoming stockgrowers organized a voluntary roundup system that depended, for its enforcement, on a refusal to cooperate with those who did not belong to the association. Other associations followed suit.

The associations effectively controlled entry into the grazing commons by not allowing nonmembers to participate. If a new entrant put stock on what was seen as someone else's range, the ranchers would refuse to allow the newcomer to join the roundup. Such sanctions were quite effective. In 1885 John Conrad moved 6,000 head of cattle onto a range east of Musselshell River in Montana Territory. The Niobrara Cattle Company was already running livestock in that district and believed that the range was fully stocked. At their next meeting, the local stockmen "condemned Conrad for his violation of range law and warned him that they would not handle his stock or cooperate with him in any way. He got the message and withdrew his herd."[13]

Even someone as illustrious as Theodore Roosevelt felt association pres-

sures when he attempted to expand his herd. When Roosevelt tried to expand his operation by purchasing a second ranch in Dakota Territory in
1884, he also expanded his herd by a thousand head, far beyond the number
allowed under the range rights associated with the new ranch.[14] The expansion brought a visit from a representative of the Marquis de Mores, one of
the leading ranchers in the area. The representative warned Roosevelt's foreman "that he should tell their boss his cattle were trespassing on range that
by right belonged to the Marquis. Roosevelt might purchase grazing rights
for a substantial sum; otherwise, he must clear out."[15] Roosevelt abided by
the warning.

Local newspapers also often carried announcements that cooperation
would not be forthcoming if additional cattle were placed on a range that
was considered fully stocked:

> Notice is hereby given that at the fall meeting of the Little Missouri River's
> Stockgrowers' Association, September, 1886, it was decided that as the
> ranges on the Little Missouri River and Beaver Creek and their tributaries
> are fully stocked with cattle and horses, and that as any additional herds
> placed upon such ranges would entail severe losses, not only to present oc-
> cupants but also to any new herds that may be up on said ranges, the mem-
> bers of the association, therefore, would refuse to aid or assist in any man-
> ner any party who may place cattle or horses upon said ranges after said
> meeting.[16]

And a notice published in a Helena, Montana, paper in 1883, asserted: "We
the undersigned, stockgrowers of the above described range, hereby give notice that we consider said range already overstocked; therefore we positively
decline allowing any outside parties or any parties locating herds upon this
range the use of our corrals, nor will they be permitted to join us on any
roundup on the said range from and after this date."[17]

These efforts succeeded in creating economically valuable customary
range rights that were bought and sold along with the base property and cattle that formed a ranch. R. Taylor Dennen found numerous instances of
range rights being exchanged in the marketplace. In 1884 the Swan Land
and Cattle Company purchased a 160-acre ranch with improvements and
stock from the National Cattle Company for $768,850. The same company

purchased another 320-acre ranch with improvements and cattle for
$984,023 of which the range rights constituted over $200,000. The Arkansas
Valley Land and Cattle Company carried on its books a valuation of $85,000
for the range rights that it owned.[18]

THEN CAME SHEEP

The roundup as an exclusionary mechanism broke down when cattle grazing interfaced with sheep grazing. The first sheep in the northern ranges
were trailed in from California, Utah, and Oregon in the 1870s. By 1881 in
Montana and by 1886 in Wyoming the number of sheep exceeded the number of cattle.[19] The usual reason given for the antipathy between the cattle
growers and the sheep growers is that sheep ruined the range for cattle by
cropping the grass too close and by fouling the water.[20]

A more plausible explanation for the conflicts between cattlemen and
sheepmen, however, was the threat that the sheepman brought to the customary property-rights system enforced by the cattlemen's associations. As a
rancher explained:

> The idea that cattle can't graze on the same ranch with sheep . . . is com-
> pletely untrue. If they belong to the same owner or, as the saying used to be,
> "they wear the same brand," they get along very well. In later years, we had
> winter and fall cattle pastures. In certain times, we had a band of sheep
> camped in some of the same pastures. . . . The problem came when a "float-
> ing" sheepman brought his sheep into an area already the "accustomed
> range" of someone else, whether a cattleman or another sheepman. . . . The
> so-called cattleman-sheepman wars derived from the same root cause as the
> conflict of long-established cattleman versus the newcomer cattleman. . . .
> All of these conflicts arose because of the absence of any legal way to regu-
> late the available grazing.[21]

Roundups were essential to cattle operations, and access to the roundup
was an effective method of controlling the number of entrants and the total
herd size in a given area. But when a sheepman arrived, he did not need to
be included in the roundup to have a viable economic operation. Sheep were
controlled on the open range by herders, and there was no need to rely on

TABLE 9.2

Production and Sale of Barbed Wire, 1874–1880

	Pounds Sold
1874	10,000
1875	600,000
1876	2,840,000
1877	12,863,000
1878	26,655,000
1879	50,377,000
1880	80,500,000

SOURCE: Webb 1931, 309.

neighbors for any cooperative work. Therefore the cattleman warred with the sheepman not because of any natural dissonance between cattle and sheep but rather because of the institutional incompatibility of the two modes of operation. In the words of Osgood, "against the sheep herder, fences or force were the only successful protective measures."[22]

BARBED WIRE: A FENCING REVOLUTION

To deal with the conflicts between grazers on the open range, to avoid some of the collective costs of roundups, and to reduce the costs of manning line camps, cattlemen were constantly searching for cheaper ways to define and enforce their property rights. Because conventional fencing was not an option on the Great Plains, where trees and stones were scarce, line camps were the answer. Ultimately, however, inventors of barbed wire responded to the demand for less expensive ways to define and enforce property rights, filing for 368 patents between 1866 and 1868.[23] The most successful wire was developed by Joseph Glidden in 1873. As a lower-cost way of establishing property rights, barbed wire skyrocketed in popularity, as shown in Table 9.2. The 80.5 million pounds of barbed wire sold in 1880 was sufficient to construct 500,000 miles of fence with four strands of wire.

Wherever it was possible to establish clear title to land, barbed wire was in great demand. Texas, which was not governed by homestead laws because it had entered the nation with independent status, was one of the biggest users of barbed wire. In 1881 Joseph Glidden, in partnership with Henry Sanborn, purchased 125,000 acres in the Texas Panhandle and added another 125,000 acres of Texas public-school land. They fenced the entire area with 150 miles of Glidden wire and stocked it with 1,500 cattle.[24] Another famous ranch, the XIT, was created when three million acres of state land was traded to a syndicate in return for the building of the state capitol. Upon securing title to the land, the owners immediately began building fences, hiring 300 fence-builders in order to secure the property before the 50,000 cattle that were to stock the range arrived. By 1885, they had fenced 476,000 acres into one large pasture. Eventually, 1,500 miles of fence enclosed the XIT.[25]

Barbed wire was also used to fence land where customary rights evolved through first possession and local extralegal agreements. Table 9.3 shows the extent of these illegal enclosures in the eleven far-western states. Economist Gary Libecap concludes that this fencing "increased ranch values: pasture and water holes could be protected; the drift of livestock could be constrained to prevent straying into areas with poisonous plants, alkali water, or diseased animals; and breeding could be controlled to improve herd quality."[26]

Artificially Induced Tragedy

The methods for disposing of the public domain roused great controversy throughout the late eighteen and nineteenth centuries.[27] Until 1862 public lands were disbursed primarily through sale at auction, although states and individuals received some land through grants, and over time, squatters were allowed preemption rights.[28] Continual pressure to make "free" land available led to the passage of the first Homestead Act in 1862. This act allowed settlers to claim 160 acres if they resided on the land for five years and cultivated it.[29] Several more acts followed the Homestead Act. The Timber Culture Act of 1873 permitted settlers to claim an additional 160 acres if they planted and cultivated 40 acres in trees. The Desert Land Act of 1877 allowed up to 640 acres to be claimed if the land was irrigated. The Enlarged

TABLE 9.3
Illegal Enclosures in the Eleven Far-Western States,
1883–1908

	Total Acreage
1883	2,157,000[a]
1884	2,975,000[a]
1885	1,221,000[b]
1886	6,400,000[b]
1887	8,579,000[b]
1888–1900	Not reported
1901	2,488,000[b]
1902	3,953,000[b]
1903	2,605,000[b]
1904	1,355,000[b]
1905	363,000[b]
1906	2,000,000[b]
1907	800,000[b]
1908	1,323,000[b]

SOURCE: Libecap 1981, 20.
[a] Colorado only.
[b] Includes Nebraska, North and South Dakota, and Kansas.

Homestead Act of 1909 expanded the basic acreage available to 320 acres. Finally, the Stock Raising Homestead Act of 1916 further expanded the acreage to 640 acres.

Although all these acts created property rights in land, they also supplanted existing customary rights enforced by local institutions and artificially raised the costs of defining and enforcing property rights. The fencing of the public domain was an effort to secure control of property rights in a less costly way than through homesteading. However, in response to such fencing, legislation was passed in 1885 that states:

No person, by force, threats, intimidation, or by any fencing or enclosing, or any other unlawful means, shall prevent or obstruct, or shall combine and confederate with others to prevent or obstruct, any person from peaceably entering upon or establishing a settlement or residence on any tract of public land subject to settlement or entry into the public land laws of the United States, or shall prevent or obstruct free passage or transit over or through public lands.[30]

This law essentially codified open access to the public domain. Fourteen months after the passage of the 1885 anti-fencing act, "375 unlawful enclosures of public lands containing 6,410,000 acres had been brought to the attention of the officers, proceedings to compel removal of fences had been recommended in 83 cases, involving 2,250,000 acres, and final decrees ordering removals had been obtained in 13 cases involving 1 million acres."[31] In several cases, the military was called out to remove illegal fences.[32]

The homestead acts also artificially raised the costs of definition and enforcement in several ways: by specifying a claim size that was generally inappropriate given the aridity of land on the frontier, by requiring residence on the land for five years, and by requiring improvements to land that were not economical.[33] If the land had been put up for sale, it would have been purchased when its discounted present value became positive (see Chapter 2),[34] but it would not have been put into production until the annual rents from production turned positive (t^* in Figure 2.1). However, the homesteading rules required claimants to bid for the land on the basis of their residence upon and improvement of the land rather than on the basis of dollars paid for it. Hence under the homestead acts, the time for moving to and producing from the land was not when the annual rents turned positive but before that, when the net discounted value of the land turned positive.[35] In other words, the homestead acts encouraged premature settlement, which dissipated at least some of the value of the property rights to land and,[36] in the limit, potentially dissipated the entire value of the land through the race for property rights.

The exact calculation of these values was anybody's guess, varying according to expectations about land productivity, rainfall, appropriate crops, output prices, and transportation costs. But whatever the best estimates about those unknowns, the race for property rights required settlement before the net value of output from the land turned positive. And if homesteaders were unjustifiably optimistic about the productive potential of the land, as many

Homesteader Cabin. Homesteading encouraged a race for property rights that induced premature settlement and undue hardship until the farms and ranches became economically viable. This homestead cabin was typical of rudimentary structures where people lived as they attempted to "prove up" on their homesteads. No. 81-78, "Sodbuster's Place," Thain White Collection, K. Ross Toole Archives, University of Montana, Missoula.

were (meaning they thought the rents would turn positive sooner), they would bid even more in terms of hardship. Gary Libecap and Barbara Hansen conclude that this optimism "led too many to migrate to the region and settle on too many small dry land wheat farms."[37] As a result, the homestead acts created a "starving time" for many homesteaders.

The uncertainty inherent in the process and the pressure to establish property rights prematurely is evident in the homesteading failure rates. Fletcher reports that 80 percent of the original homesteads in the Benchland District north of central Montana's Musselshell River were relinquished.[38] Of the 70,000 to 80,000 who homesteaded in Montana between 1909 and 1918, "by 1922, about 66,000 or 88 percent had starved out or given up."[39]

And fewer than half of the 88,687 homestead entries filed in Wyoming between 1910 to 1934 were completed.[40] In the words of preeminent land historian Benjamin Hibbard, "The great weakness of the Homestead Act was, and is, its utter inadaptability to the parts of the country for which it was not designed. The idea of the farms small in acres within the semi-arid region was tenacious, but untenable. It was even vicious in its operation."[41]

A quintessential example of racing for property rights is the Oklahoma Land Rush of 1893.[42] The Outlet, also known as the Cherokee Strip,[43] was an area 226 miles long and 58 miles wide (8.4 million acres) in what is now northwest Oklahoma.[44] Because of previous allotments to Indian tribes, only 6 million of the 8.4 million acres were available for claiming. The Outlet had been created as part of an 1828 treaty with the Cherokee tribe in order to give them access to hunting grounds, but after 1866 the tribe's access was limited by a subsequent treaty.[45] The tribe did, however, retain property rights to the area and attempted to defend those rights against intrusion, first by trail herds passing through and then by neighboring ranchers.[46] The Cherokees collected nominal taxes on cattle in the Outlet for the first few years, and entered into leases with ranchers after 1878.

In an effort to lower negotiation and enforcement costs, the ranchers formed the Cherokee Strip Livestock Association in 1883 and empowered it to enter into a lease with the tribe and then sublease to member ranchers.[47] The original lease between the association and the tribe had a five-year term and carried an annual payment of $100,000.[48] Believing that their property rights were relatively secure, the ranchers erected fences and made other improvements in the Outlet.

The federal government announced in 1888 that it would no longer recognize leases between the Cherokees and the ranchers, and in 1889 Congress passed legislation to purchase the Outlet for $1.25 an acre. In October of that year the secretary of the interior told the ranchers that their cattle had to be removed from the Outlet.[49] The tribe agreed to sell their rights to the federal government for $8.6 million.[50] They did so despite the fact that by this time they had received bids from the ranchers of $30 million. Evidently the Cherokees recognized that expropriation by the government was a strong possibility, and the $8.6 million sale was better than having the land taken.

The government wanted to gain control of the Outlet because of political pressure to open the land for settlers who wished to claim it through homesteading.[51] As soon as the purchase was complete, pressure mounted to open the land for settlement. However, the fact that already settled land surrounded the large block of available land meant that rules had to be established as to who could enter and when. On August 19, 1893, President Grover Cleveland issued a 15,000-word proclamation that detailed the conditions for claiming land within the Outlet.[52] The area would become available at noon on September 16, and no claims were allowed before that time.

The proclamation specified that the land must be entered from either the northern or the southern borders of the strip. It also provided for nine registration booths, four on the southern border and five on the northern border. These booths were necessary because potential claimants needed to obtain a certificate in order to enter the race. After finding a claim, the individual was to report to a land office and register his or her claim and surrender the certificate. Several railroads with tracks crossing the Outlet were allowed to run trains for claimants as long as they did not exceed fifteen miles per hour and stopped at points not more than five miles apart.[53] The race for land was big news, and reporters came from a wide area, thus ensuring that knowledge of the race was widespread.

As soon as the registration booths were set up, they were besieged with applicants. Irene Lefebvre reports:

> The booths opened for business at seven o'clock on Monday morning, before the run on Saturday, the sixteenth. At Arkansas City people had been forming in line and had held their places throughout the two previous days and nights. . . .
> The line at Orlando, in Oklahoma Territory, numbered at least fifteen hundred at the time of the opening of the booth for registration with hundreds pouring in every hour. . . . Each day the numbers increased until some 10,000 men and women were standing in the sweltering heat and thick dust.[54]

According to D. Earl Newsom, "By early September, the Strip border was almost one vast encampment. Living conditions were barely tolerable. Water was two miles away. Many home-seekers had meager food supplies and little money. Toilet facilities were primitive. The sun and dust continued to bear down unmercifully."[55] One newspaper reported several deaths: "At Arkansas City over fifty were overcome by heat on that day, six of whom died before night; at Caldwell, twenty were sunstruck, two of whom died; at Orlando, twenty-two sunstrokes were reported and two deaths; at Hennessey, eighteen, with one death."[56]

Waiting in line was only one way that some of the rents were dissipated; there were also efforts to gain an advantage in the race. Trainloads of fast horses were shipped in. To dissuade others, rumormongers told of potential dangers and rule changes that raised the cost of racing. The military was kept busy evicting settlers who attempted to sneak into the region prior to the start of the race to find the best land.

Finally, on the morning of September 16, between 100,000 and 150,000 racers—three to four times the number of available claims[57]—gathered along the border. Soldiers with rifles stood guard every 600 yards to stop anyone taking off before the signal. A deaf person thought the signal had occurred and was shot from his saddle when he started early. When the signal was given at noon, the racers surged forward, and the trains, with passengers filling the cars and clinging to the outsides, released their brakes. Bedlam ensued as people on horseback and wagon raced for their claims. Horses broke their legs, and wagons overturned on the rough terrain. Across the prairie, wagon contents such as stoves, buckets, and boxes lay scattered. Those who thought they could race on foot were trampled by horses and run over by wagons. Those who boarded trains risked breaking their legs as they jumped from moving trains trying to beat the others.[58] "E. C. (Evalyn) Aldrich from Chambersville, Mo., charged across the line on a cow pony. After a mile and half, he paused to count 40 race horses that had collapsed and died from heat, thirst, and over-exertion."[59] Those who tried to jump the gun risked being shot as they heard shouts of "Sooner! Sooner! Shoot the S. O. B."[60]

The Oklahoma Land Rush differed from homesteading in that the race occurred after the land could generate positive annual returns (t^* in Figure 2.1), but the process clearly dissipated some of the land's value. The important lesson, similar to that from the homestead acts, is that rules for establishing property rights are more likely to dissipate the value of the property if they are dictated by individuals or groups without a direct stake in the outcome. With property rights to the Cherokee Strip already well-established, there was no reason to encourage broken legs, uncivil behavior, and death.

Conclusion

The waste of resources incurred by the rules for defining and enforcing property rights under the national land laws contrasted starkly with the economies realized by the rules for establishing property rights under land-claims clubs and cattlemen's associations. These groups conserved on the investment in definition and enforcement activity. The reason for the difference between the locally determined informal property institutions and the nationally determined formal laws is that the former were created by individuals with a stake in the outcome and therefore an incentive to conserve on resources invested in the definition and enforcement process. The homestead acts, on the other hand, were created by members of Congress with little claim on any rents that might be saved by more efficient definition and enforcement processes. On the contrary, politicians gained popularity by advocating "free land,"[61] and the local land bureaucracies that pressured them stood to extract some value through the homesteading process.[62] Jonathan Raban describes how local government workers could gain from the federal land allocation system: "a spell on a survey team could lead to a profitable career in real estate; and most of the locators, who showed up in their buggies at railroad stations whenever an emigrant was expected, had done time on the Land Survey. For an ex-chain man, the locating business was money for jam at $25 for a light morning's work."[63]

Because the federal land laws artificially increased the transaction costs of establishing property rights, it is not surprising that pressure to move to a more efficient system grew. The ranchers realized that the homestead acts were not likely to be repealed, but did hope for a leasing system that would give them control over land still in the public domain. In 1884 the National Cattle Growers' Association lobbied Congress to "enact such laws as will enable the cattlemen of the West to acquire by lease the right to graze on unoccupied lands."[64] Eastern political power prevailed, however, and Congress failed to pass any leasing legislation until the Taylor Grazing Act of 1934. At that point there were still 165 million acres in eleven western states of unappropriated and unreserved public lands, testimony to the difficulty of establishing property rights through homesteading.[65]

In part, the West was saddled with an inefficient system for establishing property rights because lawmakers in the East did not have the same information and incentives possessed by the property-right entrepreneurs on the frontier. As Walter Prescott Webb saw it,

> when he [the Westerner] began to talk about his needs and wants to his Eastern neighbor and lawmaker of the humid region, he often spoke a strange language. The Westerner talked in terms that the Eastern man could not understand because the Easterner and his fathers lacked the experience that enabled them to appreciate the new problems; the Easterner was therefore reluctant to approve any proposal made by the Westerner for new institutions for the West.[66]

Not only did the national land laws foster a return to the tragedy of the commons, they encouraged a race for property rights that dissipated at least a portion of the gains from privatization that had been captured previously through voluntary associations.

TEN

Making the Desert Bloom

As agrarian settlement pushed into the region west of the hundredth meridian during the latter half of the nineteenth century, it became obvious that the aridity of the region was its single most defining characteristic. Many observers questioned whether the West—particularly the Great Plains region, dubbed the Great American Desert—had any economic possibilities. In 1837 Washington Irving wrote:

> The great Chippewyan chain of mountains, and the sandy and volcanic plains which extend on either side, are represented as incapable of cultivation. The pasturage which prevails there during a certain portion of the year, withers under the aridity of the atmosphere, and leaves nothing but dreary waste. An immense belt of rocky mountains and volcanic plains, several hundred miles in width, must ever remain an irreclaimable wilderness, intervening between the abodes of civilization, and affording a last refuge to the Indian. Here roving tribes of hunters, living in tents or lodges, and fol-

lowing the migrations of game, may lead a life of savage independence, where there is nothing to tempt the cupidity of the White man.[1]

Even as late as 1875, W. B. Hazen, an army officer who served in the West, claimed that all the land between the hundredth meridian and the Sierra Nevada was uninhabitable. "Hereafter, let emigration to these places known not to be arable, be emphatically discouraged," he declared.[2]

Despite this pessimism, many saw the potential for productive agriculture, especially if the lands could be irrigated. Some of the optimism was driven by promoters such as the federal government and the railroads, which encouraged farmers to take advantage of "free" land and even used fraudulent claims to attract settlers. One agricultural scientist went so far as to claim that frequent, gentle rains would come if farmers would settle the region and water 10 out of every 160 acres, thus turning the area into a cornucopia of agricultural produce.[3]

Though the race to claim the land undoubtedly caused premature settlement (see Chapter 8), farming did eventually become economical, especially where settlers irrigated the land. For this reason, rents from agriculture were as closely tied to the ownership of water as to the ownership of the land. Not surprisingly, therefore, institutional entrepreneurs devoted considerable effort to defining, reorganizing, and redistributing water rights.

Water Rights from the Ground Up

Because of the transitory nature of water, the rules governing ownership of that resource evolved in ways very different from those governing other resources. Writing from his vantage point in humid England, the great common-law jurist William Blackstone asserted, "Water is a moving, wandering thing, and must of necessity continue common by the law of nature; so that I can only have a temporary, transient, usufructuary property therein."[4] Hence the riparian doctrine that evolved under English common law gave landowners along a stream a right to an undiminished quantity and quality of water. The riparian doctrine worked well where water was used mainly for domestic purposes, for livestock, or for driving water wheels, and where diversion for irrigation was unnecessary. Under these conditions, riparian

Miners Working on a Flume. Miners invested considerable sums diverting water from streams, in order to wash gravel in their sluice boxes and to power the hydraulic lines that dislodged gold ore from rocks. Capital investment in flumes and sluice boxes necessitated a legal system that would allow diversion and guarantee water rights. Therefore the miners replaced the riparian doctrine from the East with the prior-appropriation doctrine that governs most western water today. Courtesy of Doris Whithorn.

owners could exercise their right to use water without harming downstream owners.

In an arid region, however, water use required diversion, and diversion in quantities greater than necessary for domestic and livestock consumption impaired downstream riparians. This constraint first became apparent in mining, where large quantities of water had to be diverted considerable distances to sluice boxes and to high-pressure hoses for hydraulic mining. Such diversions from a stream deprived downstream users of their enjoyment of an undiminished quantity and quality of water. Moreover, since water levels varied considerably from year to year, times were sure to come when supply would be too short to meet everyone's demands.

From this setting, the doctrine of prior appropriation developed as an alternative to the riparian doctrine in the West:

These miner's rules and regulations . . . were very simple and as far as property rights were concerned related to the acquisition, working, and retention of their mining claims, and to the appropriation and diversion of water to be used in working them. . . . There was one principle embodied in them all, and on which rests the "Arid Region Doctrine" of the ownership and use of waters, and that was the recognition of discovery, followed by prior appropriation, as the inception of the possessor's title, and development by working the claim as the condition of its retention.[5]

This doctrine constituted a marked departure from English common law in four ways. First, it granted to the first appropriator an exclusive right to the water and conditioned other rights upon those prior rights. Second, it permitted diversion of water to nonriparian lands. Third, it limited the amount of water that could be claimed to that which could be put to beneficial use. Finally, it allowed voluntary exchange of water rights. These changes all represented new attributes of property rights that became important as water became more valuable.

The importance of water scarcity as a driving force in the adoption of the prior-appropriation doctrine is illustrated in Map 5. The states that fully adopted the prior-appropriation doctrine clearly lay in the arid Great Plains, and those that adopted a modified version of the riparian doctrine had higher rainfall.[6]

Mixing Water and Capital

Diverting water in small amounts for a small sluice box or for irrigating riparian fields needed little infrastructure, but larger-scale diversions required coordination of labor and capital. To realize scale economies with larger sluices or hydraulic mining, miners had to build dams to store and divert the water and build flumes to deliver the water to the sluices or hoses. In some cases they even diverted entire streams from their natural channels so that the stream beds could be mined. Similarly, farmers who wanted to cultivate land some distance from the stream had to build diversion dams and ditches.

The search for the appropriate organization for water storage and delivery, especially for irrigation, entailed three important transaction costs. First,

MAP 5. The Evolution of Water Law

an irrigation company selling water along a delivery canal had to contract with many irrigators and had to convince those irrigators that it would not get them committed to buy water from the irrigation company and then raise the price of water. Second, a company wishing to build a canal across properties owned by disparate individuals would have its returns from the project jeopardized by any property owner who threatened to deny a right-of-way unless he received a higher price for the right-of-way. And finally, individuals trying to coordinate operation and maintenance of an irrigation facility faced the free-rider problem because upstream users had little incentive to worry about downstream delivery.

Institutional entrepreneurs responded to the challenge posed by these transaction costs, building diversion and storage dams and hundreds of miles of flumes, canals, and ditches.[7] As shown in Table 10.1, millions of acres were irrigated by private water development, far exceeding the acreage irrigated by governmental projects. The organizational forms for these private projects varied considerably.

Private Irrigation Firms

The simplest organizational form was the private firm that owned irrigation facilities. In the 1880s numerous private irrigation companies were established in western states.[8] These firms constructed and maintained diversion dams, delivery canals, and feeder canals and contracted to deliver water to farmers bordering the canals.

This simple contractual arrangement encountered problems for both the firm and the farmer. First, the irrigation firm had to secure rights-of-way for its canals. Without the power of eminent domain, companies faced a holdout problem: a landowner whose property a canal would have to cross could extract an exorbitant price for the right-of-way by withholding permission to cross his land. The irrigator without alternative access to water faced a monopoly problem: a firm with exclusive control over water delivery in the area could price its services unchecked by competition and threaten recalcitrant landowners with loss of water.

By integrating ownership of irrigation facilities with ownership of land, entrepreneurs could overcome these problems.[9] If a single firm owned the land over which the canal would be built, no holdout problems or negotiation costs would arise in locating irrigation facilities. If it also owned the land that would be irrigated, the rents from that land and the rents from the water would accrue to the same firm so that there would be no incentive to restrict the flow of water to obtain a higher monopoly price.

Numerous attempts to solve the coordination problems via integration succeeded, including several in California. In 1857, for example, fifty German settlers formed a joint-stock company and purchased a large ranch formed under a Spanish land grant. Known as the Anaheim Colony, this company was one of the more successful large-scale irrigation efforts in early

TABLE 10.1

Irrigation Development in Seventeen Western States, 1890–1950 (acres)

	Irrigated with Government Water	Irrigated via Private Development	Total Irrigated
1890	—	3,631,381	3,631,381
1900	—	7,527,690	7,527,690
1902	—	8,875,090	8,875,090
1910	568,558	13,456,774	14,025,332
1920	2,388,199	16,204,769	18,592,988
1930	3,049,970	15,894,886	18,944,856
1940	3,800,239	16,594,804	20,395,043
1950	5,700,000	19,169,000	24,869,000

SOURCE: Golze 1952, 14.

California agriculture. The joint-stock company owned and operated the ir-rigation facilities, while the property was distributed by lottery to the colony members.[10]

The Southern California Colony Association at Riverside was also cre-ated to integrate ownership of land and irrigation facilities. In 1870, Judge John Wesley North purchased large tracts of land from the Roubidoux Ran-cho and the Gurapo Rancho.[11] The association developed the irrigation project with water from the Santa Ana River and then sold the land to set-tlers.

Several other projects followed. In 1872, a group of investors purchased 8,000 acres of the Cucamonga Rancho and obtained rights to water from San Antonio Creek.[12] In 1875, another group purchased 5,600 acres from the Rancho San Jose. The San Gabriel Orange Grove Association, under the leadership of D. N. Berry, purchased 2,800 acres of land four miles from Los Angeles, developed irrigation facilities, and again assigned tracts to members by lottery.[13]

Homogeneous religious and quasi-religious organizations provided an-other private mechanism for lowering transaction costs associated with private water development. The Mormon experience in Utah was the most notable. Having reached the Salt Lake valley in the summer of 1847, the Mormons had 5,000 acres of crops under irrigation by 1848 and 150,000 acres under irrigation by 1865.[14] The cohesiveness and hierarchical structure of the Mormon community helped overcome the transaction costs:

> Dams and ditches were constructed on a community basis, rights to use the water were associated with the utilization of land, and a public authority was appointed to supervise the appropriation of water for culinary, industrial, and agricultural purposes. . . . When a group of families found themselves in need of water (or additional water) to irrigate their farms and gardens, the bishop arranged for survey and organized the men into a construction crew. Each man was required to furnish labor in proportion to the amount of land he had to water. Upon completion of the project, the water would be distributed by a ward water master in proportion to his labor. The labor necessary to keep the canal in good repair was handled the same way, in accordance with assignments made in regular Sunday services or priesthood meetings.[15]

Irrigation activities were developed communally to capture economies of scale, but the land was owned privately to preserve production incentives.[16]

Other religious organizations had less success with irrigation projects because they did not pay attention to incentives. For example, in 1898 the Salvation Army established two irrigation colonies, one at Fort Amity in the Arkansas River Valley of Colorado, 267 miles east of Denver, and one near Soledad in the Salinas Valley in California.[17] Because these irrigation colonies were designed to provide farming opportunities for destitute families rather than members of the faith as with the Mormons, they quickly attracted indigents. The urban poor who came to the projects lacked both agricultural experience and homogeneity of purpose. As a result, both projects were abandoned by 1907.

Horace Greeley instigated another private social experiment, in what later became Greeley, Colorado. In 1869, Nathan Cook Meeker, an agent for Greeley, led the establishment of an irrigation colony about fifty miles north of Denver at the delta of the South Platte and Cache la Poudre Rivers.[18] Greeley published a prospectus for the community in the *New York Tribune*,

TABLE 10.2

Irrigated Acreage in California, by Type of Enterprise, 1920–1950
(thousands of irrigated acres)

	1920[a]	1930[a]	1940[b]	1950[b]
Single farm	1503	1735	2353	4260
Mutual irrigation	1216	854	898	889
Commercial	813	312	392	296
Public irrigation district	577	1599	1779	1821

SOURCE: Smith 1983, 172.
[a] U.S. Department of Agriculture (1930, 87).
[b] U.S. Department of Agriculture (1950, 85).

for which he served as agricultural editor. The colony purchased 12,000 acres of private land from the Denver Pacific Railroad and laid out a town and an irrigation system for adjoining farms. The community quickly attracted settlers, and land sales were rapid. However, because the founders underestimated the cost of canals to deliver water, the colony did not prosper.

Mutual Irrigation Companies

To raise capital for large-scale irrigation facilities and to overcome the problems of market power on the part of an irrigation facility owner, individual farmers formed mutual irrigation companies.[19] Table 10.2 shows the relative importance of various organizational forms of irrigation enterprises in California from 1920 to 1950. Excluding single-farm enterprises, mutual irrigation companies were the dominant form of organization in 1920, but this changed dramatically during the ensuing decade as public irrigation districts came to dominate.

In addition to raising capital, mutual companies helped farmers overcome the free-rider problem associated with the operation and maintenance of irrigation facilities. Once the delivery canal was built, those at the head of the canal had little incentive to contribute to its operation and maintenance, as Elwood Mead describes:

> Enthusiasm or the press of need would suffice to build partnership ditches, but friction would disrupt their subsequent operation. Human selfishness would then assert itself. The man whose land was near the head of the ditch did not need to keep it in repair; so long as water for all others had run past his lateral, the people below him would have to attend to this or do without. The irrigator having this fortunate location showed equal ingenuity in manipulating his head gates so as to take more than his share of the water, while the unfortunate irrigator at the lower end of the ditch found himself doing more work and getting less for it than the other members of the partnership. Until farmers learned that they must place the control of their ditch in the hands of one individual, there was either murder or suicide in the heart of every member of the partnership.[20]

Economist Rodney Smith concludes that mutual irrigation companies effectively amassed capital, overcame the free-rider problem, and contracted to avoid potential monopoly pricing problems.[21] Despite their efficiency-enhancing potential, however, mutual irrigation companies lost ground to public irrigation districts. Smith's explanation for the relative decline in mutual irrigation companies is that the public irrigation district's "ability to tax land for cross-subsidizing water use created income redistribution powers for the local government, the exercise of which proved to be an important incentive for some landholders preferring public ownership."[22]

Irrigation Districts

Irrigation districts, created by state governments in the 1880s and 1890s, were granted taxing and bonding power for the purpose of building, operating, and maintaining irrigation facilities. California first established the procedure for creating irrigation districts with passage of the Wright Act in 1887. Other states, including Washington in 1890; Kansas and Nevada in 1891; Idaho, Nebraska, and Oregon in 1895; and Colorado in 1901, followed rapidly with similar legislation.[23] Under the California law, which was typical, when fifty or more of the landowners within an area wanted to form a district, they would petition their county board of supervisors. A special election would be called in which all eligible voters, not just landholders, could vote, with a two-thirds majority required for the creation of an irrigation district. Once the district was formed, a simple majority of the voters could approve the issuance of irrigation bonds. All land in the district, not just that under irrigation, would then be taxed to retire the debt.[24]

Irrigation districts offered a way of lowering transaction costs where landownership was fragmented. A few vertically integrated projects had been tried, as discussed earlier, but these were possible only where large Spanish land grants lowered the transaction costs of putting together large blocks of land. With numerous small farms, however, transaction costs were much higher, making irrigation districts a useful institution for overcoming free-rider and holdout problems.

Lower transaction costs also allowed irrigation districts to resolve externality problems. For instance, as an irrigation project grew, drainage from one field could affect another field and could affect water quality. Irrigation also raised water tables and lowered the costs of pumping from wells. In addition, irrigation storage reservoirs provided the public good of flood control. By centralizing decision making and using taxing powers, districts could internalize the costs and benefits associated with irrigation.

Despite these advantages, very little land was brought under irrigation by the early districts because of constraints on bond financing. The California legislation, for example, set the coupon rate at 6 percent and specified that the bonds could not be sold at less than 90 percent of face value. In 1897, the restrictions became even more onerous when the coupon rate was lowered to 5 percent and no sales were allowed at less than the face value.[25] Furthermore, bonds were not backed by a lien on the irrigation works or other property; instead, the bondholders could claim only lands on which irrigation district taxes had not been paid.[26]

The success of the irrigation district as an organization for promoting irrigation changed dramatically in the early twentieth century. By 1930 California had 169 districts irrigating 3,110,305 acres.[27] Irrigation districts in California between 1910 and 1930 owed their success in part to a substantial increase in the price of irrigated crops and to the formation of the Bond Certifications Committee (BCC) by the California legislature in 1911.[28]

The BCC lowered the costs of obtaining capital by providing information about the reliability of bonds of different irrigation districts. This information was valuable because private rating services such as Moody's did not begin to rate irrigation bonds until well into the 1920s.[29]

Another reason for the increased success of irrigation districts was governmental regulation of private irrigation companies. The California State Railroad Commission, established in 1911, regulated prices charged by public utilities, including those charged by private irrigation companies, but did not regulate prices of mutual irrigation companies or irrigation districts.[30] The greater flexibility in pricing and fee structures of irrigation districts made these districts more attractive.

The above arguments suggest that irrigation districts exemplify the lowering of transaction costs by governmental power, but that same power also had the potential for redistribution of rents created by irrigation projects. When district-wide taxes are used to support irrigation, payment for the irrigation facility is disconnected from benefits received. Rodney Smith argues that this taxing power led to redistribution of costs from one group of landowners to another,[31] especially when landowners differed in their water demands per acre. On the other hand, if irrigation districts were small and homogeneous, the potential for redistribution was reduced because members were residual claimants and because it was easier to monitor agents working for the collective.

Evidence that redistribution may not have been great is found in the voting records of irrigation districts. James Buchanan and Gordon Tullock argue that the potential for coercive redistribution is reduced as collective agreement approaches unanimity.[32] Table 10.3 lists the irrigation district voting results for 46 districts that were formed between 1915 and 1925. The average "yes" vote favoring the formation of a district was 92.2 percent, indicating a high degree of consensus for the irrigation district. Moreover, there is no negative trend in the percentage of "yes" votes, which one would expect if people who were not benefiting from the projects were learning that they were subsidizing other landowners.[33]

Another factor militating against redistribution was the potential for land to be excluded from a district. Enabling legislation provided that if landowners petitioned and could show that their lands were not going to benefit from irrigation, the district directors would be required to exclude that land from the district and its taxes. In the formation of the Glenn-Colusa District, for example, the organizing committee actually asked several opposing landowners to exclude 10,000 acres (out of a total of 121,592 acres) to increase the likelihood that the irrigation district would be created.[34] The fact that similar exclusion options were exercised in numerous cases suggests that landowners could and did avoid redistribution by opting out.

Artificial Transaction Costs

As we have seen, institutional entrepreneurs wishing to develop water rights and irrigation projects in the West faced high transaction costs associated with holdout problems in obtaining construction rights-of-way, with free-rider problems in the construction and maintenance of delivery systems, and with controlling monopoly power. If land was held in large parcels, these costs were lower because these problems were internalized; a single landowner developing a project cannot withhold a right-of-way from himself, cannot free-ride on himself, and cannot charge high prices to himself.[35] As the number of landowners wishing to irrigate their land jointly increases, however, the transaction costs also increase. Unfortunately, this fragmentation of ownership was exacerbated by a number of governmental policies that artificially raised transaction costs.

THE HOMESTEAD ACTS

Beginning in 1862, a series of homestead acts imposed upon the West a vision of small family farms (see Chapter 9). In the words of historian Benjamin Hibbard, "the idea of the farm small in acres within the semi-arid region was tenacious, but untenable."[36] Homesteading included a residency requirement that encouraged a race for property rights and acreage limitations that were generally too small for efficient agricultural production.

The requirements made raising capital for irrigation projects more costly because individuals wishing to irrigate their land had to make investments without secure property rights to the land or wait through the residency requirement before making the investments. Title was not conveyed until the land was "proved up on."[37] Therefore someone wishing to develop irriga-

TABLE 10.3
Irrigation District Voting Results

Irrigation District	Date of Formation	Gross Acres	"Yes" Vote	"No" Vote	Percent "Yes"
Alpaugh	1915	8175	71	14	83.5
Anderson-Cottonwood	1914	32113	483	17	96.5
Banta Carbona	1921	14349	73	22	76.8
Beaumont	1919	4141	307	114	72.9
Byron-Bethany	1919	17200	173	14	92.5
Carmichael	1916	3121	45	3	93.7
Citrus Height	1920	3076	65	0	100.0
Compton Devel	1920	2652	10	0	100.0
Consolidated	1921	149047	1121	62	94.7
Corcoran	1919	51606	111	2	98.2
Cordua	1919	5461	7	0	100.0
El Camino	1921	7548	7	2	77.7
El Dorado	1925	30703	679	141	82.8
Fairoaks	1917	3900	184	16	92.0
Fallbrook	1925	10216	186	0	100.0
Foothill	1920	50687	356	3	99.1
Fresno	1920	241300	1438	184	88.6
Glenn-Colusa	1920	121592	287	12	95.9
Grenada	1921	4948	74	1	98.6
Hot Springs	1919	9497	21	0	100.0
Imperial	1911	605000	1304	360	78.3
Island No. 3	1921	4620	88	13	87.1
Jacinto	1917	11554	103	28	78.6
James	1920	26265	8	0	100.0
Laguana	1920	34858	251	4	98.4
La Mesa	1913	18000	397	3	99.2
Lindsay-Strathmore	1915	15250	150	20	88.2
Lucerne	1925	33407	138	26	84.1
Madera	1920	352000	1642	47	97.2
Maxwell	1918	8819	9	0	100.0
Merced	1919	189682	1967	922	68.0

TABLE 10.3 *(continued)*

Irrigation District	Date of Formation	Gross Acres	"Yes" Vote	"No" Vote	Percent "Yes"
Montague	1925	26117	198	2	99.0
Naglee Burk	1920	2871	13	0	100.0
Nevada	1921	268500	636	168	79.1
Oakdale	1909	74240	349	27	92.8
Potter Valley	1924	5042	110	3	97.3
Provident	1918	22805	13	0	100.0
South San Joaquin	1909	71112	376	87	81.2
Table Mountain	1922	955	7	0	100.0
Thermalito	1922	3110	135	6	95.7
Tranquility	1918	10750	68	0	100.0
Tule-Baxter	1917	24351	6	0	100.0
Waterford	1913	14100	70	1	98.5
West Stanislaus	1920	21400	115	4	96.6
Woodbridge	1924	12430	23	6	79.3

Summary of Results

	Number of Irrigation Districts	Average "Yes" Vote (%)
San Joaquin Valley		
IDs with > 50,000 gross acres	8	89.98
IDs with < 50,000 gross acres	12	90.70
All irrigation districts	20	90.41
Sacramento Valley		
IDs with > 50,000 gross acres	2	87.40
IDs with < 50,000 gross acres	14	93.97
All irrigation districts	16	93.16

SOURCE: McDevitt 1994, Table 3.4.

tion did not have the option of providing the lender with a legal lien on his property. If irrigation was necessary for successful farming and if outside capital was required for this irrigation, the farmer faced an intractable problem. He could not satisfy the residency and farming requirements until he irrigated the land, and he could not irrigate the land until he had adequate capital, which required some security for a loan.

When the requirements of homesteading were combined with the beneficial-use requirement of the prior-appropriation doctrine, the transaction costs of forming independent irrigation firms went even higher. Beneficial use required that farmers use the water, so irrigation companies that did not own the land to be irrigated found it difficult to have a clear property right to the resource they wanted to market. Mead captures the essence of the problem: "Theoretically, the right of the canal company is based on a beneficial use of the water, and this use must be made by the purchaser. The canal company is, therefore, selling something which it does not possess."[38]

Vertical integration provided a way around this ownership problem, but it was almost impossible to carry out under the homestead acts, with their residency requirements and acreage restrictions. Someone who wished to consolidate holdings faced the high transaction costs of negotiating agreements with numerous private landowners or engaging in fraudulent transactions by using dummy entrymen, who settled on the land, fulfilled the homesteading requirements, and then transferred title to the person for whom they were working.[39] In contrast, the irrigation efforts in California described above were facilitated by Spanish land grants that provided large blocks of consolidated land. In the case of the Mormons in Utah, the homestead acts did not apply, and there was not even a General Land Office in Utah until 1869. When it opened, the Mormons exerted enough pressure to get existing titles recognized by the federal government.[40]

Had railroad land grants been more contiguous, they might have helped lower the transaction costs of private water development. Railroad land grants, however, were mainly for alternate sections along the rail line, preventing "railroads from securing the unbroken tracts needed for comprehensive water projects."[41] In one case where the Northern Pacific Railroad did control a significant contiguous acreage, it carried out a major irrigation project. The railroad formed the Northern Pacific, Yakima, and Kittitas Irrigation Company in 1889 to irrigate land in the Yakima Valley.⁴² By 1892, the company had built 42 miles of aqueduct and irrigated 15,000 acres, and planned to irrigate 85,000 acres eventually. When the railroad sold the land under irrigation from the aqueduct, it granted one share of stock to the owner for each ten acres of land, with the understanding that control of the ditch was to pass to the farmers. The depression of 1893, however, slowed settlement in the area and left the project idle until the turn of the century, when the federal government absorbed it into its Yakima Project.⁴³

By the 1870s, there was a growing recognition that the homestead acts were stifling private irrigation in the West. In his annual message in 1876, President Ulysses S. Grant noted that the national land laws were "very defective" and that "land must be held in larger quantities to justify the expense of conducting water upon it to make it fruitful or to justify utilizing it as pasturage."⁴⁴

To rectify the problem, Congress passed the Desert Land Act in 1877. The act applied to California, Oregon, Nevada, and to the territories of Washington, Idaho, Montana, Utah, Wyoming, New Mexico, and Dakota. Under the act, an applicant could pay 25 cents per acre for 640 acres and then, if the applicant diverted water to and reclaimed the land within three years, all rights could be purchased for one dollar an acre. The act was unclear regarding how much irrigation was necessary, but the commissioner of the Land Office, J. A. Williamson, chose to interpret it as requiring irrigation on all 640 acres.⁴⁵ This raised the costs of acquiring title and also encouraged fraud. "Hundreds of ditches were built solely for this purpose by parties who had no intention at the time of cultivating the lands, but irrigated them in order to acquire title."⁴⁶

Despite its efforts to encourage irrigation through expanded opportunities for claiming land, Congress still had preconceived notions about the form that irrigated agriculture should take. "Strictly speaking, the Desert Land Act made no provision for reclamation except by individual effort, and it was on the basis of this assumption that Congress had designated 640 acre units."⁴⁷ Donald Pisani argues that "a spread of 640 acres was too much land for one farmer to irrigate but not enough for a ditch company, unless it used fraud to acquire multiple sections."[48]

Like the homestead acts, the Desert Land Act made the use of land for securing loans problematic. "As title to the land resided in the Government until final proof and it could not be made until water was actually delivered, no lien could be placed until after irrigation. Consequently, this method of raising money to build projects was eliminated."[49]

In 1891, Congress revised the Desert Land Act, but rather than lowering transaction costs, the legislation placed additional restrictions that increased those costs:

> Persons filing entries were, after 1891, required to show their plans for irrigating the land, including the canals and ditches projected and the source of water; they were required to expend $1 per acre in each of the first 3 years upon construction of irrigation works and on leveling the land; they were permitted to associate together in planning the construction but must affirm that they were not making the entries for others, corporate or individual.[50]

Moreover, the revised act repeated earlier limitations on land acquisition by foreigners and thus limited foreign investment, which had been so important in the development of the western cattle industry.[51] Hence the law that was supposed to rectify the problems created by the homestead acts did little to promote private irrigation on the great American desert.

THE POWELL SURVEYS AND RESERVOIR RESERVATIONS

John Wesley Powell was one of the most influential of the nineteenth-century explorers of the West. He led expeditions to previously unmapped regions in 1867 and 1868, and in 1869 completed a famous trip down the Green and Colorado rivers. In 1879 he issued his *Report on the Lands of the Arid Region of the United States*. In it Powell showed an understanding of the nature of feasible agriculture on the Great Plains and recommended that the homestead acts be amended to allow individuals to claim 2,560 acres. He recognized that there were vast differences in the productivity of different lands and suggested adjustments in claims based upon that productivity. Powell also had a sense of the necessity of involving settlers in decision making and early on had recommended that local initiatives should be recognized in developing irrigation.

However, Powell's ultimate faith in science and his belief that only centralized information gathering could provide adequate knowledge basically negated the role that local residual claimants would play in irrigation development. In 1888 Congress provided $100,000 to the Geological Survey headed by Powell, who believed that "he had to complete the topographical mapping, make a survey of reservoir sites, catchment basins, stream flow, canal lines, and the lands to which water could most economically and efficiently be brought, and conduct an exploratory engineering survey to determine the practicability of head works and canals."[52] Powell feared that without adequate identification of land and water characteristics, settlers would irrigate the wrong lands, and that haphazard development would occur. Powell wanted his work to serve as the master plan for irrigation and argued that development projects already installed or planned by private enterprise should be ignored. If the survey process overrode already established private rights, that was part of the cost of a well-ordered irrigation plan.[53]

Hence the Geological Survey was to specify which lands were appropriate for irrigation and for reservoir sites and was to withdraw those lands from the public-domain land that was available for homesteading. Though generating this information was an enormous labor that took many years, Powell undertook the task with great enthusiasm. Within two years of the formation of the Geological Survey, 30 million acres of arid lands capable of irrigation and 150 reservoir sites had been selected for withdrawal.[54] The Land Office cooperated by withdrawing an additional 850 million acres from the public domain as it awaited the results of Powell's classification efforts. It also directed local land offices to cancel all claims filed after October 2, 1888, on reservoir, ditch, or canal sites.[55]

In 1889 the U.S. attorney general ruled that new homestead applications for land designated as potentially irrigable would no longer be allowed and that any post-1882 homestead claims to land that was later designated irrigable would be invalid. These measures threw the whole privatization plan of the homestead acts into question and made the transaction costs of establishing rights inordinately high.

The closing of almost all the public domain to further settlement created enough of an uproar that in 1890 Congress voted to repeal the general withdrawal of irrigable lands from the public domain. It retained withdrawals of potential reservoir sites, however, making large-scale private irrigation reservoirs unlikely. This was particularly important because by this time most of the lands that could be irrigated without storage facilities had already been developed.

CESSION OF LANDS TO THE STATES

Another federal act, the Carey Act of 1894, also attempted to promote irrigation. In addition to 500,000 acres reserved by Congress in 1841 for each state admitted to the United States,[56] the Carey Act ceded one million acres to each western state that would develop irrigation on the land before the land was patented.[57] Unfortunately, the process of choosing and segregating the lands that were to be ceded to the states was very costly. "The objection to it [the law] lies in the delay and expense involved in segregating the tracts to be irrigated. Maps and plans have to be approved, first by the State and then by the Secretary of the Interior. There is in this procedure an almost endless round of red tape, involving delays and expenses, which restricts the usefulness of the Act to large projects."[58]

Seven states opted to obtain lands under the Carey Act under the condition that they would develop irrigation of the ceded lands. Of the seven states, five replicated the Desert Land Act provisions requiring actual settlement and cultivation of the land before ownership was finally granted. They also specified that if cooperative irrigation endeavors were undertaken, ownership rights in any irrigation companies had to remain in the hands of the farmers, thus precluding separate ownership of irrigation facilities.[59] The ineffectiveness of the Carey Act in promoting irrigation is evident from the fact that by 1902, only one state, Wyoming, had patented a single acre of land under the act.[60]

Redistribution Through Reclamation Act

Although private projects had brought 7.5 million acres under irrigation in seventeen western states by 1900 (see Table 10.1), citizens in the western states were turning their attention to Washington for help in developing irrigation projects. In 1891 the first National Irrigation Congress met in Salt Lake City, supported by James J. Hill, president of the Great Northern Railroad, and by many other railroads, state land commissioners, lawyers, and civil engineers.[61] Participants in the congress agreed that federal subsidies for irrigation were needed, but they debated over the appropriate mechanism for delivering such subsidies. Some argued for federal construction of large irrigation projects, while others favored cession of federal lands to the states, with the proceeds from sales of those lands going to support irrigation projects. The National Irrigation Congress met again in Los Angeles in 1893 and in Denver in 1894, generating further pressure for government involvement in irrigation.[62] By 1900, supporters of government irrigation development had generated enough political support that both the Republican and the Democrat party platforms contained planks favoring western water development by the federal government.[63] In 1901, in his State of the Union message, President Theodore Roosevelt made the case for a federal reclamation policy:

> Great storage works are necessary to equalize the flow of streams and to save the flood waters. Their construction has been conclusively shown to be an undertaking too vast for private effort, nor can it be best accomplished by the individual States acting alone. Far-reaching inter-state problems are involved; and the resources of single States would often be inadequate. It is probably a national function, at least in some of its features. . . . These irrigation works should be built by the National Government. . . . No reservoir or canal should ever be built to satisfy selfish personal or local interests; but only in accordance with the advice of trained experts, after long investigation.[64]

Roosevelt captured well the sentiment that private irrigation efforts were inadequate and that federal involvement was necessary to "make the desert bloom like a rose." In 1902 Congress passed the Reclamation Act, which provided for the planning, construction, and maintenance of dams and other irrigation works in western states. As discussed below, the evidence indicates that almost all of the federal reclamation projects subsidized individual farmers without passing a simple cost-benefit test regarding their economic viability.[65]

Under this subsidization, a relatively small number of people in the West gained at the expense of a large number living in the East. How did this redistribution of costs come about? Legislation similar to the Reclamation Act had failed in 1901 because eastern and midwestern legislators feared the redistributive aspects of the reclamation bill. But in 1902 President Roosevelt put his considerable weight behind the legislation, and those concerned about the potential redistribution secured a clause that said those receiving irrigation waters would be obligated to pay the full cost of construction of the projects.[66] All 26 representatives from the arid states voted in favor of the Reclamation Act, and support from other sections of the country sufficed to make the final vote 146 to 55 in the House of Representatives.[67]

Not all members of Congress, however, celebrated the legislation. Representative Hepburn, of Iowa, captured the essence of the opposition:

> the proposition involved in this bill is the most insolent and impudent attempt at larceny that I've ever seen embodied in a legislative proposition. These gentlemen do what? They ask us . . . to give away an empire in order that their private property may be made valuable. . . . I insist now, as I have before, that this is a thinly veneered and thinly disguised attempt to make the Government, from its general fund, pay for this great work—great in extent, great in expenditure, but not great in results. . . . Certainly there can be no return to the general government.[68]

Nonetheless, the legislation easily passed both houses of Congress, and President Roosevelt signed it into law on June 17, 1902.

The attempt to prevent redistribution by requiring full repayment of the costs of irrigation projects by recipients of the benefits failed from the start. Funding for reclamation projects was to come from the sale of public lands in sixteen western states with arid land.[69] Previously, receipts from public land sales had gone into the U.S. Treasury to pay for a variety of federal initiatives. With receipts going to reclamation, funding for other federal efforts had to come from other sources at least until the costs of reclamation projects were paid off with interest.

Not surprisingly, they were never paid off with interest. In the first place, the Reclamation Act specified payback over a ten-year period, but it was silent on the issue of interest. Hence payback was assumed to be without interest. The implicit subsidy from the no-interest loans was large, varying from 48 percent to 95 percent of the original costs.[70]

The interest subsidy was increased by the fact that Congress extended the payback period beyond the 10 years, eventually making it 20 years in 1914 and 40 years in 1926.[71] During bad times for agriculture, especially in the 1920s and 1930s, Congress also deferred payments and eventually, in 1939, allowed the Bureau of Reclamation to use an "ability to pay" plan to determine when and if repayment would occur.[72]

Congress tried to limit the extent and distribution of subsidies by limiting individuals to 160 acres that could be irrigated under the Reclamation Act. Individuals could, however, easily skirt the provision by having spouses own 160 acres, by deeding land to children, and by selling land and leasing it back. And, of course, bureau officials happily accommodated delivery to more acreage because doing so expanded the size and budget of the agency.[73]

Finally, the extent of subsidies was increased when the Army Corps of Engineers began competing with the Bureau of Reclamation to supply dams and irrigation water. The Corps of Engineers had been involved in the West for some time, facilitating navigation by clearing driftwood, dredging, and removing sunken ships from rivers and harbors. But the corps's functions in the West expanded significantly during the Great Depression as it began building dams.[74] Communities that wanted dams built for flood control and for irrigation could play the Bureau of Reclamation off against the Corps of Engineers. In several cases, irrigators actually got the two agencies to bid repeatedly for the privilege of providing the greatest subsidy and the largest expenditure.[75]

Just as settlers on the frontier chose to raid rather than trade with Indians once they had the U.S. Army behind them (see Chapter 4), farmers in the West found ample opportunity to raid other taxpayers when the federal government involved itself in water development. Because the laws were created at the state and national levels, where rule makers did not bear the full costs of their actions, there was little incentive for institutional efficiency.

Conclusion

The scarcity of water in the American West, as compared to England and the eastern United States, led to the evolution of secure and transferable property rights under the prior-appropriation doctrine. Under this doctrine, institutional entrepreneurs developed numerous organizational forms to store and deliver water to mines and agricultural fields.

Federal policies, however, limited the potential for private water development. In particular, artificial transaction costs made it more difficult for entrepreneurs to capture the economies of scale inherent in large irrigation projects and to vertically integrate to overcome free-rider and holdout problems. Withdrawal of public lands and reservoir sites from privatization further limited the potential for private water development. Given these federal restrictions, it is amazing that the private sector was able to irrigate 3 million acres by 1890.

Beginning in 1902, the federal government began to affect the allocation of western water directly, through the Reclamation Act. This act was not just a misguided effort to overcome perceived market failure but an opportunity for large-scale rent seeking by western landowners. The entry of the Corps of Engineers into western water development in the 1930s provided additional redistribution opportunities, and the centralization of water allocation through legislatures and administrative agencies further increased rent-seeking opportunities. In summary, the history of water in the West evolved from an era of creation and reorganization of water rights to an era dominated by redistribution of those rights.

ELEVEN

New Frontiers

The nineteenth-century Western frontier was a crucible for the evolution of property rights. Both Indians and whites had to create new rights to land, wildlife, minerals, water, and livestock in the face of new technologies and a physical environment that was very different from the East and from England, and had to restructure social organizations to coordinate production. For example, when the horse came to the plains, Indians stopped living in the large groups that had enabled them to capture the scale economies of hunting buffalo on foot. Instead they formed smaller groups capable of following the buffalo migrations and harvesting animals from horseback. Those who owned horses and had the skill to ride and shoot in stampeding buffalo herds rose to the top of the social hierarchy. Similarly, the organization of wagon trains was necessary to govern groups of people and equipment trying to cross the Great Plains in search of riches farther west. Because mining technology required water to be moved from streams to sluice boxes and hydraulic lines, miners hammered out the prior-appropriation doctrine to replace the older riparian doctrine carried over from water-rich England. Branding and brand registration evolved as effective means of defining ownership to livestock on the open range, and ranchers formed cattlemen's associations to manage the range before it was enclosed with barbed wire.

Studying this crucible, we have learned important lessons about how property rights evolve and what impact they have on resource stewardship and prosperity. By rewarding owners for good stewardship, property rights thwart the tragedy of the commons. Instead of leaving rents from natural resources up for grabs and thereby encouraging wasteful rent seeking, property rights promote voluntary, positive-sum exchange. Because defining and enforcing property rights is costly, people will not engage in definition and enforcement activity until it is economical to do so. Thus when land was readily available, only minimal effort was put into defining boundaries with signs declaring ownership, but as land values rose, more effort was put into recording boundaries and protecting them with fences. Where group action was called for, the tendency was to minimize wasteful rent dissipation because members of small groups had a larger stake in the efficiency of the outcome. Not surprisingly, small, privately organized irrigation districts produced more cost-effective irrigation projects than the massive ones built by the Bureau of Reclamation. Small groups also could capitalize on their more homogeneous cultures to enforce property rights and promote cooperation among group members, as evidenced by cattlemen's associations. On the other hand, when the federal government began to dictate institutional change, it fostered a tendency to dissipate resources in the process of creating property rights. The homestead acts offer the quintessential example of how people competed in a race to capture rents.

This institutional history of the West provides a very different image from that of Hollywood movies and most academic histories. These tend to depict the West as a place either of triumphant individualism or of domination by powerful capitalists. Unlike the imagined wild and woolly region where the fastest gun or the biggest landowner exploited everyone else, the real West was generally peaceful because of the stable institutional environment that was carved out by the early pioneers. To be sure, the federal government did employ its standing army to seize massive amounts of land from Indians. But when smaller groups of private individuals determined the evolution of property rights, such takings were far from the norm. Indeed the first two centuries of Indian-white relations were characterized by relatively peaceful trading, in contrast to the violence of the Indian Wars. In the mining camps and on the open range, the six-gun seldom served as the arbiter of disputes. Instead, miners established rules in camp meetings, and cattlemen used their associations to carve up the range, round up their cattle, and enforce brand registration. Though not all attempts at dispute resolution succeeded, institutional entrepreneurs found ways to define and enforce property rights that created rather than destroyed wealth. In short, the West was really not so wild.

The lessons from the American West not only are usefully applied to history but also provide insights into how property rights are evolving and will evolve on new frontiers. Though the western frontier may have closed at the end of the nineteenth century, new frontiers are continually opening. Environmental debates are essentially about property rights, about who owns the land, air, water, and wildlife, and about how property rights will or will not evolve to establish ownership to these resources. For example, the oceans have long been a commons, but as the value of their bounty rises, institutional entrepreneurs will have a choice between crafting new property rights or watching the tragedy of the commons destroy ocean resources. New technologies are continually changing the ways in which property rights are defined and enforced. Just as barbed wire made it possible to fence land, satellites make it possible to explore and monitor remote places on earth. The internet has created an electronic frontier where information can be exchanged or exploited. As the music industry discovered with the Napster case, the new technology of the Internet can weaken traditional copyrights to music. And outer space perhaps will be the ultimate frontier for centuries to come.

Let us see how the insights from the American West apply to these new frontiers.

Frontiers in the Developing World

Developing countries are much like the frontier of the American West. In many cases, indigenous people inhabit remote lands far from modern technologies and modern institutions. As we saw in the American West, customs and culture often form the basis of property rights among homogeneous indigenous societies, but as the frontier of the developed world moves toward indigenous territories, local customs and cultures are not well suited for interactions among heterogeneous people and do not allow for the exchange of property rights.

Consider the Amazonian frontier in Brazil. With little pressure on forest resources, indigenous people used customs and culture to allocate rights to those parts of the rain forest that were valuable to them. Government policies, however, have subsidized modern agriculture in the Amazon basin and subsidized transportation to move agricultural products to urban markets. By artificially increasing the rents to land, these policies have encouraged a race for property rights, rights that require settlement and land development reminiscent of homesteading in the American West.[1] The process of land allocation is highly politicized, and squatters are able to organize and expropriate private farms, thus increasing the uncertainty of land title.[2] Economists Lee Alston, Gary Libecap, and Bernardo Mueller conclude that "conflicting government and bureaucratic jurisdictions have confused the provision of definitive property rights to land" and that "inconsistencies between civil law and its protection of title, and populist constitutional law and its emphasis on land redistribution, have set the stage for violent confrontation between owners and squatters, with the accompanying dissipation of land rents."[3] As in the American West, top-down policies for establishing property rights on the Amazon frontier are promoting neither efficiency nor equity.

In many developing economies, property rights in urban areas are evolving at the local level because of artificially high transaction costs imposed by formal government entities.[4] Hernando de Soto and his colleagues calculated the cost of setting up a one-worker garment workshop in Lima, Peru. All together it took 289 days of "filling out the forms, standing in the lines, and making the bus trips into central Lima to get all the certification required to operate."[5] They estimate that in Peru generally, "15 percent of gross income from manufacturing in the extralegal sector is paid out in bribes, ranging from 'free samples' and special 'gifts' of merchandise to outright cash."[6] The lack of registered and enforceable property rights means that the poor have little incentive to improve their property and also find it difficult to use their homes and their land as equity for borrowing to start small businesses. In most cases, local, informal institutions such as the church or community organization have records of who owns what property. Insecure as these titles might be, de Soto estimates that "the total value of the real estate held but not legally owned by the poor of the Third World and former communist nations is at least $9.3 trillion." This is "nearly as much as the total value of all the companies listed on the main stock exchanges of the world's twenty most developed countries."[7]

De Soto's research on property-rights systems goes beyond Peru to detail formal and informal rules in Haiti, Egypt, and the Philippines. In all of these countries, de Soto finds that the legal system has failed to acknowledge and enforce property rights, especially for the poor. A lack of formal records limits enforcement, creates artificially high transaction costs, and raises the cost of creating new contractual forms to produce goods and services and adapt modern technology.

In addition to his research and writing on property rights, de Soto is himself an institutional entrepreneur. He is helping local people in Peru and Indonesia to formalize their local, informal systems of property rights by codifying them in much the same way that cattlemen codified brand registration. Once these rights are officially titled and enforced through the court systems, owners can make long-term investments using their property as collateral. In this regard the contrast between the developed and the developing world is dramatic. Nearly 70 percent of new businesses in the U.S. get their collateral from mortgages.[8] But with 80 percent of owners lacking formal or up-to-date land titles in the countries de Soto studied, capital secured by land mortgages is difficult to obtain.

The lack of secure property rights and the control of institutions by central governments without regard for local conditions have also been major causes of stagnation and conflict throughout Africa.[9] During the colonial period, governments established and enforced property rights that ignored indigenous institutions and hence earned the enmity of the local populations. English, French, and Belgian colonial rulers extracted wealth through the slave trade and the exportation of precious metals, nearly always violating indigenous property rights.

Even after African countries earned their independence in the 1950s and 1960s, centralized control of institutions has remained the norm. In George Ayittey's words:

True freedom never came to much of Africa after independence. Despite the rhetoric and vituperations against colonialism, very little changed in the years immediately following independence. For many countries independence meant only a change in the color of the administrators from white to black. The new leaders began to act in the same manner as the colonialists. In fact in many places they were worse than the colonialists.[10]

For instance, Nkrumah of Ghana, immediately upon coming to power, abrogated numerous constitutional rights. Likewise Julius Nyerere, upon becoming president of Tanzania, declared the country a one-party state and jailed opposition leaders. Perhaps the most notorious was Mobutu Sese Seko, who ruled Zaire from 1965 through 1997. In that time he extracted over four billion dollars for himself, most of which he sent out of the country.[11]

Well-defined and secure property rights for intellectual property are a key to economic growth in the modern world, but are seldom enforced in developing countries. By not recognizing and enforcing intellectual property rights, the governments of developing countries discourage intellectual investment in and technology transfers to their countries. For example, in 1997 in China, 96 percent of software being used was pirated, in Bulgaria 93 percent, and in El Salvador and Russia 89 percent.[12] A survey of U.S. chemical and pharmaceutical companies in 1995 revealed that, because of insecure intellectual property rights, 55 percent refused to transfer their latest and best technology to Colombia, 51 percent refused transfers to Venezuela, 49 percent to Argentina, 45 percent to Mexico, and 42 percent to Chile.[13] Estimated losses for U.S. companies due to Chinese software piracy alone was $1.4 billion in 1997. In Latin America, "the United States loses an estimated $3.45 billion annually due to inadequate enforcement of intellectual property rights in information-intensive sectors—such as pharmaceuticals, entertainment software, and motion pictures."[14] Though it is easy for governments of developing countries to dismiss losses to foreign businesses as simply a redistribution away from rich capitalists, insecure intellectual property rights are a major impediment to economic growth.

Who Owns the Environment?

The increased amenity value of natural resources—that is, their value as sources of recreation and enjoyment—affords institutional entrepreneurs an opportunity to capture amenity rents. As early as the late nineteenth century, entrepreneurs noticed these values. Railroad tycoons were always looking for ways of capturing land rents, and not just from traditional production such as crops, timber, and minerals. They were the first to recognize the amenity values of Yellowstone National Park, for example.[15] As one Northern Pacific Railroad official put it:

> We do not want to see the Falls of the Yellowstone driving the looms of a cotton factory, or the great geysers boiling pork for some gigantic packing-house, but in all the native majesty and grandeur in which they appear to-day, without, as yet, a single trace of that adornment which is desecration, that improvement which is equivalent to ruin, or that utilization which means utter destruction.[16]

Contrary to popular myth, Yellowstone, the nation's first national park, was not created because far-sighted conservationists feared that private development would destroy the area's spectacular natural wonders. Rather, it was created mainly because railroad entrepreneurs recognized the profit opportunities available from transporting tourists to the park and providing them with accommodations.[17] Knowing that its transcontinental route would pass near Yellowstone, the Northern Pacific Railroad financed many of the early expeditions to the region. Fearing that homesteaders would claim attractions such as Mammoth Hot Springs or Old Faithful and charge entrance fees to those sites that might eat into the railroad's share of potential rents, the Northern Pacific lobbied Congress to set aside the region as a national park and to give Northern Pacific or its subsidiaries monopoly control of transportation and accommodations within the park. With no competition from alternative modes of transportation to Yellowstone and with monopoly control on internal services, the Northern Pacific could effectively capture the amenity rents in the fees it charged early visitors. Because the homestead acts created artificially high transaction costs, the railroad could not obtain title to Yellowstone, but it was able to circumvent these artificial transaction costs and capture the rents through its monopoly on transportation and on services within the park.

Amenity values recognized by early railroad tycoons have risen even more since World War II, thus providing a greater return to institutional entrepreneurs who can reorganize property rights to land. Tom Bourland, a wildlife manager for International Paper (IP) in the 1980s and 1990s, is one such entrepreneur.[18] Working for one of the largest timber producers in the United States, he recognized that the relative values of timber and recreation had shifted and that creating new rights for hunting and camping would increase profits for the company. In the early 1980s Bourland became responsible for wildlife management on IP's 1.2 million acres of timber-producing land in its mid-south region. At that time little effort was put into charging for access to hunting, fishing, and camping on any IP lands. Under Bourland's leadership, the company created and marketed rights to these activities, so that by the late 1990s recreational revenues constituted 25 percent of IP's total profits for the region.

For centuries, common-law courts have adjudicated disputes over the use of resources and hence contributed to the evolution of property rights. For example, when neighboring property owners disagree about the boundary line, they may end up in a civil law suit in which the plaintiff claims that the defendant has caused harm by encroaching on the plaintiff's property. As far back as 1611, an English court ruled on *William Aldred's Case*, in which a homeowner, Mr. Aldred, claimed that odor from a neighboring hog farm was creating a harm. The court found in Aldred's favor, stating that "One should use his property in such a manner as not to injure that of another."[19]

Since then, courts have followed this logic to settle complex property-rights disputes involving various kinds of pollution. In *Carmichael v. City of Texarkana* (1899), for instance, the court found in favor of the Carmichael family, which claimed harm by the city for the sewage the city was dumping in the family's water supply. The court found that the "cesspool is a great nuisance because it fouls, pollutes, corrupts, contaminates, and poisons the water of [the creek] . . . depriving them [the Carmichaels] of the use and benefit of said creek."[20]

Though the evolution of property rights through common law has been somewhat supplanted by environmental statutes,[21] common-law courts offer a venue for settling environmental disputes, especially when new technologies make it easier to prove the cause and effect of damages. In 1982 a Rhode Island court overturned a 1934 ruling in *Wood v. Picillo*. The earlier ruling disallowed the plaintiff's claim that the defendant's dump was polluting the groundwater, because groundwater was "indefinite and obscure." In other words, the costs of defining and enforcing property rights to groundwater were so high as to make such definition and enforcement impossible. The court reversed the opinion in 1982 because "the science of groundwater hydrology as well as societal concern for environmental protection has developed dramatically. As a matter of scientific fact the course of subterranean waters is no longer obscure and mysterious."[22]

Better science and technology can improve the potential for defining and enforcing property rights to air and water and hence for reducing pollution. In an effort to determine the source of air pollution in the Grand Canyon area, a consortium of governmental agencies and utility companies used tracer analysis. It established a battery of air-monitoring stations in the area and injected deuterated methane, a gas that mimics sulfur dioxide, into the stack of the Navajo Generating Station. The experiment found that the generating facility was responsible for 70 to 80 percent of the haze caused by sulfur. After studying various methods of identifying the sources of contaminants, environmental engineer Anna Michalak concluded, "contaminant source identification can help define and enforce the property rights of all parties affected by contamination, but not without some costs."[23] Her work shows that science and technology are lowering these costs and improving the prospects for the evolution of environmental property rights.

Property rights to ocean fisheries are also evolving, in this case through establishment of individual transferable quotas (ITQs). Each quota enables the holder to catch a specific percentage of a total allowable catch, generally specified by a government agency, but preferably with input from fishers with a stake in the fishery. ITQs give quota holders certainty about their total catch and thereby avert a tragedy of the commons. Further, because they are transferable, ITQs tend to end up in the hands of the most efficient fishers. Both New Zealand and Iceland have used ITQs to manage nearly all of their fisheries, and Australia and Canada are using them more and more. Fisheries-management expert Donald Leal concludes, "Overall, ITQs have generated higher incomes for fishers and improved product quality for consumers, reduced fleet excesses, and nearly eliminated instances in which the actual harvest exceeded the total allowable catch."[24]

Battles over the use of public lands in the modern West exemplify what can happen when property rights are continually reallocated in the political arena. These battles are couched in terms of development versus conservation, but are more properly viewed as conflicts over whose demands for land use should be met. Should we have logging, grazing, mining, hiking, hunting, wildlife habitat, wilderness, or any number of other uses? Without secure and transferable property rights, one special-interest group's gain is another's loss. Not surprisingly, the conflicts grow.[25]

To see how an institution from the frontier might help, consider debates over grazing on federal lands. Environmentalists have called for cattle and sheep to be removed from federal grazing allotments or, at least, for higher fees to be charged for ranchers whose cattle graze on those allotments, but they have been largely unsuccessful. A "not so wild" solution to the conflict over land use would recognize the grazing permits as secure property rights and allow them to be traded to environmentalists who oppose grazing. Indeed one environmental group has attempted to use this strategy to retire grazing on hundreds of thousands of acres in Utah, but federal restrictions on the transfer of permits to nongrazing uses have stifled this willing buyer–willing seller solution.[26] As a result, political rent seeking and conflict continues when gains from trade and cooperation could be realized.

New Technologies

The enforcement of customary grazing rights on the frontier changed dramatically with the invention of barbed wire. Similarly, new technologies today continue to change the way property rights are defined and enforced throughout the world. For instance, geographic information systems (GIS), combined with aerial photographs and satellite imagery, are cost-reducing tools for adjudicating water rights and settling disputed claims. GIS enables users to layer several kinds of spatially referenced information in a visual map format. Computer technology has lowered the price of such mapping and has made it easier to detect violations and prove water rights claims.[27] The state of Oregon, for example, has used GIS technology to produce maps of surface rights, ground-water rights, and instream-flow rights as well as physical and natural features. This information, combined with data on diversion points, pump sites, and priority dates make it less costly to define and enforce claims.

Technology is also lowering the costs of enforcing the individual transferable quotas (ITQs) mentioned above. Global positioning satellites (GPS) can monitor the location and activity of fishing fleets, and on-vessel measuring devices, such as sealed video cameras, can record harvest data. By lowering the cost of enforcement, this technology has induced fishers with a stake in fisheries to put more effort into securing their claims.[28]

The increased use of cellular telephones has extended the question of property rights to the electromagnetic spectrum. Initially property rights were created in a political process that led to rent dissipation.[29] The Federal Communications Commission assigned spectrum licenses in hearings in which the worthiness of the applicants was determined. Applicants put much effort into attempting to appear "worthy," dissipating rents in the process. Congress replaced that process with a lottery, assigning each license randomly among the applicants. Because no limit was placed on the number of applications, however, rents were further dissipated as applicants went to the trouble of submitting multiple applications for licenses that might someday be valuable. At one point, the commission received over 400,000 applications for the potential cellular licenses.[30] Eventually an auction system was implemented, which curtailed the rent dissipation.

Conclusion

Just as the American West provides abundant examples of how property rights encouraged resource stewardship and discouraged rent dissipation, modern examples of new frontiers suggest that institutional entrepreneurs still hold the key to cooperation and prosperity. In developing countries, in common-law courts, and through some governmental programs, property rights are evolving to resolve conflicts over resource use.

But property rights do not always evolve peacefully and productively, as the Indian Wars demonstrated. Though less bloody, the homestead acts and the expensive water projects under the Reclamation Act of 1902 encouraged a competition for property rights that wasted resources. Today rent dissipation continues as governments try to dole out property rights or, worse yet, continually reallocate them through the political process. A quintessential example is the battle among irrigators, environmentalists, and Indian tribes for the water of the Klamath River in Oregon. In 2001, with extreme water shortages in the Klamath, property rights to water were continually reallocated through government fiat.[31]

New frontiers will continue to arise, and we will continue to face important choices about institutional design. Today Mars is much like the West that Lewis and Clark explored. Just as many people in the early nineteenth century found it inconceivable that the upper reaches of the Missouri River would ever be settled and developed, most people today cannot imagine economically viable development of Mars. But undoubtedly Mars and other planets will become the frontiers of the twenty-first century, as technology improves and resource values change. As that happens, we can speculate how property rights will evolve. On September 11, 2002, Reuters News Service quoted a leading British astronomer who said, "Mars could resemble the lawless Wild West if privately funded adventurers seeking to exploit the planet get there before governments." Our history of the American West suggests a much more positive prediction about what might evolve in the "lawless" vacuum of outer space. Indeed if governments get there before "privately funded adventurers," the value of the new frontier may be dissipated through conflict rather than conserved through cooperation.

The western frontier had its heroes in the institutional entrepreneurs who hammered out the property rights to land, water, livestock, minerals, and even national parks. New frontiers will have their entrepreneurial heroes as well. The lesson we should learn from the "not so wild, wild West" is that secure and transferable property rights may not be easy to develop, but they are a necessity for supplanting conflict with cooperation. Whether we are contemplating traditional resource use in the developing world, environmental issues in the developed world, or a space race, we have a choice between wild and not so wild.

Notes

CHAPTER I

1. Turner 1894, 199.
2. Dippie 1991, 114.
3. For a more complete discussion of Turner's view of the role of violence in the West and its relationship to other settings, see Faragher 1994, 230–32.
4. For a summary of the various aspects of the new approach, see Limerick, Milner, and Rankin 1991.
5. See Limerick 1991 and Robbins 1991, 191.
6. Limerick 1987, 26.
7. For a useful summary of the new institutional economics, see Eggertsson 1990 and Furubotn and Richter 1997.
8. Hardin 1968.
9. See Gwartney and Lawson 2002 and O'Driscoll, Holmes, and O'Grady 2002.
10. Norton 1998, 44.
11. De Soto 2000, 148–49.

CHAPTER 2

1. Tocqueville 1835.
2. This definition is an economic one and differs from the traditional understanding of the frontier as the place where settlement is starting to occur (Turner 1894). Under our definition, the frontier occurs when the value of the land turns positive. In our conception, substantial settlement can occur before the value is positive—in other words, on land beyond what is defined as the frontier. Whether this happens will depend on the institutions that govern how property rights to land are determined. As discussed later, inappropriate rules for establishing ownership can encourage premature settlement.
3. Whether the value is spiritual or productive is not particularly important for our analysis.

4. While recognizing that the species is technically bison, we use the term "buffalo jump" since it is the common designation for the cliffs over which the bison were stampeded to their deaths.

5. For complete discussion of how rents can be dissipated in the formation of property rights, see T. Anderson and Hill 1983.

6. For a complete discussion, see T. Anderson and Hill 1990.

7. For a complete discussion of the frontier between Indians and non-Indians, see T. Anderson and McChesney 1994.

8. For a thorough discussion of transaction costs, see Eggertsson 1990, 15.

9. For an interesting discussion of the evolution of moral constraints, see Ridley 1997 and Ellickson 2001.

10. Novak Kapor, discussed above in Chapter 1, was an active member in his Serbian Lodge, an organization that bound together fellow Serbs with a pledge to help one another.

11. The reduction of enforcement costs will be discussed more thoroughly below in this chapter.

12. See T. Anderson and Snyder 1995.

13. See Schumpeter 1934, 66.

14. Williamson 1985.

15. See Wellman 1967 [1939], 111.

16. See Skaggs 1973, 123.

17. For a more complete discussion of the evolution of property rights, see T. Anderson and Hill 1975.

18. Baumol 1990, 894.

19. In this context, the term "institutional entrepreneur" is intended to encompass a wide variety of actors who alter the rules governing property rights. So, for example, a bureaucrat or politician engaged in institutional change is as much an entrepreneur as a member of the private sector who uses contractual innovations to create or partition rights. Thus the use of the term "institutional entrepreneur" in and of itself carries no evaluative content; the institutions created by such an entrepreneur can either improve or worsen resource allocation and encourage or discourage social cooperation.

20. Rent seekers can use government both to secure transfers of property rights and to restrict competition for profits. For example, taxi services are not unique, but entry into the taxi business is often restricted governmentally so that profits may be earned only by a limited field of operators. The profits are the result not of unique ideas, products, or resources but of restrictions on competition enforced by governmental regulations.

21. See Rucker and Fishback 1983.

22. For an excellent discussion of this, see Libecap 1981.

23. See McChesney 1997.

24. See Kirzner 1973 for the best discussion of entrepreneurship.

25. T. Anderson 1995, 57; see also Holder 1970, chap. 3.

26. See T. Anderson 1995, 55–58.

27. Denig 1930, 533; Henry and Thompson 1965, 520.

28. See T. Anderson 1995, 58–64.

29. For details of the tradeoffs, see Haddock 1997.

30. Production methods depend heavily on existing technology. Therefore the geographic size is influenced by technology.

31. For a discussion of the potential impact of the tragedy of the commons caused by the interface between tribal and buffalo territories, see Martin and Szuter 1999. Also, see Lueck 1989 for a discussion of how the optimal size of production units affects transaction costs.

32. See Ellickson 1993 for an excellent discussion of the influence of the optimal size of the collective.

33. The use of force against one another within the collective is necessary to prevent what economists call the free-rider problem, as discussed above in this chapter.

34. For a formal rendition of this argument applied to mining camps, see Umbeck 1981.

35. See T. Anderson and McChesney 1994, 68–71.

36. In technical terms this would mean that the discounted value of the negative rents prior to t^* would just equal the discounted positive rents after t^*. For a formal discussion of this possibility, see T. Anderson and Hill 1990.

37. For a more complete discussion of the role that norms can play in the definition and enforcement of property rights, see Ellickson 1991.

38. The costs of adjudicated disputes are also likely to be lower in a culturally homogeneous group. Norms specify right and wrong and provide low-cost ways of resolving disputes. And as individuals within a group confront conflicts over property rights, tradition becomes a way of economizing on adjudication costs. Hence the common law evolves by categorizing similarities between different conflicts and using those similarities to create property and liability rules.

39. See Libecap 1989, 20–21, for additional discussion of the distributional consequences of group homogeneity.

CHAPTER 3

1. See chaps. 3 and 4 in T. Anderson 1995.

2. For a complete account of the Chief Seattle myth, see Wilson 1992.

3. Wilson 1992, 1457.

4. Timmons 1980, ix.

5. Farb 1968, 6.

6. Bailey 1992, 183.

7. Huffman 1992, 907.
8. Goldsmidt 1951, 511.
9. Hoebel 1954, 294.
10. Posner 1980, 53.
11. Copper 1949, 1.
12. Steward 1938, 253. As we shall see in the next chapter, Indian societies lacked property rights to natural resources because natural resources in their "raw" state were not scarce. Because resources were abundant, defining property rights to them was not worth the effort. Eagle nests were an exception probably because they were scarce and therefore demanded husbanding.
13. Ibid.
14. Ellis 1979, 355.
15. Kennard 1979, 554.
16. Forde 1931, 367.
17. Ibid., 369. Forde's article provides an extensive discussion of Hopi agriculture and land ownership.
18. Ibid., 399.
19. See Kennard 1979, 554–57, and Forde 1931 for details.
20. Fowler 1986, 65.
21. Steward 1941, 240.
22. Ibid., 254.
23. Steward 1934, 252.
24. Steward 1938, 258.
25. Lowie 1940, 303.
26. Ibid.
27. Reported in Steward 1934, 305. For a more complete discussion of property rights to piñon trees, see Lowie 1940.
28. Steward 1934, 253.
29. See Demsetz 1967.
30. Basso 1970, 5.
31. Langdon 1989, 306.
32. For a more complete discussion, see Higgs 1982.
33. Netboy 1958, 11.
34. Higgs 1982, 59.
35. See Oberg 1973 and De Laguna 1972.
36. De Laguna 1972, 464.
37. See Olson 1967.
38. Higgs 1982, 59.
39. *United States v. Washington*, 384 F. Supp. 312, 352–53 (1974).
40. Speck 1939, 258–59.
41. Ibid., 259. This principle is similar to the Lockean proviso. The ironic point,

however, is that when Locke first propounded his theory, he conspicuously ignored its application to Indian culture, proclaiming that America was in a state of nature before the white man arrived, just waiting for him to come and homestead it, to claim his share. See Chase 1986, 110–11.

42. Freed 1960, 351.

43. Fowler 1986, 82. Though no anthropological evidence seems to be available to explain why organizers, leaders, or net owners might have received a larger share, it is likely that the differential reflected the greater contribution that these people made to the hunt. This suggests that Indians were not necessarily egalitarian and that rewards for effort were based on the value of the person's contribution.

44. Bailey 1992, 187. Since the last point is more applicable in Africa, where predatory animals, especially large cats, are more likely to take the product of the hunt, it will be ignored here.

45. This point dovetails with Posner's (1980) theory of information cost as it applies to primitive societies.

46. Bailey 1992, 188.

47. In the context of this discussion, the firm can be thought of as a communal institution, though the residual claimant is generally clearer than in more traditional communal institutions. For a discussion of the firm in this context see Alchian and Demsetz 1972.

48. Barsness 1985, 53.

49. Sass 1936, 5.

50. Ewers 1969, 303.

51. The pedestrian stalk also avoided some of the coordination costs of the communal hunt, in that the smaller number of people involved in the stalk were less likely than a larger communal hunting group to scare off the buffalo herd. If the pedestrian stalk involved too many hunters, they would be likely to scare the herd before any were killed.

52. See Arthur 1975, 64, and Hornaday 1889, 423.

53. See Simpson 1843, 404, and Denig 1961, 160.

54. See Barsness 1985, 45–46.

55. See Reher and Frison 1980, 8.

56. Barsness 1985, 44.

57. Ibid., 37.

58. See Schaeffer 1978, 247, and Henry and Thompson 1965, 725.

59. Carter 1990, 27.

60. Grinnell 1962, 234.

61. The literature generally does not differentiate the community size for Plains Indians from that for other North American groups. John White (1979, 76) gives the inclusive figure of 100–300 persons. But earlier he writes: "The most comfortable size of a band was usually felt to be about 100–150 persons, but it was often much

smaller. When it began to swell in size, and approached the 200 mark, the problem of feeding it became serious, and the usual solution was fission" (J. White 1979, 55). Wissler (1966, 261) writes: "An Indian community rarely consisted of more than a hundred persons of all ages."

62. These congregations were not always for hunting. The Shoshoni organized in composite bands only to deter Blackfoot aggression. When Blackfoot power waned by 1850, the seasonal congregations ended (Madsen 1980, 24–25).

63. See Wissler 1966, 261.

64. See Roe 1955, 191.

65. Wyman 1945, 70.

66. Steckel and Prince (2001) report that nineteenth-century Plains Indians were possibly the tallest people in the world. The high protein content of their buffalo-dominated diet was a major contributor to their nutritional status.

67. Ewers 1969, 168–69. Also see Baden, Stroup, and Thurman 1981 for a discussion of Indian responses to relative prices.

68. Faegre 1979, 152.

69. Barsness 1985, 50.

70. See J. White 1979, 71–72, and Wissler 1966, 289.

71. See Barsness 1985, 50.

72. Lavender 1992, 22.

73. Ewers 1969, 304.

74. Ibid., 305.

75. Lowie 1982, 42.

76. See Maximilian 1902, 351, and Farnham 1843, 82.

77. Carter 1990, 27.

78. Wyman 1945, 74.

79. Carter 1990, 35.

80. Shimkin 1986, 309.

81. Ewers 1969, 172.

82. Ibid., 175.

83. Barsness 1985, 53.

84. Steward 1938, 248–49. It should be noted that these warfare institutions evolved out of necessity and hence disappeared when the Indians were subjugated by the whites. "The office and its duties, having no precedence in native institution and concerning principally warfare negotiations with the white man, were limited in scope and duration. They survived too briefly to have won general respect and support. When the wars ceased the need for organization largely vanished and the chiefs lost authority" (ibid., 249).

85. Schultz 1907, 152.

86. Ewers 1969, 22.

CHAPTER 4

1. See T. Anderson and McChesney 1994.

2. For a more rigorous and complete discussion of the analysis that follows, see T. Anderson and McChesney 1994.

3. Of course, we realize that there was not a single collective unit of Indians that controlled the land between the coasts. Indeed, the same analysis can be used to think about zones of conflict between various groups of Indians.

4. Hughes 1976, 35.

5. Russell 1973, 42.

6. Roosevelt 1889, 90.

7. Quoted in Prucha 1962, 139.

8. Kickingbird and Ducheneaus 1973, 7.

9. Quoted in Washburn 1971, 56.

10. Jefferson, quoted in Washburn 1971, 39.

11. Jefferson 1955 [1787], 96.

12. Roback 1992, 11.

13. Washburn 1971, 49.

14. Utley 1984, xx.

15. Quoted in Prucha 1962, 139.

16. Ibid., 143.

17. Ibid., 145.

18. Cohen 1947, 32.

19. Debo 1970, 16.

20. Quoted in Utley 1984, 61.

21. Ibid., 11.

22. Roback 1992, 5.

23. Utley 1984, 7–8.

24. Ibid., 44.

25. The 1862 Sioux uprising in Minnesota began when a group of Indian youths murdered five whites. "The deed had not been planned. One had dared another to prove his courage" (Utley 1984, 78). The Washita massacre occurred because Black Kettle, a Cheyenne chief who persistently argued for peace with whites, "had a hard time keeping his young men under control" (ibid., 125). When a group of braves slipped away to raid white settlements, their trail in the snow led back to Black Kettle's village. Cavalry under General Custer followed the trail, stormed the village, and killed over one hundred Cheyenne, including Black Kettle.

26. Quoted in Prucha 1962, 156.

27. Webb 1971, 169.

28. Quoted in Debo 1970, 221.

29. Utley 1967, 7.

30. Axtell 1988, 140.

31. Utley 1984, 105.

32. For a discussion of Custer's faulty information regarding Indian strength, see Connell 1988, 263–264.

33. Chapel 1961, 259.

34. Quoted in Webb 1971, 174.

35. Ibid., 175.

36. Beers 1975, 173.

37. Utley 1967, 2–3.

38. Ibid., 110–11.

39. Quoted in Debo 1970, 215.

40. Russell 1973, 47.

41. For further discussion, see Utley 1967, 14–17.

42. The test might seem subject to the criticism that while the army was away fighting, Indians took advantage of this absence to increase attacks on whites, with the army ultimately returning to subdue the tribes. However, the number of troops in the West actually increased during the Civil War.

43. For a detailed discussion of this regression analysis, see T. Anderson and McChesney 1994.

44. Carlson 1992, 74.

45. Hurt 1987, 230.

46. Ibid., 75.

47. Quoted in Otis 1973, 10–11.

48. Bethell 1998 or Pipes 1999.

49. De Soto 2000.

50. Carlson 1981, 10, comments: "The cession of surplus lands to the government was to be approved by the tribe, although in practice the government had a strong position in such negotiations. The role of the tribes was reduced further in 1903, when the courts held that tribal approval was not necessary for the disposal of surplus lands. The proceeds from the land sales were held in trust for the tribe."

51. Ibid., 18.

52. Ibid., 44.

53. Ibid., 174.

54. Ibid., 43.

55. Ibid.

56. Ibid., 44.

57. Prucha 1984, 716.

58. Ibid., 671.

59. McChesney 1992, 114–15.

60. Niskanen 1971 argued that budget maximization by bureaucracies makes them self-perpetuating, and more recent literature has contended that staff size, salaries, and power may all be a part of what bureaucrats maximize. See Johnson and

Libecap 1994 for an excellent summary of competing theories of bureaucratic growth.

61. Quoted in McChesney 1992, 127.

62. Prucha 1984, 864.

63. Schemeckebier 1927, 81.

64. McChesney 1992, 125, 127.

65. Ibid., 123.

66. Ibid., 135.

67. The theory and data in this section come mainly from T. Anderson and Lueck 1992.

68. Libecap and Johnson 1980, 83.

69. This point was first made by Trosper (1978).

70. Given the mean of 0.54 and the standard deviation of 0.495, the hypothesis that trust land and private land are equally productive can be rejected with 99 percent confidence.

71. T. Anderson and Lueck 1992.

72. For details of this regression analysis, see T. Anderson and Lueck 1992, 446–48.

CHAPTER 5

1. See Lueck 1995.

2. See Martin and Szuter 1999.

3. Higgs 1982.

4. "Furs" here refers to pelts from many species of small animals, such as foxes, minks, badgers, and so on, but beavers were the main source. "Robes" refers to buffalo hides with the hair on; "hides" refers simply to the leather from buffalo or deer, whether raw or tanned.

5. Wishart 1979, 212.

6. The records of various trading posts and forts from the 1820s and 1830s record sales of the pelts of foxes, prairie dogs, bears, muskrats, otters, wolves, badgers, hares, minks, and martins, as well as beavers (Wishart 1979, 58–59). Chittenden (1954, 2: 826) lists fox, otter, mink, raccoon, squirrel, polecat, and muskrat pelts as a regular part of the fur trade with St. Louis.

7. Utley 1997, 11–12.

8. Wishart 1979, 45.

9. Maguire, Wild, and Barclay 1997, 2–3.

10. See Wishart 1979, 161, and Sunder 1965, 11–12.

11. Wishart 1979, 166.

12. Wishart estimates that "the movement of furs and letters from St. Louis to New York took about four weeks, and the round-trip passage between New York and Liverpool averaged 56.2 days in 1839" (ibid., 79).

13. The first steamboat to make it to Fort Union (where the Yellowstone River joins the Missouri River) was in 1832. After that the steamboat was a regular and important component of the fur trade, hauling supplies upriver and returning to St. Louis with furs and robes.

14. Utley 1997, 45.

15. Ibid.

16. Quoted in ibid., 64.

17. Sandoz 1964, 233–34.

18. Ibid., 234–35.

19. Ibid., 235.

20. For a discussion of the effectiveness of the Hudson's Bay Company at overcoming the tragedy of the commons, see Carlos and Lewis 1995.

21. See Utley 1997, 135.

22. Ibid., 135.

23. Ibid.

24. Wishart 1979, 64.

25. See ibid., 100–102.

26. Quoted in Utley 1997, 64, italics in original.

27. T. Anderson and McChesney 1994.

28. Ashley's party was attacked by the Arikaras on the upper Missouri. With support from 230 infantrymen and 750 Sioux led by Colonel Leavenworth, the Arikara offensive was subdued.

29. Utley 1997, 65.

30. See Martin and Szuter 1999.

31. Sandoz 1964, 242.

32. For an excellent account of the efforts to establish forts at the Three Forks, see Sandoz 1964, chap. 4.

33. Wishart 1979, 29 and 45.

34. Ibid., 46.

35. Ibid., 119.

36. Ibid., 50.

37. Ibid., 79.

38. See ibid., 81.

39. See Wimmer 2001.

40. Wishart 1979, 82.

41. Utley 1997, 86.

42. See Wishart 1979, 125, and Utley 1997, 87–88.

43. Beck and Haase 1989, 26.

44. Wishart 1979, 194.

45. South Pass, a wide depression to the south of the Wind River Mountains, afforded important and easy access to the trapping grounds farther west. Robert Stuart crossed it in 1812, becoming probably the first white American to use the pass,

but it became a part of the regular route through the Rockies only after Smith's re-discovery in 1824.

46. Wishart 1979, 195.

47. Gowans 1985, 106.

48. See Maguire, Wild, and Barclay 1997, 165–91, and Gowans 1985.

49. Chittenden 1954, 1: 68.

50. Morgan 1953, 307.

51. Quoted in Utley 1997, 175.

52. Quoted in Wishart 1979, 65.

53. Ibid., 143 and 161.

54. Quoted in Maguire, Wild, and Barclay 1997, 194–95.

55. Utley 1997, xiv.

56. Wishart 1979, 142.

57. Sunder 1965, 10.

58. Wishart 1979, 149.

59. Quoted in ibid., 150.

60. Quoted in ibid., 32.

61. Carlos and Lewis 1993 and 1995.

62. Sandoz 1964, 272.

63. Quoted in D. White 1996, 1: 296.

64. Quoted in Utley 1997, 97.

65. See ibid., 71.

66. Weber 1971, 206–7.

67. See Utley 1997, 109.

68. Wishart 1979, 54.

69. Ibid., 71.

70. Sandoz 1964, 273.

71. See, for example, Burt and Cummings 1970.

72. The prices presented in Table 5.1 are for all furs. No consistent series exists for beaver prices, but there are scattered observations, all of which indicate that the price drop in Table 5.1 understates the actual fall in prices of beaver pelts (Wishart 1979, 125, 140–41, 161; Burger 1968, 168).

73. Quoted in Wishart 1979, 66.

74. Flores (1991) uses the 1910 agriculture census of cattle on the Great Plains to arrive at his estimate of twenty-eight to thirty million. Earlier estimates based on contemporary estimates of the great herds put the number much higher—between sixty and a hundred million. See Roe 1970 and Hornaday 1889.

75. Isenberg 2000, 163.

76. Ibid., 197–98.

77. See Hornaday 1889, 441–42, and Hanner 1981, 246. Some have argued that during this time the Indians did not overexploit the buffalo and that extermination occurred only when the white hunters entered the market. Frank Roe (1970) has

been the leading exponent of that position. For a similar argument, see Branch 1929. For a more general argument about the Indians' harmony with nature, see Barreiro 1988, vii–xi. More recent work holds that once Indians had the horse and rifle, the buffalo was doomed (see Flores 1991 and Isenberg 2000, 94).

78. Sunder 1965, 17.

79. Rister 1929, 44.

80. Hornaday 1889, 499.

81. Hanner 1981, 239.

82. Hornaday 1889, 512.

83. Ibid., 509.

84. Isenberg 2000, 157.

85. See Smits 1994.

86. Ibid., 332.

87. Hanner 1981, 269.

88. Geist 1996, 96.

89. See Diamond 1999 for a discussion of the importance of domesticated large mammals for economic development.

90. Roe 1970, 712–13.

91. Seton 1927, 671.

92. Hanner 1981, 247.

93. Bison and cattle hides were evidently good substitutes for one another (Hanner 1981, 253–54). And since the number of cattle hides used by tanners far exceeded the number of buffalo hides, when the buffalo hide harvest decreased dramatically in 1884 the impact on hide prices was not significant (ibid., 253, Table 1).

94. Hanner (1981, 253) reports that buffalo-hide prices in the north ranged between $2.85 and $3.34 from 1880 through 1884, with the average at $3.07. The U.S. Department of Agriculture collected statistics on the farm values of livestock per head in the latter part of the nineteenth century, and according to these data, cattle in Montana in 1883, the earliest date reported, were worth $25.10 (U.S. Department of Agriculture 1927). Indices of national cattle prices from 1880 through 1884 (Strauss and Bean 1940, 110) indicate that cattle prices varied considerably during this time, with the lowest price at 82 percent of the 1883 price. Eighty-two percent of $25.10 is $20.58.

95. Isenberg 2000, 141.

96. Hanner 1981, 261.

97. Isenberg 2000, 182.

98. Ibid., 189.

CHAPTER 6

1. McGrath 1984, 247.

2. Gates 1968, 701.

3. Ibid., 702.

4. Shinn 1948, 50.

5. Umbeck 1981, 69.

6. Gates 1991, 251.

7. Davis 1902, 11.

8. Shinn 1948, 168.

9. Robinson 1948, 134.

10. Paul 1947, 25.

11. Ibid., 43.

12. Quoted in Zerbe and Anderson 2001, 114.

13. Quoted in ibid., 115.

14. For a discussion of the calculus for the decision to battle over property rights or settle disputes peacefully, see T. Anderson and McChesney 1994. Their analysis parallels that used by Umbeck (1981) to explain why miners generally chose peaceful settlement of property rights disputes.

15. For an excellent survey of this literature, see Cooter and Rubinfeld 1989.

16. Umbeck 1981.

17. Umbeck 1977, 430.

18. Zerbe and Anderson 2001, 115–16.

19. See Lueck 2003.

20. Umbeck 1981, 88.

21. Paul 1947, 198.

22. Robinson 1948, 138–39; Umbeck 1981, 92–98.

23. See Umbeck 1981, 94.

24. Quoted in Davis 1902, 20.

25. Umbeck 1981.

26. Ibid., 108–9.

27. Davis 1902, 22.

28. Umbeck 1981, 123–25.

29. Rohrbough 1997, 89.

30. Shinn 1948, 168–69.

31. Paul 1947, 203; Davis 1902, 31.

32. Shinn 1948, 105.

33. Paul 1947, 224.

34. Rohrbough 1997, 203.

35. Paul 1947, 164.

36. Ibid., 127.

37. Umbeck 1981, 89.

38. Davis 1902, 33.

39. Leshy 1987, 18; *Sparrow v. Strong*, 70 U.S. (3 Wall.) 97, 104 (1865).

40. Gates 1968, 720.

41. Leshy 1987, 26–27.

42. See Royce 1886, 366–67; Caughey 1948, 194; Shinn 1948, 234.

43. Quoted in Paul 1947, 108–9.

44. Choy 1971, 270.

45. Though the Foreign Miners' Tax was eventually lowered to $3 per month and was selectively enforced, mainly against Chinese miners, it still provided 20 percent of state receipts from 1853 through 1859 (Clay and Wright 1998, 21).

46. Shinn 1948, 164.

47. Zerbe and Anderson 2001, 115.

48. Libecap 1978, 342.

49. Gates 1968, 711.

50. Libecap 1978, 339.

51. Preemption Acts, which were usually specific to a state or territory, gave first rights to purchase the land to people who settled a region before it was officially opened.

52. Leshy 1987, 10.

53. Libecap 1978, 343.

54. Leshy 1987, 170.

55. Davis 1902, 14.

56. Libecap 1978, 345–46.

57. Libecap 1989, 41.

58. Libecap 1978, 346.

59. Leshy 1987, 21.

60. Libecap 1978, 347.

61. Ibid., 361, 356.

62. In 1870, the value of gold and silver production was ten times that of agricultural production (Libecap 1978, 33). Hence most state legislators had an interest in creating efficient institutions for governing mining.

CHAPTER 7

1. Unruh 1979, 403.

2. As discussed above in Chapter 5, throughout the 1820s and 1830s, annual rendezvous in the Rockies brought trackers together to trade furs for supplies. Entrepreneurs carrying trade goods to the rendezvous sites established what became the first part of the Oregon and California trail.

3. See Reid 1997a, 1.

4. See Unruh 1979, 408–9.

5. Reid 1997a, 157.

6. Quoted in Hansen 1937, 1.

7. Ibid., Appendix.

8. See Reid 1997a, 128–36.

9. See Hansen 1937, 20.

10. See ibid., 30.

11. Reid 1997a, 131.

12. Quoted in ibid.

13. Ibid., 133–34.

14. See ibid., 128, and Unruh 1979, 97.

15. Quoted in Reid 1997a, 287.

16. Unruh 1979, 106.

17. Reid 1997a, 84.

18. Hansen 1937, 105–6.

19. See Reid 1997b, 91, 94, 96.

20. Quoted in Reid 1997b, 104.

21. Ibid., 157.

22. Reid 1997a, 171.

23. Buchanan and Tullock 1962, 68–72.

24. Reid 1997b, 103.

25. Hansen 1937, 123.

26. Reid 1997a, 174–75.

27. Ibid., 186.

28. Ibid., 200.

29. Unruh 1979, 120.

30. See Lamar 1998, 738.

31. Stegner 1981 [1964], 174.

32. See Reid 1997a, 29, 177, 188, 18, and Unruh 1979, 105, 139.

33. Quoted in Reid 1997b, 19–20.

34. Unruh 1979, 156–57.

35. Reid 1997a, 329.

36. Unruh 1979, 244.

37. Quoted in ibid., 245.

38. Ibid., 247.

39. Ibid., 110.

40. Reid 1997a, 117.

41. See ibid., 116–17, and Unruh 1979, 110–11.

42. Unruh 1979, 111.

43. Reid 1997a, 324.

44. Unruh 1979, 347.

45. Ibid., 260, 281.

46. Ibid., 303.

47. Reid 1997a, 213.

CHAPTER 8

1. Jordan 1993, 222.
2. Osgood 1929, 33, 32.
3. Quoted in ibid.
4. Wellman 1967 [1939], 114.
5. McCoy 1932 [1874], 56.
6. Quoted in Osgood 1929, 33.
7. Wellman 1967 [1939], 113.
8. See Barzel 1984.
9. Wellman 1967 [1939], 130; McCoy 1932 [1874], 78–79; Dale 1960, 33; Skaggs 1973, 30.
10. Wellman 1967 [1939], 96–97.
11. Ibid., 100.
12. Skaggs 1973, 10.
13. Ibid., 54.
14. Ibid., 123.
15. Ibid., 53.
16. Wellman 1967 [1939], 111.
17. Ibid.
18. Brayer and Brayer 1952, 89.
19. Dale 1960, 51.
20. The fever was only a temporary phenomenon, caused by the arrival of cattle in a region. Once the cattle wintered there, the ticks they brought in were killed by freezing weather and no longer represented a danger.
21. Reported in Skaggs 1973, 106.
22. McCoy 1932 [1874], 44.
23. Wellman 1967 [1939], 133.
24. McCoy 1932 [1874], 115.
25. Wellman 1967 [1939], 139.
26. Dykstra 1968, 83.
27. McCoy 1932 [1874], 73.
28. Dykstra 1968, 79.
29. McCoy 1932 [1874], 64–65.
30. Quoted in ibid., 65.
31. Osgood 1929, 37.
32. McCoy 1932 [1874], 125.
33. Dykstra 1968, 155.
34. Dykstra says that it is not clear "whether this was a bond filed with the state in compliance with the 1867 quarantine law, or only a local voluntary measure" (ibid., 154).
35. Ibid.

36. Skaggs 1973, 107.

37. See ibid., 96, and Osgood 1929, 162-64. During this period the federal government also sought to control another health problem, pleuro-pneumonia. In the 1880s Britain threatened to embargo U.S. cattle because of the perceived threat from the disease. As a result, the federal Bureau of Animal Industry was created in 1884 to regulate the movement of diseased cattle (Osgood 1929, 172).

38. See above, hypotheses 6 and 7, Chapter 2.

39. Osgood 1929, 170.

40. Ibid.; Meiners and Morriss 2003, 24.

41. Cheney 1990, 1-7.

42. See Osgood 1929, 125-26.

43. Ibid., 137.

44. Ibid., 151-52.

45. Fletcher 1960, 142.

46. Stuart 1967 [1925], 2: 166.

47. Osgood 1929, 136.

48. Stuart 1967 [1925], 2: 196. Although Stuart argued for a severe penalty, he also opposed efforts to raise an army and attack the rustlers. He thought such action foolhardy and likely to lead to much bloodshed. However, he later supported the actions of Montana Stockgrowers described below when they organized a more discrete group of "detectives" who sought out and killed several of the cattle thieves.

49. Quoted in Fletcher 1960, 59.

50. Stuart 1967 [1925], 2: 209.

51. H. Smith 1966, 224.

52. Osgood 1929, 28.

53. Fulton 1982, 112 and 135.

54. The author is referring to the continual gathering and working of cattle that interrupted their grazing so much and kept them so physically active that they lost weight.

55. Quoted in Osgood 1929, 120.

56. Abbott and Smith 1939, 86.

57. Fletcher 1960, 75-78.

58. Quoted in Brown and Felton 1956, 173.

59. Meiners and Morriss 2003. The control of glanders was not an entirely private operation since the state compensated ranchers for infected horses that were destroyed.

60. Osgood 1929, 140.

61. The work of a roundup fell into a clear hierarchy of tasks, and this was used to provide incentives for appropriate skills. Cheney (1990, 19) reports that ropers had to call out the appropriate brand for a calf when it was pulled to the fire. If a calf got up and followed a cow of a different brand, meaning the roper had wrongly identified it, he was assigned to the least desirable job, namely, holding the herd.

62. Cheney 1990, 31.

63. Ibid., 79; Fletcher 1960, 54.

64. Gressley 1966.

65. Ibid., 37, 71.

66. Ibid., 109.

67. Ibid., 137–39. For a period of time, the cattlemen's associations instituted a similar rule for hired hands, prohibiting them from owning cattle. The associations believed that this stricture would reduce the incentives for rustling. However, several ranchers protested that this rule discriminated against cowhands who were enterprising enough to try to save their wages and start a herd of their own. Consequently, the rule was short-lived (Osgood 1929, 148).

68. In 1880, only 56,000 acres of Montana land were planted with hay, but by 1900, the figure had increased to 712,000 acres (Fletcher 1960, 111).

69. Quoted in Fletcher 1960, 115.

70. Gressley 1966, 111.

71. Fletcher 1960, 139.

CHAPTER 9

1. See Shambaugh 1900.

2. Bogue 1963, 51.

3. After the homestead acts were passed, land-claims clubs ceased to be a viable option for establishing property rights to land since their function had been to establish prior claims under a system of purchase.

4. Osgood 1929, 182–83.

5. Stuart 1967 [1925], 2: 185–88.

6. Osgood 1929, 105.

7. Ibid., 183.

8. In 1910 a sheriff from Belle Fourche, South Dakota, was called upon to adjudicate a dispute between sheep herders and cattle ranchers on the open range. He decided that the cattlemen had been there first and that the sheep would therefore have to leave (Rumph 1993, 7).

9. Quoted in Osgood 1929, 183.

10. See Wellman 1967 [1939], 229.

11. See Stuart 1967 [1925], 2: 146–49, and Roosevelt 1968, 29–30.

12. Osgood 1929, 115.

13. Malone and Roeder 1976, 124.

14. Brands 1997, 186.

15. Ibid., 183.

16. Quoted in Dennen 1976, 426–27.

17. Quoted ibid., 427.

18. Ibid., 434.

19. Osgood 1929, 189, 230.

20. See Thaden 1989, 5.

21. Fulton 1982, 42–43.

22. Osgood 1929, 189.

23. McCallum and McCallum 1965, 27.

24. Ibid., 111.

25. Ibid., 124–27.

26. Libecap 1981, 23.

27. For a history of the land-disposal controversies, see Gates 1968 and G. Anderson and Martin 1987.

28. See Kanazawa 1996c.

29. See Gates 1968, 395.

30. Quoted in McCallum and McCallum 1965, 177–78.

31. Gates 1968, 468.

32. See Libecap 1981, 33–34.

33. The original Homestead Act required that the land be plowed in order for full title be granted. Later acts required irrigation or tree planting. Even when the maximum size was increased to 320 acres in the 1909 act and to 640 acres in 1916, the laws did not recognize that much of the land was suitable only for grazing, not farming. The allowed acreage never reached the size of a viable unit. On much of the Great Plains, 20 to 30 acres is required to sustain one cow for one year. Thus even under the Stock Raising Homestead Act of 1916, a homestead could support only 20 to 30 cows, far below the number required for the survival of a ranch.

34. In the context of our definition of the frontier, the present value turns positive before the annual rent from the land turns positive. Therefore the land would be purchased before it would be put into production.

35. This value is determined by computing the discounted value of the negative rents incurred when the land is settled prior to t^* and subtracting that from the discounted value of the positive rents from t^* onward. For a formal presentation of this calculation, see T. Anderson and Hill 1990.

36. Squatting on the land in hopes of gaining a preemption right also dissipated rents because of premature entry by claimants who found it necessary to be on the land before t^* in order to establish their claim (see Kanazawa 1996c). However, squatting often occurred in the context of land-claims clubs or other joint action designed to limit the amount of premature activity and hence the rent dissipation inherent in a race for property.

37. Libecap and Hansen 2000, 33.

38. Fletcher 1960, 146.

39. Fulton 1982, 66.

40. Gates 1968, 505.

41. Hibbard 1924, 409.

42. The one discussed here is the largest and most famous of the "runs." An ear-

lier one involved 50,000 people and 1.9 million acres in the Unassigned District (Campbell 1997, 1).

43. The name "Cherokee Strip" originally referred to a narrow piece of land (2.5 miles wide and 276 miles long) ceded to Oklahoma as an adjustment following a survey controversy along the Kansas-Oklahoma border (Newsom 1992, 1). However, the terms "Outlet" and "Strip" came to be used interchangeably to describe the larger area discussed here.

44. Lefebvre 1993, 87.

45. See Newsom 1992, 2, and Savage 1990, 19.

46. Newsom 1992, 18, estimates that 4.8 million Texas cattle passed through the Outlet from 1866 through 1884.

47. Savage 1990, 47.

48. Ibid., 60.

49. Savage 1990, 108–16.

50. Ibid., 123.

51. See Alston and Spiller 1992, 94.

52. Newsom 1992, 29.

53. See ibid., 31. The restrictions were designed to prevent unfair competition with those who were riding horses.

54. Lefebvre 1993, 74–75.

55. Newsom 1992, 38.

56. Quoted in Lefebvre 1993, 76.

57. Each settler could claim 160 acres. With 5,740,000 acres available (Newsom 1992, 29), there were only 35,875 potential claim sites.

58. See Newsom 1992 and Lefebvre 1993.

59. Newsom 1992, 50.

60. Ibid., 43.

61. See G. Anderson and Martin 1987.

62. See McChesney 1992 and 1997.

63. Raban 1996, 59.

64. Webb 1971, 201.

65. Gates 1968, 612. This does not include the land managed by the U.S. Forest Service.

66. Webb 1971, 386.

CHAPTER 10

1. Quoted in Pisani 1992, 70.

2. Quoted in ibid.

3. See ibid., 74, and Raban 1996, 30–33.

4. Quoted in Webb 1971, 434.

5. Kinney 1912, sect. 598.

6. Webb 1971, 438. Kanazawa (1996b) argues that in cases where riparian rules remained but impeded efficient use of water, the courts allowed the rule of reasonable use (a part of the riparian doctrine) to evolve so as to permit more diversions.

7. The first organizational efforts occurred in mining, followed by similar institutional innovations in agriculture. For instance, in the winter of 1852, mining entrepreneurs along the Yuba River in California organized twenty companies along a four-mile stretch of the stream. Membership in the companies varied from eight to thirty members, and diversion dams cost from $50,000 to $80,000 (Pisani 1992, 16). Larger and larger reservoirs were built with longer flumes to provide a year-round water supply and to develop pressure for hydraulic mining. The California mining camps used partnerships and joint-stock ventures for most of their water companies. By 1870, nearly 7,000 miles of ditches moved water to claims (Pisani 1992, 18).

8. Ganoe 1937.

9. Demsetz 2002.

10. Winther 1953, 95. Note that the lottery eliminates rent seeking associated with the distribution of property rights to land by eliminating any opportunity to gain an advantage in the distribution.

11. Ibid.

12. Ibid., 96.

13. Ibid., 97.

14. Wahl 1989, 13.

15. Arrington 1958, 53.

16. Early in its history, the Mormon church experimented with a much more extensive regime of communal ownership. In 1831 it used the Law of Consecration and Stewardships to govern property ownership within the church. This law required that all property be dedicated to the church, although much of it was allocated back to the original owner as a stewardship. Nevertheless, the law mandated an annual socialization of all surpluses above the family's "just wants and needs." The Law of Consecration and Stewardship was suspended in 1834, and private property, with a strong requirement of tithing from income, became the dominant form of ownership (Bullock and Baden 1977).

17. Pisani 1992, 82–83.

18. Ibid., 79.

19. In fact, the vertically integrated irrigation companies described above faced the market-power problem once landownership was distributed to individuals. Long-term contracts created when land was distributed to new owners could reduce this potential, but such contracts still allowed market power when they expired. To avoid this problem, irrigators formed mutual irrigation districts to purchase irrigation companies.

20. Mead 1907, 52–53.

21. R. Smith 1983.

22. Ibid., 173.

23. Pisani 1992, 103.

24. Ibid., 102.

25. McDevitt 1994, 190.

26. Ibid., 191.

27. Ibid., table 3.1.

28. Ibid., 194.

29. Ibid., 98.

30. McDevitt argues that the rules against a two-part tariff—that is, an initial fixed fee for service and a second variable fee for water used—reduced the economic viability of the private firms (ibid., 173).

31. R. Smith 1983.

32. Buchanan and Tullock 1962.

33. A trend regression of the percentage of "yes" votes over the time period shows a slope coefficient of 0.1509 with a t value of 0.421, suggesting the trend is not significantly different from zero.

34. McDevitt 1994, 88–89.

35. For a discussion of the relationship between transaction costs and firm size, see Demsetz 2002. Also see Lueck 1995 for a discussion of how parcel size relates to the transaction cost of organizing economic activities as related to wildlife.

36. Hibbard 1924, 409.

37. Under the original Homestead Act, this required five years of residence, although the period was later lowered to three years, and various commutation provisions allowed for purchase after a more limited period of time.

38. Mead 1907, 93.

39. For a discussion of entrymen in the case of timber lands, see Libecap and Johnson 1979.

40. Arrington 1958, 249; Gates 1968, 421, 428.

41. Pisani 1992, 87.

42. Ibid., 86.

43. Ibid., 87.

44. Quoted in ibid., 88.

45. Gates 1968, 639.

46. Ibid., 641.

47. Ganoe 1937, 151.

48. Pisani 1992, 89.

49. Ganoe 1937, 152.

50. Gates 1968, 642.

51. For a discussion of foreign investment in cattle ranching, see Gressley 1966.

52. Stegner 1953, 305–6.

53. Ibid., 309.

54. Gates 1968, 642.

55. Stegner 1953, 318-19.
56. Hibbard 1924, 190.
57. Ibid., 436.
58. Mead 1907, 26.
59. Gates 1968, 648.
60. Kanazawa 1996a.
61. Gates 1968, 648.
62. Ibid.
63. Mayhew and Gardner 1994, 71.
64. Quoted in Gates 1968, 652.
65. Mayhew and Gardner 1994.
66. Gates 1968, 655; Mayhew and Gardner 1994, 76.
67. See Golze 1952, 25.
68. *Congressional Record* 1902, 6742, 6762.
69. Gates 1968, 655.
70. Wahl 1989, table. 2.1.
71. Ibid., 30.
72. Ibid., 28-33.
73. See Rucker and Fishback 1983, 63-79.
74. Reisner 1993, 173.
75. Ibid., 174-90.

CHAPTER II

1. Alston, Libecap, and Mueller 1999; Mahar 1989.
2. Alston, Libecap, and Mueller 1999, 20.
3. Ibid., 195.
4. De Soto 2000.
5. De Soto 2000, 18.
6. Ibid., 155.
7. Ibid., 35.
8. Ibid., 84.
9. Ayittey 1992.
10. Ayittey 1992, 100.
11. *Facts on File, World News Digest* 1997.
12. Buscaglia and Ratliff 2000, 20.
13. Ibid., 26.
14. Ibid., 21.
15. T. Anderson and Hill 1994.
16. Quoted in Runte 1990, 23.
17. Yellowstone National Park was not the only park whose value was recognized

and partially captured by railroads. Major railroads were behind Mt. Rainier, the Grand Canyon, Yosemite, Rocky Mountain, and Crater Lake, to mention a few. See Runte 1990.

18. T. Anderson and Leal 1997, 4–8.
19. Quoted in Yandle 1997, 89.
20. Quoted in ibid., 96.
21. Ibid., chap. 6.
22. Quoted in ibid., 112.
23. Michalak 2001, 143.
24. Leal 2002, 9.
25. Nelson 1995.
26. Thayer 2003.
27. Landry 2001, 23–37.
28. Huppert and Knapp 2001, 79–100.
29. McMillan 1994, 145–62.
30. Ibid., 146.
31. Meiners and Kosnik 2003.

Bibliography

Abbott, E. C., and Helena Huntington Smith. 1939. *We Pointed Them North: Recollections of a Cowpuncher*. Norman: University of Oklahoma Press.

Alchian, Armen A., and Harold Demsetz. 1972. Production, Information Costs, and Economic Organization. *American Economic Review* 62 (5): 777–95.

Alston, Lee J., Gary D. Libecap, and Bernardo Mueller. 1999. *Titles, Conflict, and Resource Use*. Ann Arbor: University of Michigan Press.

Alston, Lee J., and Pablo Spiller. 1992. A Congressional Theory of Indian Property Rights: The Cherokee Outlet. In *Property Rights in Indian Economies*, ed. Terry L. Anderson. Lanham, Md.: Rowman and Littlefield.

Anderson, Gary M., and Dolores T. Martin. 1987. The Public Domain and Nineteenth Century Transfer Policy. *Cato Journal* 6 (3): 905–23.

Anderson, Terry L. 1995. *Sovereign Nations or Indian Reservations? An Economic History of American Indians*. San Francisco: Pacific Research Institute for Public Policy.

Anderson, Terry L., and Peter J. Hill. 1975. The Evolution of Property Rights: A Study of the American West. *Journal of Law and Economics* 18: 163–79.

———. 1980. *The Birth of a Transfer Society*. Stanford, Calif.: Hoover Institution Press.

———. 1983. Privatizing the Commons: An Improvement? *Southern Economic Journal* 50 (2): 438–50.

———. 1990. The Race for Property Rights. *Journal of Law and Economics* 33 (April): 177–97.

———. 1994. Rents from Amenity Resources: A Case Study of Yellowstone National Park. In *The Political Economy of the American West*, ed. Terry L Anderson and Peter J. Hill. Lanham, Md.: Rowman and Littlefield.

Anderson, Terry L., and Donald R. Leal. 1997. *Enviro-Capitalists: Doing Good While Doing Well*. Lanham, Md.: Rowman and Littlefield.

———. 2001. *Free Market Environmentalism: Revised Edition*. New York: Palgrave.

Anderson, Terry L., and Dean Lueck. 1992. Land Tenure and Agricultural Productivity on Indian Reservations. *Journal of Law and Economics* 35 (October): 427–54.

Anderson, Terry L., and Fred McChesney. 1994. Raid or Trade? An Economic Model of Indian-White Relations. *Journal of Law and Economics* 37 (April): 39–74.

Anderson, Terry L., and Pamela A. Snyder. 1995. *Water Markets: Priming the Invisible Pump.* Washington, D. C.: Cato Institute.

Arrington, Leonard J. 1958. *Great Basin Kingdom: An Economic History of the Latter-Day Saints, 1830–1900.* Cambridge, Mass.: Harvard University Press.

Arthur, George W. 1975. An Introduction to the Ecology of Early Historic Communal Bison Hunting Among the Northern Plains Indians. National Museum of Man Mercury Series, Archaeological Survey of Canada, Paper No. 37. Ottawa: National Museums of Canada.

Axtell, James. 1988. Through Another Glass Darkly: Early Indian Views of Europeans. In *After Columbus: Essays in the Ethno-History of Colonial North America.* New York: Oxford University Press.

Ayittey, George B. N. 1992. *Africa Betrayed.* New York: St. Martin's.

Baden, John, Richard Stroup, and Walter A. Thurman. 1981. Myths, Admonitions, and Rationality: The American Indian as a Resource Manager. *Economic Inquiry* 19 (1): 132–43.

Bailey, Martin J. 1992. Approximate Optimality of Aboriginal Property Rights. *Journal of Law and Economics* 35 (April): 183–98.

Barreiro, Jose, ed. 1988. *Indian Roots of American Democracy.* Ithaca, N.Y.: American Indian Program, Cornell University.

Barsness, Larry. 1985. *Heads, Hides, and Horns.* Fort Worth: Texas Christian University Press.

Barzel, Yoram. 1984. The Entrepreneur's Reward for Self-Policing. *Economic Inquiry* 25: 103–16.

Basso, Keith H. 1970. *The Cibecue Apache.* New York: Holt, Rinehart and Winston.

Baumol, William J. 1990. Entrepreneurship: Productive, Unproductive, and Destructive. *Journal of Political Economy* 98 (5, pt. 1): 893–921.

Beck, Warren A., and Ynez D. Haase. 1989. *Historical Atlas of the American West.* Norman: University of Oklahoma Press.

Beers, Henry P. 1975. *The Military Frontier 1815–46.* Philadelphia: Porcupine.

Bethell, Tom. 1998. *The Noblest Triumph: Property and Prosperity Through the Ages.* New York: St. Martin's.

Blue, Ted Franklin. 1996. *The Long Hunt: Death of the Buffalo East of the Mississippi.* Mechanicsburg, Pa.: Stackpole Books.

Bogue, Allan G. 1963. The Iowa Claim Clubs: Symbol and Substance. In *The Public Lands,* ed. Vernon Carstensen. Madison: University of Wisconsin Press.

Branch, Douglas E. 1929 *The Hunting of the Buffalo.* New York: D. Appleton.

Brands, H. W. 1997. *T. R.: The Last Romantic.* New York: Basic Books.

Brayer, Garnet M., and Herbert O. Brayer. 1952. *American Cattle Trails 1540–1900.*

Bayside, N.Y.: Western Range Cattle Industry Study, in cooperation with the American Pioneer Trails Association.

Brown, Mark H., and W. R. Felton. 1956. *Before Barbed Wire*. New York: Bramhall House.

Buchanan, James M., and Gordon Tullock. 1962. *The Calculus of Consent*. Ann Arbor: University of Michigan Press.

Bullock, Kari, and John Baden. 1977. Communes and the Logic of the Commons. In *Managing the Commons*, ed. Garrett Hardin and John Baden. San Francisco: W. H. Freeman.

Burger, Carl. 1968. *Beaver Skins and Mountain Men*. New York: E. P. Dutton.

Burt, Oscar, and Ronald G. Cummings. 1970. Production and Investment in Natural Resource Industries. *American Economic Review* 60 (4): 576–90.

Buscaglia, Edgardo, and William Ratliff. 2000. *Law and Economics in Developing Countries*. Stanford, Calif.: Hoover Institution Press.

Campbell, Noel D. 1997. There Goes the Neighborhood: White Settlement in the Unassigned District. Ph.D. diss., George Mason University, Fairfax, Virginia.

Carlos, Ann M., and Frank D. Lewis. 1993. Indians, the Beaver and the Bay: The Economics of Depletion in the Lands of the Hudson's Bay Company, 1700–1763. *Journal of Economic History* 53: 465–94.

———. 1995. Strategic Pricing in the Fur Trade: The Hudson's Bay Company, 1700–1763. In *Wildlife in the Marketplace*, ed. Terry L. Anderson and Peter J. Hill. Lanham, Md.: Rowman and Littlefield.

Carlson, Leonard A. 1981. *Indians, Bureaucrats, and the Land: The Dawes Act and the Decline of Indian Farming*. Westport, Conn.: Greenwood.

———. 1992. Learning to Farm: Indian Land Tenure and Farming Before the Dawes Act. In *Property Rights and Indian Economies*, ed. Terry L. Anderson. Lanham, Md.: Rowman and Littlefield.

Carter, Sarah. 1990. *Lost Harvests: Prairie Indian Reserve Farmers and Government Policy*. Montreal and Kingston: McGill-Queen's University Press.

Caughey, John Walton. 1948. *Gold Is the Cornerstone*. Berkeley: University of California Press.

Chapel, Charles Edward. 1961. *Guns of the Old West*. New York: Coward-McCann.

Chase, Alston. 1986. *Playing God in Yellowstone*. Boston: Atlantic Monthly Press.

Cheney, Truman McGiffin. 1990. *So Long, Cowboys of the Open Range*. Helena, Mont.: Falcon.

Chittenden, Hiram Martin. 1954. *The American Fur Trade of the Far West*. Vols. 1 and 2. Stanford, Calif.: Academic Reprints.

Choy, Philip P. 1971. Golden Mountains of Lead, the Chinese Experience in California. *California Historical Quarterly* 50 (3): 267–76.

Clay, Karen, and Gavin Wright. 1998. Property Rights in California Gold. Unpublished manuscript. Stanford University, Stanford, Calif.

Cohen, Felix. 1947. Original Indian Title. *Minnesota Law Review* 32: 28–59.

Congressional Record. 1902. 57th Cong., first sess., vol. 35.

Connell, Evan S. 1988. *Cavalier in Buckskin.* Norman: University of Oklahoma Press.

Cooter, Robert D., and Daniel L. Rubinfeld. 1989. Economic Analysis of Legal Disputes and Their Resolution. *Journal of Economic Literature* 27 (1989): 1067–97.

Copper, John M. 1949. Indian Land Tenure Systems. In *Indians of the United States: Contributions by Members of the Delegation, and by Advisers to the Policy Board of the National Indian Institute, for the Second Inter-American Conference on Indian Life, Convened at Cuzco, Peru, June 24–July 4, 1949.* N.p.

Dale, Edward Everett. 1960. *The Range Cattle Industry: Ranching on the Great Plains from 1865 to 1925.* Norman: University of Oklahoma Press.

Davis, John F. 1902. *Historical Sketch of the Mining Law in California.* Los Angeles: Commercial Printing House.

Debo, Angie. 1970. *A History of the Indians of the United States.* Norman: University of Oklahoma Press.

De Laguna, Frederica. 1972. *The Story of a Tlingit Community.* Bureau of American Ethnology Bulletin 1972. Washington, D.C.: Government Printing Office.

Demsetz, Harold. 1967. Toward a Theory of Property Rights. *American Economic Review* 57 (2): 347–59.

———. 2002. Ownership and the Externality Problem. In *Property Rights: Cooperation, Conflict, and Law,* ed. Terry L. Anderson and Fred S. McChesney. Princeton, N.J.: Princeton University Press.

Denig, Edwin T. 1930. Indian Tribes of the Upper Missouri. In *46th Annual Report (1928–29), Bureau of American Ethnology,* ed. J. N. B. Hewitt. Washington, D.C.: U.S. Government Printing Office.

———. 1961. *Five Indian Tribes of the Upper Missouri,* ed. John C. Ewers. Norman: University of Oklahoma Press.

Dennen, R. Taylor. 1976. Cattlemen's Associations and Property Rights in Land in the American West. *Explorations in Economic History* 13: 423–36.

de Soto, Hernando. 2000. *The Mystery of Capital: Why Capitalism Triumphs in the West and Fails Everywhere Else.* New York: Basic Books.

Diamond, Jared. 1999. *Guns, Germs, and Steel.* New York: W. W. Norton.

Dippie, Brian W. 1991. American Wests: Historiographical Perspectives. In *Trails: Toward a New Western History,* ed. Patricia Nelson Limerick, Clyde A. Milner II, and Charles E. Rankin. Lawrence: University Press of Kansas.

Dykstra, Robert R. 1968. *The Cattle Towns.* Lincoln: University of Nebraska Press.

Eggertsson, Thráinn. 1990. *Economic Behavior and Institutions.* Cambridge, Eng.: Cambridge University Press.

Ellickson, Robert C. 1991. *Order Without Law: How Neighbors Settle Disputes.* Cambridge, Mass.: Harvard University Press.

———. 1993. Property in Land. *Yale Law Journal* 102 (April): 1315–1400.

————. 2001. The Market for Social Norms. *American Law and Economic Review* 1: 1–49.

Ellis, Florence Hawley. 1979. Isleta Pueblo. In *Handbook of North American Indians* 9. Washington, D.C.: Smithsonian Institution.

Ewers, John C. 1969. *The Horse in Blackfoot Indian Culture*. Washington, D.C.: Smithsonian Institution Press.

Faegre, Torvald. 1979. *Tents: Architecture of the Nomads*. Garden City, N.Y.: Anchor Press/Doubleday.

Faragher, John Mack. 1994. Afterword. In *Rereading Frederick Jackson Turner*. New York: Henry Holt.

Farb, Peter. 1968. *Man's Rise to Civilization as Shown by the Indians of North America*. New York: Dutton.

Farnham, Thomas J. 1843. *Travels in the Great Western Prairies, the Anahuac and Rocky Mountains, and in the Oregon Territory*. New York: Greeley and McElrath.

Fletcher, Robert H. 1960. *Free Grass to Fences: The Montana Cattle Range Story*. New York: University Publishers Incorporated.

Flores, Dan. 1991. Bison Ecology and Bison Diplomacy: The Southern Plains from 1800 to 1850. *Journal of American History* 78 (September): 465–85.

Forde, C. Daryll. 1931. Hopi Agriculture and Land Ownership. *Journal of the Royal Anthropological Institute of Great Britain and Ireland* 61: 357–405.

Fowler, Catherine S. 1986. *Handbook of North American Indians—Great Basin* 11. Washington, D.C.: Smithsonian Institution.

Freed, Stanley A. 1960. Changing Washo Kinship. *Anthropological Records* 14 (6): 349–418.

Fulton, Dan. 1982. *Failure on the Plains: A Rancher's View of the Public Lands Problem*. Bozeman: Big Sky Books, Montana State University.

Furubotn, Eirik G., and Rudolf Richter. 1997. *Institutions and Economic Theory*. Ann Arbor: University of Michigan Press.

Ganoe, John T. 1937. The Desert Land Act in Operation, 1877–1891. *Agricultural History* 9: 142–57.

Gates, Paul W. 1968. *History of Public Land Law Development*. Washington, D.C.: Public Land Law Review Commission.

————. 1991. *Land and Law in California: Essays on Land Policies*. Ames: Iowa State University Press.

Geist, Valerius. 1996. *Buffalo Nation: History and Legend of the North American Bison*. Stillwater, Minn.: Voyageur.

Goldsmidt, Walter. 1951. Ethics and the Structure of Society: An Ethnological Contribution to the Sociology of Knowledge. *American Anthropologist* 53: 506–24.

Golze, Alfred R. 1952. *Reclamation in the United States*. New York: McGraw Hill.

Gowans, Fred R. 1985. *Rocky Mountain Rendezvous: A History of the Fur Trade Rendezvous, 1825–1840*. Layton, Utah: Peregrine Smith Books.

Gressley, Gene M. 1966. *Bankers and Cattlemen*. Lincoln: University of Nebraska Press.

Grinnell, George Bird. 1962. *Blackfoot Lodge Tales*. Lincoln: University of Nebraska Press.

Gwartney, James, and Robert Lawson. 2002. *Economic Freedom of the World: Annual Report 2002*. Vancouver, B.C.: The Fraser Institute.

Haddock, David D. 1997. Must Water Regulation Be Centralized? In *Water Marketing—The Next Generation*, ed. Terry L. Anderson and Peter J. Hill. Lanham, Md.: Rowman and Littlefield.

Hanner, John. 1981. Government Response to the Buffalo Hide Trade, 1871–1883. *Journal of Law and Economics* 24 (October): 239–71.

Hansen, Barbara Julia. 1937. *Wagon Train Governments*. Master's thesis, University of Colorado.

Hardin, Garrett 1968. The Tragedy of the Commons. *Science* 162: 1243–48. The American Association for the Advancement of Science.

Henry, Alexander, and David Thompson. 1965. *New Light on the Early History of the Greater Northwest: The Manuscripts and Journals of Alexander Henry and David Thompson, 1799–1814*, vol. 2, ed. Elliott Coues. Minneapolis: Ross and Haines.

Hibbard, Benjamin H. 1924. *A History of the Public Land Policies*. New York: Macmillan.

Higgs, Robert. 1982. Legally Induced Technical Regress in the Washington Salmon Fishery. *Research in Economic History* 7: 55–86.

Hoebel, E. Adamson. 1954. *The Law of Primitive Man*. Cambridge, Mass.: Harvard University Press.

Holder, Preston. 1970. *The Hoe and the Horse on the Plains: A Study of Cultural Development Among North American Indians*. Lincoln: University of Nebraska Press.

Hornaday, William T. 1889. *The Extermination of the American Bison*. Washington, D.C.: Report of the National Museum.

Huffman, James L. 1992. An Exploratory Essay on Native Americans and Environmentalism. *University of Colorado Law Review* 63 (4): 901–20.

Hughes, Jonathan R. T. 1976. *Social Control in the Colonial Economy*. Charlottesville: University of North Carolina Press.

Huppert, Daniel, and Gunnar Knapp. 2001. Technology and Property Rights in Fisheries Management. In *The Technology of Property Rights*, ed. Terry L. Anderson and Peter J. Hill. Lanham, Md.: Rowman and Littlefield.

Hurt, F. Douglas. 1987. *Indian Agriculture in America: Prehistory to the Present*. Lawrence: University of Kansas Press.

Isenberg, Andrew C. 2000. *Destruction of the Bison: An Environmental History, 1750–1920*. New York: Cambridge University Press.

Jefferson, Thomas. 1955 [1787]. *Notes on the State of Virginia (1787)*. Ed. William Peden. Chapel Hill: University of North Carolina Press.

Johnson, Ronald N., and Gary Libecap. 1994. *The Federal Service System and the*

Problem of Bureaucracy: The Economics and Politics of Institutional Change. NBER Series. Chicago: University of Chicago Press.

Jordan, Terry G. 1993. *North American Cattle-Ranching Frontiers: Origins, Diffusion, and Differentiation*. Albuquerque: University of New Mexico Press.

Kanazawa, Mark T. 1996a. Federal Reclamation versus Cession: The Origins of the Reclamation Act. Unpublished manuscript. Carleton College, Northfield, Minn.

———. 1996b. Financing Water Development and the Growth of Irrigated Agriculture in California, 1900–1929. Unpublished manuscript. Carleton College, Northfield, Minn.

———. 1996c. Possession Is Nine Points of Law: The Political Economy of Early Public Land Disposal. *Explorations in Economic History* 33: 227–49.

Kennard, Edward A. 1979. Hopi Economy and Subsistence. In *Handbook of North American Indians* 9. Washington, D.C.: Smithsonian Institution.

Kennett, David. 2001. *A New View of Comparative Economic Systems*. Fort Worth, Tex.: Hartcourt.

Kickingbird, Kirke, and Karen Ducheneaus. 1973. *One Hundred Million Acres*. New York: Macmillan.

Kinney, Clesson S. 1912. *A Treatise on the Law of Irrigation and Water Rights*. San Francisco: Bender-Moss.

Kirzner, Israel M. 1973. *Competition and Entrepreneurship*. Chicago: University of Chicago Press.

Lamar, Howard R., ed. 1998. *The New Encyclopedia of the American West*. New Haven: Yale University Press.

Landry, Clay J. 2001. Technology and Property Rights in Fisheries Management. In *The Technology of Property Rights*, ed. Terry L. Anderson and Peter J. Hill. Lanham, Md.: Rowman and Littlefield.

Langdon, Steve. 1989. From Communal Property to Common Property of Limited Entry: Historical Ironies in the Management of Southeast Alaska Salmon. In *A Sea of Small Boats*, ed. John Cordell. Cambridge, Mass.: Cultural Survival.

Lavender, David Sievert. 1992. *Let Me Be Free: The Nez Perce Tragedy*. New York: Doubleday.

Leal, Donald R. 2002. *Fencing the Fishery: A Primer on Ending the Race for Fish*. Bozeman Mont.: PERC—The Center for Free Market Environmentalism.

Lefebvre, Irene Sturm. 1993. *Cherokee Strip in Transition*. Enid, Okla.: Cherokee Strip Centennial Foundation.

Leshy, John D. 1987. *The Mining Law: A Study in Perpetual Motion*. Washington, D.C.: Resources for the Future.

Libecap, Gary D. 1978. Economic Variables and the Development of the Law: The Case of Western Mineral Rights. *Journal of Economic History* 38 (2): 338–62.

———. 1981. *Locking Up the Range: Federal Land Controls and Grazing*. San Francisco: Pacific Institute for Public Policy Research; Cambridge, Mass.: Ballinger.

———. 1989. *Contracting for Property Rights*. New York: Cambridge University Press.

Libecap, Gary D., and Zeynep Kocabiyik Hansen. 2000. "Rain Follows the Plow" and Dryfarming Doctrine: The Climate Information Problem and Homestead Failure in the Upper Great Plains, 1890–1925. Unpublished manuscript. Department of Economics, University of Arizona, Tucson, Arizona.

Libecap, Gary D., and Ronald N. Johnson. 1979. Property Rights, Nineteenth-Century Federal Timber Policy, and the Conservation Movement. *Journal of Economic History* 39 (1): 129–42.

———. 1980. Legislating Commons: The Navaho Tribal Council and the Navaho Range. *Economic Inquiry* 18: 69–86.

Limerick, Patricia Nelson. 1987. *The Legacy of Conquest*. New York: W. W. Norton.

———. 1991. What on Earth Is the New Western History? In *Trails: Toward a New Western History*, ed. Patricia Nelson Limerick, Clyde A. Milner II, and Charles E. Rankin. Lawrence: University Press of Kansas.

Limerick, Patricia Nelson, Clyde A. Milner II, and Charles E. Rankin, eds. 1991. *Trails Toward a New Western History*. Lawrence: University Press of Kansas.

Lowie, Robert H. 1940. Ethnographic Notes on the Washo. *American Archaeology and Ethnology* 36: 301–51.

———. 1982. *Indians of the Plains*. Lincoln: University of Nebraska Press.

Lueck, Dean. 1989. The Economic Nature of Wildlife Law. *Journal of Legal Studies* 18 (2): 291–324.

———. 1995. The Economic Organization of Wildlife Institutions. In *Wildlife in the Marketplace*, ed. Terry L. Anderson and Peter J. Hill. Lanham, Md.: Rowman and Littlefield.

———. 2003. First Possession as the Basis of Property. In *Property Rights: Cooperation, Conflict and Law*, ed. Terry L. Anderson and Fred S. McChesney. Princeton, N.J.: Princeton University Press.

Madsen, Brigham D. 1980. *The Northern Shoshoni*. Caldwell, Idaho: Caxton Printers.

Maguire, James H., Peter Wild, and Donald A. Barclay, eds. 1997. *A Rendezvous Reader: Tall, Tangled, and True Tales of the Mountain Men 1805–1850*. Salt Lake City: University of Utah Press.

Mahar, Dennis J. 1989. *Government Policies and Deforestation in Brazil's Amazon Region*. Washington, D.C.: World Bank.

Malone, Michael P., and Richard B. Roeder. 1976. *Montana: A History of Two Centuries*. Seattle: University of Washington Press.

Martin, Paul S., and Christine R. Szuter. 1999. War Zones and Game Sinks in Lewis and Clark's West. *Conservation Biology* 13 (1): 36–45.

Maximilian, Prince of Wied. 1902. Travels in the Interior of North America, 1833–1834. In *Early Western Travels* 23, ed. Reuben Gold Thwaites. Cleveland, Ohio: A. H. Clark.

Mayhew, Stewart, and B. Delworth Gardner. 1994. The Political Economy of Early

Federal Reclamation in the West. In *The Political Economy of the American West*, ed. Terry L. Anderson and Peter J. Hill. Lanham, Md.: Rowman and Littlefield.

McCallum, Henry D., and Frances T. McCallum. 1965. *The Wire That Fenced the West*. Norman: University of Oklahoma Press.

McChesney, Fred S. 1992. Government as Definer of Property Rights: Indian Lands, Ethnic Externalities, and Bureaucratic Budgets. In *Property Rights and Indian Economies*, ed. Terry L. Anderson. Lanham, Md.: Rowman and Littlefield.

———. 1997. *Money for Nothing: Politicians, Rent Extraction, and Political Extortion*. Cambridge, Mass.: Harvard University Press.

McCoy, Joseph G. 1932 [1874]. *Historic Sketches of the Cattle Trade of the West and Southwest*. Reprint, Washington, D.C.: The Rare Book Shop.

McDevitt, Edward Paul. 1994. The Evolution of Irrigation Institutions in California: The Rise of the Irrigation District. Ph.D. diss., Department of Economics, University of California, Los Angeles.

McGrath, Roger D. 1984. *Gunfighters, Highwaymen, and Vigilantes: Violence on the Frontier*. Berkeley: University of California Press.

McMillan, John. 1994. Selling Spectrum Rights. *Journal of Economic Perspectives* 8 (Summer): 145–62.

Mead, Elwood. 1907. *Irrigation Institutions*. New York: McMillan.

Meiners, Roger, and Lea-Rachel Kosnik. 2003. *Restoring Harmony in the Klamath Basin*. PERC Policy Series PS-27. Bozeman, Mont.: PERC—The Center for Free Market Environmentalism.

Meiners, Roger, and Andrew Morriss. 2003. Agricultural Commons Problems and Responses: Sick Hogs at the Trough. In *Environmental Policy and Agriculture: Conflicts, Prospects, and Implications*, ed. Roger Meiners and Bruce Yandle. Lanham, Md.: Rowman and Littlefield

Michalak, A. M. 2001. Feasibility of Contaminant Source Identification for Property Rights Enforcement. In *The Technology of Property Rights*, ed. Terry L. Anderson and Peter J. Hill. Lanham, Md.: Rowman and Littlefield.

Morgan, Dale. 1953. *Jedediah Smith and the Opening of West*. Indianapolis: Bobbs-Merrill.

Nelson, Robert H. 1995. *Public Lands and Private Rights: The Failure of Scientific Management*. Lanham, Md.: Rowman and Littlefield.

Netboy, Anthony. 1958. *Salmon of the Pacific Northwest: Fish vs. Dams*. Portland, Ore.: Binfords and Mort.

Newsom, D. Earl. 1992. *The Cherokee Strip: Its History and Grand Opening*. Stillwater, Okla.: New Forums Press.

Niskanen, William. 1971. *Bureaucracy and Representative Government*. Chicago: Aldine, Atherton.

Norton, Seth W. 1998. Property Rights and the Environment. In *Who Owns the Environment*, ed. Peter J. Hill and Roger E. Meiners. Lanham, Md.: Rowman and Littlefield.

Oberg, K. 1973. *The Social Economy of the Tlingit Indians*. American Ethnological Society Monograph 55. Seattle: University of Washington Press.

O'Driscoll, Gerald P., Kim R. Holmes, and Mary Anastasia O'Grady. 2002. *2002 Index of Economic Freedom*. Washington, D.C.: The Heritage Foundation.

Olson, R. L. 1967. *Social Structure and Social Life of the Tlingit in Alaska*. Anthropological Records 26. Berkeley: University of California Press.

Osgood, Ernest Staples. 1929. *The Day of the Cattleman*. Chicago: University of Chicago Press.

Otis, Delos Sacket. 1973. *The Dawes Act and the Allotment of Indian Lands*. Ed. Francis Paul Prucha. Norman: University of Oklahoma Press.

Paul, Rodman. 1947. *California Gold: The Beginning of Mining in the Far West*. Cambridge, Mass.: Harvard University Press.

Pipes, Richard. 1999. *Property and Freedom: The Story of How Through the Centuries Private Ownership Has Promoted Liberty and the Rule of Law*. New York: Alfred A. Knopf.

Pisani, Donald J. 1992. *To Reclaim a Divided West: Water-Law, and Public Policy, 1848–1902*. Albuquerque: University of New Mexico Press.

Posner, Richard A. 1980. A Theory of Primitive Society with Special Reference to Primitive Law. *Journal of Law and Economics* 23 (1): 1–54.

Prucha, Francis Paul. 1962. *American Indian Policy in the Formative Years: The Indian Trade and Intercourse Acts, 1790–1834*. Cambridge, Mass.: Harvard University Press.

———. 1984. *The Great Father: The United States Government and the American Indians*. Lincoln: University of Nebraska Press.

Raban, Jonathan. 1996. *Bad Land*. New York: Vintage Books.

Reher, Charles A., and George C. Frison. 1980. The Vore Site, 48CK302, a Stratified Buffalo Jump in the Wyoming Black Hills. *Plains Anthropologist: Journal of the Plains Conference* 25 (88): 1–190.

Reid, John Phillip. 1997a. *Law for the Elephant: Property and Social Behavior on the Overland Trail*. San Marino, Calif.: Huntington Library.

———. 1997b. *Policing the Elephant: Crime, Punishment, and Social Behavior on the Overland Trail*. San Marino, Calif.: Huntington Library.

Reisner, Marc. 1993. *Cadillac Desert: The American West and Its Disappearing Water*. New York: Penguin.

Ridley, Matt. 1997. *The Origins of Virtue: Human Instincts and the Evolution of Cooperation*. New York: Penguin Book.

Rister, C. C. 1929. The Significance of the Destruction of the Buffalo in the Southwest. *Southwestern Historical Quarterly* 3: 34–49.

Roback, Jennifer. 1992. Exchange, Sovereignty, and Indian-Anglo Relations. In *Property Rights and Indian Economies*, ed. Terry L. Anderson. Lanham, Md.: Rowman and Littlefield.

Robbins, William G. 1991. Laying Siege to Western History: The Emergence of

New Paradigms. In *Trails: Toward a New Western History*, ed. Patricia Nelson Limerick, Clyde A. Milner II, and Charles E. Rankin. Lawrence: University Press of Kansas.

Robinson, W. W. 1948. *Land in California*. Berkeley: University of California Press.

Roe, Frank Gilbert. 1955. *The Indian and the Horse*. Norman: University of Oklahoma Press.

———. 1970. *The North American Buffalo*. Toronto, Canada: University of Toronto Press.

Rohrbough, Malcolm J. 1997. *Days of Gold: The California Gold Rush and the American Nation*. Berkeley: University of California Press.

Roosevelt, Theodore. 1889. *The Winning of the West* 1. New York: G. P. Putnam's Sons.

———. 1968. Ranch Life in the Far West. Flagstaff, Ariz.: Northland.

Royce, Josiah. 1886. California, from the Conquest in 1846 to the Second Vigilance Committee. In *San Francisco: A Study of the American Character*. Boston, New York: Houghton Mifflin.

Rucker, Randall R., and Price V. Fishback. 1983. The Federal Reclamation Program: An Analysis of Rent-Seeking Behavior. In *Water Rights: Scarce Resource Allocation, Bureaucracy, and the Environment*, ed. Terry L. Anderson. San Francisco: Pacific Institute for Public Policy Research.

Rumph, Dick. 1993. Biddle History Presented. *Powder River Examiner*, January 7, 6–7.

Runte, Alfred. 1990. *Trains of Discovery*. Niwot, Colo.: Robert Rinehart.

Russell, Don. 1973. How Many Indians Were Killed? *American West* 10 (4): 42–47.

Sandoz, Mari. 1964. *The Beaver Men: Spearheads of Empire*. New York: Hastings House.

Sass, H. R. 1936. Hoofs on the Prairie. *Country Gentleman* (July): 5–6 and 68–69.

Savage, William W. 1990. *The Cherokee Strip Live Stock Association*. Norman: University of Oklahoma Press.

Schaeffer, Claude E. 1978. The Bison River of the Blackfoot Indians. *Plains Anthropologist: Journal of the Plains Conference* 23 (82, pt. 2): 243–48.

Schemeckebier, Laurence R. 1927. *The Office of Indian Affairs*. Baltimore: The Johns Hopkins University Press.

Schultz, James Willard. 1907. *My Life as an Indian: The Story of a Red Woman and a White Man in the Lodges of the Blackfeet*. Boston: Houghton Mifflin.

Schumpeter, Joseph A. 1934. *The Theory of Economic Development*. Cambridge, Mass.: Harvard University Press.

Seton, Ernest Thompson. 1927. *Lives of Game Animals* III, Garden City, N.Y.: Doubleday, Doran.

Shambaugh, Benjamin F. 1900. Frontier Land Clubs, or Claim Associations. *Annual Report of the American Historical Association* 1, 67–84.

Shimkin, Demitri B. 1986. Eastern Shoshone. In *Handbook of North American Indians* 11. Washington, D.C.: Smithsonian Institution.

Shinn, Charles Howard. 1948. *Mining Camps: A Study in American Frontier Government*. New York: Alfred Knopf.

Simpson, Thomas. 1843. *Narrative of the Discoveries on the North Coast of America*. London: Richard Bentley.

Skaggs, Jimmy M. 1973. *The Cattle-Trailing Industry: Between Supply and Demand, 1866–1890*. Lawrence: University Press of Kansas.

Smith, Helena Huntington. 1966. *The War on the Powder River*. Lincoln: University of Nebraska Press.

Smith, Rodney T. 1983. The Economic Determinants and Consequences of Private and Public Ownership of Local Irrigation Facilities. In *Water Rights: Scarce Resource Allocation, Bureaucracy, and the Environment*, ed. Terry L. Anderson. San Francisco: Pacific Institute for Public Policy Research.

Smits, David D. 1994. The Frontier Army and the Destruction of the Buffalo: 1865–1883. *Western Historical Quarterly* (Autumn): 313–38.

Speck, Frank G. 1939. Aboriginal Conservators. *Bird Lore* 40: 258–61.

Steckel, Richard H., and Joseph M. Prince. 2001. Tallest in the World: Native Americans of the Great Plains in the Nineteenth Century. *American Economic Review* 91 (1): 287–94.

Stegner, Wallace. 1953. *Beyond the Hundredth Meridian: John Wesley Powell and the Second Opening of the West*. Boston: Houghton Mifflin.

———. 1981 [1964]. *The Gathering of Zion: The Story of the Mormon Trail*. Lincoln: University of Nebraska Press.

Steward, Julian H. 1934. Ethnography of the Owens Valley Paiute. *American Archaeology and Ethnology* 33 (1): 233–324.

———. 1938. *Basin-Plateau Aboriginal Sociopolitical Groups*. Smithsonian Institution, Bureau of American Ethnology, Bulletin 120. Washington, D.C.: Government Printing Office.

———. 1941. Cultural Element Distributions: XIII Nevada Shoshoni. *Anthropological Records* 4 (2): 209–59.

Strauss, Frederick, and Louis H. Bean. 1940. *Gross Farm Income and Indices of Farm Production and Prices in the United States, 1869–1937*. U. S. Department of Agriculture, Technical Bulletin No. 703, December.

Stuart, Granville. 1967 [1925]. *Forty Years on the Frontier as Seen in the Journals and Reminiscences of Granville Stuart*. Ed. Paul C. Phillips. Two volumes in one. Glendale, Calif.: Arthur H. Clark.

Sunder, John E. 1965. *The Fur Trade on the Upper Missouri, 1840–1865*. Norman: University of Oklahoma Press.

Thaden, Robert L., Jr., ed. 1989. *Faded Hoof Prints—Bygone Dreams*. Comp. Maude L. Beech. Interview with W. H. Goodspeed, Under Sheriff of Powder River

County, by Maude L. Beech in 1941. Broadus, Mont.: Powder River Historical Society.

Thayer, Toni. 2003. Grazing on Public Lands: Here to Stay or Gone Forever? *The Sierra Times*, Feb. 9. Online: http//www.sierratimes.com/03/02/09/ arpubtto20903.htm.

Timmons, Boyce D. 1980. Foreword. In *The Peace Chiefs of the Cheyennes*, ed. Stan Hoig. Norman: University of Oklahoma Press.

Tocqueville, Alexis de. 1835. *Democracy in America*. London: Saunders and Otley.

Trosper, Ronald L. 1978. American Indian Relative Ranching Efficiency. *American Economic Review* 68 (4): 503–16.

Turner, Frederick J. 1894. The Significance of the Frontier in American History. *Annual Report, American Historical Association, 1893*. Washington, D.C.: Government Printing Office.

Umbeck, John R. 1977. A Theory of Contract Choice and the California Gold Rush. *Journal of Law and Economics* 20 (2): 421–37.

———. 1981. *A Theory of Property Rights: With Application to the California Gold Rush*. Ames: Iowa State University Press.

U.S. Bureau of the Census. 1960. *Historical Statistics of the United States: Colonial Times to 1957*. Washington, D.C.

———. 1975. *Historical Statistics of the United States: Colonial Times to 1970*. Vol. 1. Washington, D.C.

U.S. Department of Agriculture. 1927. *Price of Farm Products Received by Producers*. The Mountain and Pacific States. Statistical Bulletin 17, March.

———. 1930. *Irrigation of Agricultural Lands*. Washington, D.C.: Government Printing Office.

———. 1950. *Census of Irrigation*. Washington, D.C.: Government Printing Office.

U.S. Department of Agriculture, Agricultural Economics Bureau. 1938. *Livestock on Farms, January 1, 1867–1935*. Washington, D.C.: Government Printing Office.

Unruh, John D., Jr. 1979. *The Plains Across: The Overland Emigrants and the Trans-Mississippi West, 1840–60*. Urbana and Chicago: University of Illinois Press.

Utley, Robert M. 1967. *Frontiersmen in Blue: The United States Army and the Indian, 1848–1865*. Lincoln: University of Nebraska Press.

———. 1984. *The Indian Frontier of the American West 1846–1890*. Albuquerque: New Mexico Press.

———. 1997. *A Life Wild and Perilous: Mountain Men and the Paths to the Pacific*. New York: Henry Holt.

Wahl, Richard W. 1989. *Markets for Federal Water: Subsidies, Property Rights, and the Bureau of Reclamation*. Washington, D.C.: Resources for the Future.

Washburn, Wilcomb E. 1971. *Red Man's Land/White Man's Law*. New York: Charles Scribner's Sons.

Webb, Walter Prescott. 1971 [1931]. *The Great Plains*. New York: Grosset and Dunlap; reprint, New York: Ginn.

Weber, D. J. 1971. *The Taos Trappers: The Fur Trade in the Far Southwest, 1540–1846*. Norman: University of Oklahoma Press.

Wellman, Paul I. 1967 [1939]. *The Trampling Herd: The Story of the Cattle Range in America*. Lincoln: University of Nebraska Press.

White, David A. 1996. *News of the Plains and Rockies 1803–1865*. Vol. 1. Spokane, Wash.: Arthur H. Clark.

White, John Manchip. 1979. *Everyday Life of North American Indians*. New York: Indian Head Books.

Williamson, Oliver E. 1985. *The Economic Institutions of Capitalism: Firms, Markets, Relational Contracting*. New York: Free Press.

Wilson, Paul S. 1992. What Chief Seattle Said. *Environmental Law* 22: 1451–68.

Wimmer, Linda. 2001. "Give Us Good Black Tobacco": Brazilian Tobacco, Indigenous Consumer Demand and Cross-Cultural Exchange in the Hudson's Bay Company's Fur Trade, 1750–1800. Working paper, Southwest State University, Marshall, Minnesota.

Winther, Oscar Osburn. 1953. The Colony System of Southern California. *Agricultural History* 27: 94–102.

Wishart, David J. 1979. *The Fur Trade of the American West 1807–1840*. Lincoln: University of Nebraska Press.

Wissler, Clark. 1966. *Indians of the United States*. New York: Doubleday.

Wyman, Walker D. 1945. *The Wild Horse of the West*. Lincoln: University of Nebraska Press.

Yandle, Bruce. 1997. *Common Sense and Common Law for the Environment*. Lanham, Md.: Rowman and Littlefield.

Yergin, Daniel, and Joseph Stanislaw. 1998. *The Commanding Heights*. New York: Touchstone.

Zerbe, Richard O., Jr., and C. Leigh Anderson. 2001. Culture and Fairness in the Development of Institutions in the California Gold Fields. *Journal of Economic History* 61 (1): 114–43.

Zontek, Ken. 1995. Hunt, Capture, Raze, Increase: The People Who Saved the Bison. *Great Plains Quarterly* 15 (Spring): 133–49.

Index

Abilene, Kansas, 145–47
Africa, 205–6
agency costs, 28–33, 45, 48, 131–32
agriculture: buffalo unsuitable for, 100;
cattle drives through, 144–45; crop
failure risk, 39; homestead acreage, 99,
102, 172, 189, 231n33; Indian, 38–40,
48, 59, 65–66, 72–73, 74–75*table*;
mining compared, 226n62; tractors,
153; water rights, 4, 7, 18, 23, 177–
200; vs. wildlife habitat, 78. *See also* ir-
rigation
Aldred, William, 208
Allard, Charles, 101
allotments, land, 66–71, 73–76
Alston, Lee, 204
Amazon, Brazil, 204
amenity values, environment, 207–8
American Bison Society, 101
American Fur Company, 83–84, 86, 91, 94
Anaheim Colony, 182–83
Anderson, C. Leigh, 108, 115
Anderson, Terry, 3, 64–65, 72–73
Apache, hunting, 40–41
Arikaras, 84–85, 222n28
Arkansas Valley Land and Cattle Com-
pany, 166
Army, U.S., 6; buffalo extermination, 99;
Civil War, 63, 64–65, 220n42; Corps
of Engineers, 199, 200; raid or trade
decision and, 29, 57*illus.*, 58, 63–65,
73; wars with Indians, 27, 29, 57*illus.*,
58, 63–65, 202. *See also* U.S. military
Arrowsmith, William, 34
Ashley, William H., 84–85, 88, 92,
222n28

Astor, John Jacob, 86
Atkinson, Henry, 82
auction: electromagnetic spectrum, 211;
land, 168
Ayittey, George, 205–6

Bailey, Martin, 43, 44–45
barbed wire, 24–25, 26, 99, 148, 167–68;
production and sale (1874–80),
167*table*
Barber, Amos, 152
Barlow, Samuel K., 135–36
Baumol, William, 22
beavers, 102; pelts in fur trade, 6, 44, 79–
94, 223n72; tragedy of the commons,
77, 78, 79, 90, 92, 93; trap or trade decision, 81–86
Benton, Thomas Hart, 84, 92
Berry, D. N., 183
Biddle and Ferdon Ranch, Montana, 2
bison, 214n4; buffalo jump, 12, 47,
214n4; cattle replacing, 6, 79, 95, 97*illus.*, 138–39, 224nn93,94; hide for tepees, 43, 48–49; hunting, 12, 26–27,
44–51, 94–102, 217n51, 223–24n77;
Indian diet, 48, 218n66; numbers, 94–
95, 223n74; property rights to, 6, 44,
77, 96, 97*illus.*, 98–100, 102; robe and
hide trade, 48, 96–98, 100, 102, 220n4,
224nn93,94; saving, 101–2; tragedy of
the commons, 77, 78, 94–102, 138–39,
162, 223–24n77; wars over, 50
Blackfeet: cattle, 65; fur trade, 83, 85–86;
horses, 50, 51; Shoshoni vs., 50, 218n62
Black Kettle, 60, 219n25

178, 180, 208–9, 215n38; environmental, 208–9; land, 116, 168–76, 193–94; mining, 105, 106, 112, 114–19; red man's, 34–35; rule of, 7; Spanish, 106. *See also* contracts; Homestead Acts; regulation, government
Leal, Donald, 209–10
leasing systems: land, 172, 175; mining, 105, 106
Leavenworth, Colonel, 84, 222n28
Lefebvre, Irene, 173
Leshy, John D., 118
Lewis, Frank, 92
Lewis and Clark, 77, 79, 85, 212
Libecap, Gary, 72, 118, 168, 171, 204
licensing system, fur trade, 84, 92
Lima, Peru, 204–5
Limerick, Patricia Nelson, 4
The Line Camp (L. A. Huffman), 25*illus.*
line camps, 25*illus.*, 162–63
Lisa, Manuel, 79, 86
Lockean proviso, 216–17n41
Louisiana Purchase (1803), 93
Lueck, Dean, 72–73, 78

managers, ranch, 157
Mandans: fur trade, 82, 83, 85; on trade route, 12
Marquis de Mores, 165
Mars, 11, 212
Martin, Paul, 85
Mason, Richard, 106
mavericks, cattle, 150–51
McChesney, Fred, 64–65, 68–71
McCoy, Joseph G., 140, 145–47
McDonald's, 13
McKenzie, Kenneth, 83
Mead, Elwood, 186, 192
Meek, Joe, 91
Meeker, Nathan Cook, 184–85
Mexico: and fur trade, 93; independence from Spain (1821), 106; Mexican-American War, 63, 64–65; Treaty of Guadalupe Hidalgo (1848), 93, 106
Michalak, Anna, 209
military: Indian, 50–51, 52, 61–63; technology, 58, 61–63. *See also* guns; militias, local; U.S. military; wars
militias, local, 29, 63

mining: California, 104, 106–15, 116–17, 123, 233n7; camps, 109*illus.*, 110–12, 116, 203, 233n7; claims, 3, 4, 22, 23, 104–19; coal, 2; companies, 110, 233n7; copper, 105; dispute resolution, 109*illus.*, 111–18, 203; gold, 4, 26, 104, 106–19, 123, 226n62; hydraulic, 113, 179, 180, 201, 233n7; law, 105, 106, 112, 114–19; lead, 105; leasing system, 105, 106; Nevada, 104, 115–19; placer, 112–13, 117; quartz claims, 117; reservation land, 23; silver, 104, 115, 226n62; technology, 112–14, 179, 179*illus.*, 180, 201; water rights, 7, 105, 112–15, 179–80, 201–2
Mining Law (1866/1872), 105, 114
Missouri Fur Company, 79, 86
Mobutu Sese Seko, 206
Mohler, Dr. John R., 145
Montana: buffalo extermination, 97*illus.*; cattle regulations, 149–51; homesteads, 171; horse prices, 153*table*; Jensen, 1–2; Kapor, 2; *Montana Livestock Journal*, 157; National Bison Range, 101; Stockgrowers Association, 149–50, 151, 163–64, 229n48
morality: transaction costs, 15–16, 31–32. *See also* norms
Morgan, Dale, 89
Mormons: communal and private ownership, 233n16; irrigation, 184; overland journey, 123, 131–32; river ferries run by, 135; titles to land, 192; trade, 136; and transaction costs, 16, 131–32, 184
mortality, wagon-train journey, 123
mortgages, developed and developing world, 205
mourning ceremonies, Indian, 40
Mueller, Bernardo, 204
Muir, John, 40
mutual irrigation companies, 185–86, 188, 233n19
The Mystery of Capital (de Soto), 7–8

National Bison Range, Montana, 101
National Cattle Growers' Association, 175
National Irrigation Congress, 197

neurial motivation, 24; environment/
wildlife, 85, 102, 207–8; European,
53–54; Indian, 52, 53–54, 85; overland
emigrants motivated by, 123, 124; vs.
profits, 12–13; rent extraction through
regulation and taxation, 23–24, 30;
rent seeking, 22–24, 27, 30, 52, 136–
37, 200, 210, 214n20, 233n10; residual,
33; restricted access to, 27–28, 160. *See
also* dissipation of rents; race to capture
rents
*Report on the Lands of the Arid Region of the
United States* (Powell), 194–96
reservations, 23, 53, 65, 66–76
reservoirs, 187, 195–96, 200, 233n7
revisionist historians, 4
riparian rights, 7, 10, 178–79, 180, 233n6
Roback, Jennifer, 56
robe and hide trade, 48, 96–98, 100, 102,
220n4, 224nn93,94
Rocky Mountain Fur Company, 86, 91–92
Roosevelt, Theodore, 55, 164–65, 197,
198
roundups, cattle, 7, 26, 139, 150–51,
154–56, 164, 166, 228n61
rule of law, 7
rules. *See* institutions
Russell, C. M., 51*illus.*, 57*illus.*, 133*illus.*,
155*illus.*
Russell, Don, 55
rustlers, cattle, 12, 25, 29–30, 149, 151–
52, 162, 229n48

salmon runs, 41–42, 78
Salvation Army, 184
Sanborn, Henry, 168
Sandoz, Mari, 82
San Gabriel Orange Grove Association,
183
Schemeckebier, Laurence, 69
Schultz, James Willard, 51
Serbians, Montana, 2
servants, indentured, 127
Seton, Ernest, 100
sheep, grazing rights, 7, 23, 166–68,
230n8
Sherman, General William Tecumseh,
61, 64
Shimkin, Demitri, 50

Shinn, Charles, 106, 111–12, 115
Shoshoni, 50, 218n62
silver, mining, 104, 115, 226n62
Simpson, George, 93
Sioux: vs. Arikaras, 222n28; battles
(1876–77), 62, 64, 96; Fetterman Massacre (1866), 62; uprising in Minnesota
(1862), 60, 219n25; Wagon Box Fight
(1867), 62–63; and whites hunting buffalo, 96
size of collective, 33; agency costs and,
29–32, 33; cattle drive, 20, 144; cattlemen's associations, 28; Indian, 45, 48,
49, 217–18n61; mining company,
233n7; wagon-train, 129–30, 132
sluice boxes, 179*illus.*, 180, 201
Smith, Jedediah, 88, 89, 223n45
Smith, Rodney, 186, 188
soft gold, 6, 77–103. *See also* fur trade
Southern California Colony Association,
Riverside, 183
South Pass, 88, 222–23n45
space, outer, 203
Sparrow v. Strong (1865), 114
Speck, Frank, 42
squatters: land claims, 160, 168, 204,
231n36. *See also* homesteaders
standing army. *See* Army, U.S.
steamboats, 81, 222n13
Steward, Julian, 38, 39–40, 50–51
stock detectives, 151
Story, Nelson, 141–43
Stuart, Granville, 151–52, 161–62,
229n48
Stuart, Robert, 222–23n45
Sublette, William, 89, 94
surplus lands, 66, 68–69, 220n50
Sutter's Mill, 104, 106, 116, 123
Swan Land and Cattle Company, 165–66
sweat houses, Indian communal, 40
Szuter, Christine, 85

takings clause, U.S. Constitution, 32
Tanzania, Nyere of, 206
taxation: irrigation districts, 186, 187,
188–89; irrigation subsidies, 199; rent
extraction through, 23–24, 30; war
costs, 73
Taylor Grazing Act (1934), 175